CLEP-2 COLLEGE-LEVEL EXAMINATION
PROGRAM SERIES

*This is your
PASSBOOK for...*

American History

**Test Preparation Study Guide
Questions & Answers**

COPYRIGHT NOTICE

This book is SOLELY intended for, is sold ONLY to, and its use is RESTRICTED to individual, bona fide applicants or candidates who qualify by virtue of having seriously filed applications for appropriate license, certificate, professional and/or promotional advancement, higher school matriculation, scholarship, or other legitimate requirements of education and/or governmental authorities.

This book is NOT intended for use, class instruction, tutoring, training, duplication, copying, reprinting, excerption, or adaptation, etc., by:

1) Other publishers
2) Proprietors and/or Instructors of "Coaching" and/or Preparatory Courses
3) Personnel and/or Training Divisions of commercial, industrial, and governmental organizations
4) Schools, colleges, or universities and/or their departments and staffs, including teachers and other personnel
5) Testing Agencies or Bureaus
6) Study groups which seek by the purchase of a single volume to copy and/or duplicate and/or adapt this material for use by the group as a whole without having purchased individual volumes for each of the members of the group
7) Et al.

Such persons would be in violation of appropriate Federal and State statutes.

PROVISION OF LICENSING AGREEMENTS – Recognized educational, commercial, industrial, and governmental institutions and organizations, and others legitimately engaged in educational pursuits, including training, testing, and measurement activities, may address request for a licensing agreement to the copyright owners, who will determine whether, and under what conditions, including fees and charges, the materials in this book may be used them. In other words, a licensing facility exists for the legitimate use of the material in this book on other than an individual basis. However, it is asseverated and affirmed here that the material in this book CANNOT be used without the receipt of the express permission of such a licensing agreement from the Publishers. Inquiries re licensing should be addressed to the company, attention rights and permissions department.

All rights reserved, including the right of reproduction in whole or in part, in any form or by any means, electronic or mechanical, including photocopying, recording, or by any information storage and retrieval system, without permission in writing from the Publisher.

Copyright © 2024 by
National Learning Corporation

212 Michael Drive, Syosset, NY 11791
(516) 921-8888 • www.passbooks.com
E-mail: info@passbooks.com

PUBLISHED IN THE UNITED STATES OF AMERICA

PASSBOOK® SERIES

THE *PASSBOOK® SERIES* has been created to prepare applicants and candidates for the ultimate academic battlefield – the examination room.

At some time in our lives, each and every one of us may be required to take an examination – for validation, matriculation, admission, qualification, registration, certification, or licensure.

Based on the assumption that every applicant or candidate has met the basic formal educational standards, has taken the required number of courses, and read the necessary texts, the *PASSBOOK® SERIES* furnishes the one special preparation which may assure passing with confidence, instead of failing with insecurity. Examination questions – together with answers – are furnished as the basic vehicle for study so that the mysteries of the examination and its compounding difficulties may be eliminated or diminished by a sure method.

This book is meant to help you pass your examination provided that you qualify and are serious in your objective.

The entire field is reviewed through the huge store of content information which is succinctly presented through a provocative and challenging approach – the question-and-answer method.

A climate of success is established by furnishing the correct answers at the end of each test.

You soon learn to recognize types of questions, forms of questions, and patterns of questioning. You may even begin to anticipate expected outcomes.

You perceive that many questions are repeated or adapted so that you can gain acute insights, which may enable you to score many sure points.

You learn how to confront new questions, or types of questions, and to attack them confidently and work out the correct answers.

You note objectives and emphases, and recognize pitfalls and dangers, so that you may make positive educational adjustments.

Moreover, you are kept fully informed in relation to new concepts, methods, practices, and directions in the field.

You discover that you are actually taking the examination all the time: you are preparing for the examination by "taking" an examination, not by reading extraneous and/or supererogatory textbooks.

In short, this PASSBOOK®, used directedly, should be an important factor in helping you to pass your test.

NONTRADITIONAL EDUCATION

Students returning to school as adults bring more varied experience to their studies than do the teenagers who begin college shortly after graduating from high school. As a result, there are numerous programs for students with nontraditional learning curves. Hundreds of colleges and universities grant degrees to people who cannot attend classes at a regular campus or have already learned what the college is supposed to teach.

You can earn nontraditional education credits in many ways:
- Passing standardized exams
- Demonstrating knowledge gained through experience
- Completing campus-based coursework, and
- Taking courses off campus

Some methods of assessing learning for credit are objective, such as standardized tests. Others are more subjective, such as a review of life experiences.

With some help from four hypothetical characters – Alice, Vin, Lynette, and Jorge – this article describes nontraditional ways of earning educational credit. It begins by describing programs in which you can earn a high school diploma without spending 4 years in a classroom. The college picture is more complicated, so it is presented in two parts: one on gaining credit for what you know through course work or experience, and a second on college degree programs. The final section lists resources for locating more information.

Earning High School Credit

People who were prevented from finishing high school as teenagers have several options if they want to do so as adults. Some major cities have back-to-school programs that allow adults to attend high school classes with current students. But the more practical alternatives for most adults are to take the General Educational Development (GED) tests or to earn a high school diploma by demonstrating their skills or taking correspondence classes.

Of course, these options do not match the experience of staying in high school and graduating with one's friends. But they are viable alternatives for adult learners committed to meeting and, often, continuing their educational goals.

GED Program

Alice quit high school her sophomore year and took a job to help support herself, her younger brother, and their newly widowed mother. Now an adult, she wants to earn her high school diploma – and then go on to college. Because her job as head cook and her family responsibilities keep her busy during the day, she plans to get a high school equivalency diploma. She will study for, and take, the GED tests. Every year, about half a million adults earn their high school credentials this way. A GED diploma is accepted in lieu of a high school one by more than 90 percent of employers, colleges, and universities, so it is a good choice for someone like Alice.

The GED testing program is sponsored by the American Council on Education and State and local education departments. It consists of examinations in five subject areas: Writing, science, mathematics, social studies, and literature and the arts. The tests also measure skills such as analytical ability, problem solving, reading comprehension, and ability to understand and apply information. Most of the questions are multiple choice; the writing test includes an essay section on a topic of general interest.

Eligibility rules for taking the exams vary, but some states require that you must be at least 18. Tests are given in English, Spanish, and French. In addition to standard print, versions in large print, Braille, and audiocassette are also available. Total time allotted for the tests is 7 1/2 hours.

The GED tests are not easy. About one-fourth of those who complete the exams every year do not pass. Passing scores are established by administering the tests to a sample of graduating high school seniors. The minimum standard score is set so that about one-third of graduating seniors would not pass the tests if they took them.

Because of the difficulty of the tests, people need to prepare themselves to take them. Often, they start by taking the Official GED Practice Tests, usually available through a local adult education center. Centers are listed in your phone book's blue pages under "Adult Education," "Continuing Education," or "GED." Adult education centers also have information about GED preparation classes and self-study materials. Classes are generally arranged to accommodate adults' work schedules. National Learning Corporation publishes several study guides that aim to thoroughly prepare test-takers for the GED.

School districts, colleges, adult education centers, and community organizations have information about GED testing schedules and practice tests. For more information, contact them, your nearest GED testing center, or:

GED Testing Service
One Dupont Circle, NW, Suite 250
Washington, DC 20036-1163
1(800) 62-MY GED (626-9433)
(202) 939-9490

Skills Demonstration

Adults who have acquired high school level skills through experience might be eligible for the National External Diploma Program. This alternative to the GED does not involve any direct instruction. Instead, adults seeking a high school diploma must demonstrate mastery of 65 competencies in 8 general areas: Communication; computation; occupational preparedness; and self, social, consumer, scientific, and technological awareness.

Mastery is shown through the completion of the tasks. For example, a participant could prove competency in computation by measuring a room for carpeting, figuring out the amount of carpet needed, and computing the cost.

Before being accepted for the program, adults undergo an evaluation. Tests taken at one of the program's offices measure reading, writing, and mathematics abilities. A take-home segment includes a self-assessment of current skills, an individual skill evaluation, and an occupational interest and aptitude test.

Adults accepted for the program have weekly meetings with an assessor. At the meeting, the assessor reviews the participant's work from the previous week. If the task has not been completed properly, the assessor explains the mistake. Participants continue to correct their errors until they master each competency. A high school diploma is awarded upon proven mastery of all 65 competencies.

Fourteen States and the District of Columbia now offer the External Diploma Program. For more information, contact:
External Diploma Program
One Dupont Circle, NW, Suite 250
Washington, DC 20036-1193
(202) 939-9475

Correspondence and Distance Study
Vin dropped out of high school during his junior year because his family's frequent moves made it difficult for him to continue his studies. He promised himself at the time he dropped out that he would someday finish the courses needed for his diploma. For people like Vin, who prefer to earn a traditional diploma in a nontraditional way, there are about a dozen accredited courses of study for earning a high school diploma by correspondence, or distance study. The programs are either privately run, affiliated with a university, or administered by a State education department.

Distance study diploma programs have no residency requirements, allowing students to continue their studies from almost any location. Depending on the course of study, students need not be enrolled full time and usually have more flexible schedules for finishing their work. Selection of courses ranges from vo-tech to college prep, and some programs place different emphasis on the types of diplomas offered. University affiliated schools, for example, allow qualified students to take college courses along with their high school ones. Students can then apply the college credits toward a degree at that university or transfer them to another institution.

Taking courses by distance study is often more challenging and time consuming than attending classes, especially for adults who have other obligations. Success depends on each student's motivation. Students usually do reading assignments on their own. Written exercises, which they complete and send to an instructor for grading, supplement their reading material.

A list of some accredited high schools that offer diplomas by distance study is available free from the Distance Education and Training Council, formerly known as the National Home Study Council. Request the "DETC Directory of Accredited Institutions" from:
The Distance Education and Training Council
1601 18th Street, NW.
Washington, DC 20009-2529
(202) 234-5100

Some publications profiling nontraditional college programs include addresses and descriptions of several high school correspondence ones. See the Resources section at the end of this article for more information.

Getting College Credit For What You Know
Adults can receive college credit for prior coursework, by passing examinations, and documenting experiential learning. With help from a college advisor, nontraditional students should assess their skills, establish their educational goals, and determine the number of college credits they might be eligible for.

Even before you meet with a college advisor, you should collect all your school and training records. Then, make a list of all knowledge and abilities acquired through experience, no matter how irrelevant they seem to your chosen field. Next, determine your educational goals: What specific field do you wish to study? What kind of a degree do you want? Finally, determine how your past work fits into the field of study. Later on, you will evaluate educational programs to find one that's right for you.

People who have complex educational or experiential learning histories might want to have their learning evaluated by the Regents Credit Bank. The Credit Bank, operated by Regents College of the University of the State of New York, allows people to consolidate credits earned through college, experience, or other methods. Special assessments are available for Regents College enrollees whose knowledge in a specific field cannot be adequately evaluated by standardized exams. For more information, contact the Regents Credit Bank at:

Regents College
7 Columbia Circle
Albany, NY 12203-5159
(518) 464-8500

Credit For Prior College Coursework

When Lynette was in college during the 1970s, she attended several different schools and took a variety of courses. She did well in some classes and poorly in others. Now that she is a successful business owner and has more focus, Lynette thinks she should forget about her previous coursework and start from scratch. Instead, she should start from where she is.

Lynette should have all her transcripts sent to the colleges or universities of her choice and let an admissions officer determine which classes are applicable toward a degree. A few credits here and there may not seem like much, but they add up. Even if the subjects do not seem relevant to any major, they might be counted as elective credits toward a degree. And comparing the cost of transcripts with the cost of college courses, it makes sense to spend a few dollars per transcript for a chance to save hundreds, and perhaps thousands, of dollars in books and tuition.

Rules for transferring credits apply to all prior coursework at accredited colleges and universities, whether done on campus or off. Courses completed off campus, often called extended learning, include those available to students through independent study and correspondence. Many schools have extended learning programs; Brigham Young University, for example, offers more than 300 courses through its Department of Independent Study. One type of extended learning is distance learning, a form of correspondence study by technological means such as television, video and audio, CD-ROM, electronic mail, and computer tutorials. See the Resources section at the end of this article for more information about publications available from the National University Continuing Education Association.

Any previously earned college credits should be considered for transfer, no matter what the subject or the grade received. Many schools do not accept the transfer of courses graded below a C or ones taken more than a designated number of years ago. Some colleges and universities also have limits on the number of credits that can be transferred and applied toward a degree. But not all do. For example, Thomas Edison State College, New Jersey's State college for adults, accepts the transfer of all 120 hours of credit required for a baccalaureate degree – provided all the credits are transferred from regionally accredited schools, no more than 80 are at the junior college level, and the student's grades overall and in the field of study average out to C.

To assign credit for prior coursework, most schools require original transcripts. This means you must complete a form or send a written, signed request to have your transcripts released directly to a college or university. Once you have chosen the schools you want to apply to, contact the schools you attended before. Find out how much each transcript costs, and ask them to send your transcripts to the ones you are applying to. Write a letter that includes your name (and names used during attendance, if different) and dates of attendance, along with the names and addresses of the schools to which your transcripts should be sent. Include payment and mail to the registrar at the schools you have attended. The registrar's office will process your request and send an official transcript of your coursework to the colleges or universities you have designated.

Credit For Noncollege Courses

Colleges and universities are not the only ones that offer classes. Volunteer organizations and employers often provide formal training worth college credit. The American Council on Education has two programs that assess thousands of specific courses and make recommendations on the amount of college credit they are worth. Colleges and universities accept the recommendations or use them as guidelines.

One program evaluates educational courses sponsored by government agencies, business and industry, labor unions, and professional and voluntary organizations. It is the Program on Noncollegiate Sponsored Instruction (PONSI). Some of the training seminars Alice has participated in covered topics such as food preparation, kitchen safety, and nutrition. Although she has not yet earned her GED, Alice can earn college credit because of her completion of these formal job-training seminars. The number of credits each seminar is worth does not hinge on Alice's current eligibility for college enrollment.

The other program evaluates courses offered by the Army, Navy, Air Force, Marines, Coast Guard, and Department of Defense. It is the Military Evaluations Program. Jorge has never attended college, but the engineering technology classes he completed as part of his military training are worth college credit. And as an Army veteran, Jorge is eligible for a service that takes the evaluations one step further. The Army/American Council on Education Registry Transcript System (AARTS) will provide Jorge with an individualized transcript of American Council on Education credit recommendations for all courses he completed, the military occupational specialties (MOS's) he held, and examinations he passed while in the Army. All Army and National Guard enlisted personnel and veterans who enlisted after October 1981 are eligible for the transcript. Similar services are being considered by the Navy and Marine Corps.

To obtain a free transcript, see your Army Education Center for a 5454R transcript request form. Include your name, Social Security number, basic active service date, and complete address where you want the transcript sent. Mail your request to:
AARTS Operations Center
415 McPherson Ave.
Fort Leavenworth, KS 66027-1373

Recommendations for PONSI are published in *The National Guide to Educational Credit for Training Programs;* military program recommendations are in *The Guide to the Evaluation of Educational Experiences in the Armed Forces.* See the Resources section at the end of this article for more information about these publications.

Former military personnel who took a foreign language course through the Defense Language Institute may request course transcripts by sending their name, Social Security number, course title, duration of the course, and graduation date to:

    Commandant, Defense Language Institute
    Attn: ATFL-DAA-AR
    Transcripts
    Presidio of Monterey
    Monterey, CA 93944-5006

Not all of Jorge's and Alice's courses have been assessed by the American Council on Education. Training courses that have no Council credit recommendation should still be assessed by an advisor at the schools they want to attend. Course descriptions, class notes, test scores, and other documentation may be helpful for comparing training courses to their college equivalents. An oral examination or other demonstration of competency might also be required.

There is no guarantee you will receive all the credits you are seeking – but you certainly won't if you make no attempt.

Credit By Examination

Standardized tests are the best-known method of receiving college credit without taking courses. These exams are often taken by high school students seeking advanced placement for college, but they are also available to adult learners. Testing programs and colleges and universities offer exams in a number of subjects. Two U.S. Government institutes have foreign language exams for employees that also may be worth college credit.

It is important to understand that receiving a passing score on these exams does not mean you get college credit automatically. Each school determines which test results it will accept, minimum scores required, how scores are converted for credit, and the amount of credit, if any, to be assigned. Most colleges and universities accept the American Council on Education credit recommendations, published every other year in the 250-page *Guide to Educational Credit by Examination*. For more information, contact:

    The American Council on Education
    Credit by Examination Program
    One Dupont Circle, Suite 250
    Washington, DC 20036-1193
    (202) 939-9434

Testing programs:

You might know some of the five national testing programs by their acronyms or initials: CLEP, ACT PEP: RCE, DANTES, AP, and NOCTI. (The meanings of these initialisms are explained below.) There is some overlap among programs; for example, four of them have introductory accounting exams. Since you will not be awarded credit more than once for a specific subject, you should carefully evaluate each program for the subject exams you wish to take. And before taking an exam, make sure you will be awarded credit by the college or university you plan to attend.

CLEP (College-Level Examination Program), administered by the College Board, is the most widely accepted of the national testing programs; more than 2,800 accredited schools award credit for passing exam scores. Each test covers material taught in basic

undergraduate courses. There are five general exams – English composition, humanities, college mathematics, natural sciences, and social sciences and history – and many subject exams. Most exams are entirely multiple-choice, but English composition exams may include an essay section. For more information, contact:
    CLEP
    P.O. Box 6600
    Princeton, NJ 08541-6600
    (609) 771-7865

ACT PEP: RCE (American College Testing Proficiency Exam Program: Regents College Examinations) tests are given in 38 subjects within arts and sciences, business, education, and nursing. Each exam is recommended for either lower- or upper-level credit. Exams contain either objective or extended response questions, and are graded according to a standard score, letter grade, or pass/fail. Fees vary, depending on the subject and type of exam. For more information or to request free study guides, contact:
    ACT PEP: Regents College Examinations
    P.O. Box 4014
    Iowa City, IA 52243
    (319) 337-1387
    (New York State residents must contact Regents College directly.)

DANTES (Defense Activity for Nontraditional Education Support) standardized tests are developed by the Educational Testing Service for the Department of Defense. Originally administered only to military personnel, the exams have been available to the public since 1983. About 50 subject tests cover business, mathematics, social science, physical science, humanities, foreign languages, and applied technology. Most of the tests consist entirely of multiple-choice questions. Schools determine their own administering fees and testing schedules. For more information or to request free study sheets, contact:
    DANTES Program Office
    Mail Stop 31-X
    Educational Testing Service
    Princeton, NJ 08541
    1(800) 257-9484

The AP (Advanced Placement) Program is a cooperative effort between secondary schools and colleges and universities. AP exams are developed each year by committees of college and high school faculty appointed by the College Board and assisted by consultants from the Educational Testing Service. Subjects include arts and languages, natural sciences, computer science, social sciences, history, and mathematics. Most tests are 2 or 3 hours long and include both multiple-choice and essay questions. AP courses are available to help students prepare for exams, which are offered in the spring. For more information about the Advanced Placement Program, contact:
    Advanced Placement Services
    P.O. Box 6671
    Princeton, NJ 08541-6671
    (609) 771-7300

NOCTI (National Occupational Competency Testing Institute) assessments are designed for people like Alice, who have vocational-technical skills that cannot be evaluated by other tests. NOCTI assesses competency at two levels: Student/job ready and teacher/experienced worker. Standardized evaluations are available for occupations such as auto-body repair, electronics, mechanical drafting, quantity food preparation, and upholstering. The tests consist of multiple-choice questions and a performance component. Other services include workshops, customized assessments, and pre-testing. For more information, contact:

NOCTI
500 N. Bronson Ave.
Ferris State University
Big Rapids, MI 49307
(616) 796-4699

Colleges and universities:

Many colleges and universities have credit-by-exam programs, through which students earn credit by passing a comprehensive exam for a course offered by the institution. Among the most widely recognized are the programs at Ohio University, the University of North Carolina, Thomas Edison State College, and New York University.

Ohio University offers about 150 examinations for credit. In addition, you may sometimes arrange to take special examinations in non-laboratory courses offered at Ohio University. To take a test for credit, you must enroll in the course. If you plan to transfer the credit earned, you also need written permission from an official at your school. Books and study materials are available, for a cost, through the university. Exams must be taken within 6 months of the enrollment date; most last 3 hours. You may arrange to take the exam off campus if you do not live near the university.

Ohio University is on the quarter-hour system; most courses are worth 4 quarter hours, the equivalent of 3 semester hours. For more information, contact:

Independent Study
Tupper Hall 302
Ohio University
Athens, OH 45701-2979
1(800) 444-2910
(614) 593-2910

The University of North Carolina offers a credit-by-examination option for 140 independent study (correspondence) courses in foreign languages, humanities, social sciences, mathematics, business administration, education, electrical and computer engineering, health administration, and natural sciences. To take an exam, you must request and receive approval from both the course instructor and the independent studies department. Exams must be taken within six months of enrollment, and you may register for no more than two at a time. If you are not near the University's Chapel Hill campus, you may take your exam under supervision at an accredited college, university, community college, or technical institute. For more information, contact:

Independent Studies
CB #1020, The Friday Center
UNC-Chapel Hill
Chapel Hill, NC 27599-1020
1(800) 862-5669 / (919) 962-1134

The Thomas Edison College Examination Program offers more than 50 exams in liberal arts, business, and professional areas. Thomas Edison State College administers tests twice a month in Trenton, New Jersey; however, students may arrange to take their tests with a proctor at any accredited American college or university or U.S. military base. Most of the tests are multiple choice; some also include short answer or essay questions. Time limits range from 90 minutes to 4 hours, depending on the exam. For more information, contact:

Thomas Edison State College
TECEP, Office of Testing and Assessment
101 W. State Street
Trenton, NJ 08608-1176
(609) 633-2844

New York University's Foreign Language Program offers proficiency exams in more than 40 languages, from Albanian to Yiddish. Two exams are available in each language: The 12-point test is equivalent to 4 undergraduate semesters, and the 16-point exam may lead to upper level credit. The tests are given at the university's Foreign Language Department throughout the year.

Proof of foreign language proficiency does not guarantee college credit. Some colleges and universities accept transcripts only for languages commonly taught, such as French and Spanish. Nontraditional programs are more likely than traditional ones to grant credit for proficiency in other languages.

For an informational brochure and registration form for NYU's foreign language proficiency exams, contact:

New York University
Foreign Language Department
48 Cooper Square, Room 107
New York, NY 10003
(212) 998-7030

Government institutes:

The Defense Language Institute and Foreign Service Institute administer foreign language proficiency exams for personnel stationed abroad. Usually, the tests are given at the end of intensive language courses or upon completion of service overseas. But some people – like Jorge, who knows Spanish – speak another language fluently and may be allowed to take a proficiency exam in that language before completing their tour of duty. Contact one of the offices listed below to obtain transcripts of those scores. Proof of proficiency does not guarantee college credit, however, as discussed above.

To request score reports from the Defense Language Institute for Defense Language Proficiency Tests, send your name, Social Security number, language for which you were tested, and, most importantly, when and where you took the exam to:

Commandant, Defense Language Institute
Attn: ATFL-ES-T
DLPT Score Report Request
Presidio of Monterey
Monterey, CA 93944-5006

To request transcripts of scores for Foreign Service Institute exams, send your name, Social Security number, language for which you were tested, and dates or year of exams to:

Foreign Service Institute
Arlington Hall
4020 Arlington Boulevard
Rosslyn, VA 22204-1500
Attn: Testing Office (Send your request to the attention of the testing office of the foreign language in which you were tested)

Credit For Experience

Experiential learning credit may be given for knowledge gained through job responsibilities, personal hobbies, volunteer opportunities, homemaking, and other experiences. Colleges and universities base credit awards on the knowledge you have attained, not for the experience alone. In addition, the knowledge must be college level; not just any learning will do. Throwing horseshoes as a hobby is not likely to be worth college credit. But if you've done research on how and where the sport originated, visited blacksmiths, organized tournaments, and written a column for a trade journal – well, that's a horseshoe of a different color.

Adults attempting to get credit for their experience should be forewarned: Having your experience evaluated for college credit is time-consuming, tedious work – not an easy shortcut for people who want quick-fix college credits. And not all experience, no matter how valuable, is the equivalent of college courses.

Requesting college credit for your experiential learning can be tricky. You should get assistance from a credit evaluations officer at the school you plan to attend, but you should also have a general idea of what your knowledge is worth. A common method for converting knowledge into credit is to use a college catalog. Find course titles and descriptions that match what you have learned through experience, and request the number of credits offered for those courses.

Once you know what credit to ask for, you must usually present your case in writing to officials at the college you plan to attend. The most common form of presenting experiential learning for credit is the portfolio. A portfolio is a written record of your knowledge along with a request for equivalent college credit. It includes an identification and description of the knowledge for which you are requesting credit, an explanatory essay of how the knowledge was gained and how it fits into your educational plans, documentation that you have acquired such knowledge, and a request for college credit. Required elements of a portfolio vary by schools but generally follow those guidelines.

In identifying knowledge you have gained, be specific about exactly what you have learned. For example, it is not enough for Lynette to say she runs a business. She must identify the knowledge she has gained from running it, such as personnel management, tax law, marketing strategy, and inventory review. She must also include brief descriptions about her knowledge of each to support her claims of having those skills.

The essay gives you a chance to relay something about who you are. It should address your educational goals, include relevant autobiographical details, and be well organized, neat, and convey confidence. In his essay, Jorge might first state his goal of becoming an engineer. Then he would explain why he joined the Army, where he got hands-on training and experience in developing and servicing electronic equipment.

This, he would say, led to his hobby of creating remote-controlled model cars, of which he has built 20. His conclusion would highlight his accomplishments and tie them to his desire to become an electronic engineer.

Documentation is evidence that you've learned what you claim to have learned. You can show proof of knowledge in a variety of ways, including audio or video recordings, letters from current or former employers describing your specific duties and job performance, blueprints, photographs or artwork, and transcripts of certifying exams for professional licenses and certification – such as Alice's certification from the American Culinary Federation. Although documentation can take many forms, written proof alone is not always enough. If it is impossible to document your knowledge in writing, find out if your experiential learning can be assessed through supplemental oral exams by a faculty expert.

Earning a College Degree

Nontraditional students often have work, family, and financial obligations that prevent them from quitting their jobs to attend school full time. Can they still meet their educational goals? Yes.

More than 150 accredited colleges and universities have nontraditional bachelor's degree programs that require students to spend little or no time on campus; over 300 others have nontraditional campus-based degree programs. Some of those schools, as well as most junior and community colleges, offer associate's degrees nontraditionally. Each school with a nontraditional course of study determines its own rules for awarding credit for prior coursework, exams, or experience, as discussed previously. Most have charges on top of tuition for providing these special services.

Several publications profile nontraditional degree programs; see the Resources section at the end of this article for more information. To determine which school best fits your academic profile and educational goals, first list your criteria. Then, evaluate nontraditional programs based on their accreditation, features, residency requirements, and expenses. Once you have chosen several schools to explore further, write to them for more information. Detailed explanations of school policies should help you decide which ones you want to apply to.

Get beyond the printed word – especially the glowing words each school writes about itself. Check out the schools you are considering with higher education authorities, alumni, employers, family members, and friends. If possible, visit the campus to talk to students and instructors and sit in on a few classes, even if you will be completing most or all of your work off campus. Ask school officials questions about such things as enrollment numbers, graduation rate, faculty qualifications, and confusing details about the application process or academic policies. After you have thoroughly investigated each prospective college or university, you can make an informed decision about which is right for you.

Accreditation

Accreditation is a process colleges and universities submit to voluntarily for getting their credentials. An accredited school has been investigated and visited by teams of observers and has periodic inspections by a private accrediting agency. The initial review can take two years or more.

Regional agencies accredit entire schools, and professional agencies accredit either specialized schools or departments within schools. Although there are no national accrediting standards, not just any accreditation will do. Countless "accreditation associations" have been invented by schools, many of which have no academic programs and sell phony degrees, to accredit themselves. But 6 regional and about 80 professional accrediting associations in the United States are recognized by the U.S. Department of Education or the Commission on Recognition of Postsecondary Accreditation. When checking accreditation, these are the names to look for. For more information about accreditation and accrediting agencies, contact:

    Institutional Participation Oversight Service Accreditation and State Liaison Division
    U.S. Department of Education
    ROB 3, Room 3915
    600 Independence Ave., SW
    Washington, DC 20202-5244
    (202) 708-7417

Because accreditation is not mandatory, lack of accreditation does not necessarily mean a school or program is bad. Some schools choose not to apply for accreditation, are in the process of applying, or have educational methods too unconventional for an accrediting association's standards. For the nontraditional student, however, earning a degree from a college or university with recognized accreditation is an especially important consideration. Although nontraditional education is becoming more widely accepted, it is not yet mainstream. Employers skeptical of a degree earned in a nontraditional manner are likely to be even less accepting of one from an unaccredited school.

Program Features

Because nontraditional students have diverse educational objectives, nontraditional schools are diverse in what they offer. Some programs are geared toward helping students organize their scattered educational credits to get a degree as quickly as possible. Others cater to those who may have specific credits or experience but need assistance in completing requirements. Whatever your educational profile, you should look for a program that works with you in obtaining your educational goals.

A few nontraditional programs have special admissions policies for adult learners like Alice, who plan to earn their GEDs but want to enroll in college in the meantime. Other features of nontraditional programs include individualized learning agreements, intensive academic counseling, cooperative learning and internship placement, and waiver of some prerequisites or other requirements – as well as college credit for prior coursework, examinations, and experiential learning, all discussed previously.

Lynette, whose primary goal is to finish her degree, wants to earn maximum credits for her business experience. She will look for programs that do not limit the number of credits awarded for equivalency exams and experiential learning. And since well-documented proof of knowledge is essential for earning experiential learning credits, Lynette should make sure the program she chooses provides assistance to students submitting a portfolio.

Jorge, on the other hand, has more credits than he needs in certain areas and is willing to forego some. To become an engineer, he must have a bachelor's degree; but because he is accustomed to hands-on learning, Jorge is interested in getting experience as he gains more technical skills. He will concentrate on finding schools with strong cooperative education, supervised fieldwork, or internship programs.

Residency Requirements

Programs are sometimes deemed nontraditional because of their residency requirements. Many people think of residency for colleges and universities in terms of tuition, with in-state students paying less than out-of-state ones. Residency also may refer to where a student lives, either on or off campus, while attending school.

But in nontraditional education, residency usually refers to how much time students must spend on campus, regardless of whether they attend classes there. In some nontraditional programs, students need not ever step foot on campus. Others require only a very short residency, such as one day or a few weeks. Many schools have standard residency requirements of several semesters but schedule classes for evenings or weekends to accommodate working adults.

Lynette, who previously took courses by independent study, prefers to earn credits by distance study. She will focus on schools that have no residency requirement. Several colleges and universities have nonresident degree completion programs for adults with some college credit. Under the direction of a faculty advisor, students devise a plan for earning their remaining credits. Methods for earning credits include independent study, distance learning, seminars, supervised fieldwork, and group study at arranged sites. Students may have to earn a certain number of credits through the degree-granting institution. But many programs allow students to take courses at accredited schools of their choice for transfer toward their degree.

Alice wants to attend lectures but has an unpredictable schedule. Her best course of action will be to seek out short residency programs that require students to attend seminars once or twice a semester. She can take courses that are televised and videotape them to watch when her schedule permits, with the seminars helping to ensure that she properly completes her coursework. Many colleges and universities with short residency requirements also permit students to earn some credits elsewhere, by whatever means the student chooses.

Some fields of study require classroom instruction. As Jorge will discover, few colleges and universities allow students to earn a bachelor's degree in engineering entirely through independent study. Nontraditional residency programs are designed to accommodate adults' daytime work schedules. Jorge should look for programs offering evening, weekend, summer, and accelerated courses.

Tuition and Other Expenses

The final decisions about which schools Alice, Jorge, and Lynette attend may hinge in large part on a single issue: Cost. And rising tuition is only part of the equation. Beginning with application fees and continuing through graduation fees, college expenses add up.

Traditional and nontraditional students have some expenses in common, such as the cost of books and other materials. Tuition might even be the same for some courses, especially for colleges and universities offering standard ones at unusual times. But for nontraditional programs, students may also pay fees for services such as credit or transcript review, evaluation, advisement, and portfolio assessment.

Students are also responsible for postage and handling or setup expenses for independent study courses, as well as for all examination and transcript fees for transferring credits. Usually, the more nontraditional the program, the more detailed the fees. Some schools charge a yearly enrollment fee rather than tuition for degree completion candidates who want their files to remain active.

Although tuition and fees might seem expensive, most educators tell you not to let money come between you and your educational goals. Talk to someone in the financial aid department of the school you plan to attend or check your library for publications about financial aid sources. The U.S. Department of Education publishes a guide to Federal aid programs such as Pell Grants, student loans, and work-study. To order the free 74-page booklet, *The Student Guide: Financial Aid from the U.S. Department of Education,* contact:

Federal Student Aid Information Center
P.O. Box 84
Washington, DC 20044
1 (800) 4FED-AID (433-3243)

Resources

Information on how to earn a high school diploma or college degree without following the usual routes is available from several organizations and in numerous publications. Information on nontraditional graduate degree programs, available for master's through doctoral level, though not discussed in this article, can usually be obtained from the same resources that detail bachelor's degree programs.

National Learning Corporation publishes study guides for all of these exams, for both general examinations and tests in specific subject areas. To order study guides, or to browse their catalog featuring more than 5,000 titles, visit NLC online at www.passbooks.com, or contact them by phone at (800) 632-8888.

Organizations

Adult learners should always contact their local school system, community college, or university to learn about programs that are readily available. The following national organizations can also supply information:

American Council on Education
One Dupont Circle
Washington, DC 20036-1193
(202) 939-9300

Within the American Council on Education, the Center for Adult Learning and Educational Credentials administers the National External Diploma Program, the GED Program, the Program on Noncollegiate Sponsored Instruction, the Credit by Examination Program, and the Military Evaluations Program.

College-Level Examination Program (CLEP)

1. WHAT IS CLEP?

CLEP stands for the College-Level Examination Program, sponsored by the College Board. It is a national program of credit-by-examination that offers you the opportunity to obtain recognition for college-level achievement. No matter when, where, or how you have learned – by means of formal or informal study – you can take CLEP tests. If the results are acceptable to your college, you can receive credit.

You may not realize it, but you probably know more than your academic record reveals. Each day you, like most people, have an opportunity to learn. In private industry and business, as well as at all levels of government, learning opportunities continually occur. If you read widely or intensively in a particular field, think about what you read, discuss it with your family and friends, you are learning. Or you may be learning on a more formal basis by taking a correspondence course, a television or radio course, a course recorded on tape or cassettes, a course assembled into programmed tests, or a course taught in your community adult school or high school.

No matter how, where, or when you gained your knowledge, you may have the opportunity to receive academic credit for your achievement that can be counted toward an undergraduate degree. The College-Level Examination Program (CLEP) enables colleges to evaluate your achievement and give you credit. A wide range of college-level examinations are offered by CLEP to anyone who wishes to take them. Scores on the tests are reported to you and, if you wish, to a college, employer, or individual.

2. WHAT ARE THE PURPOSES OF THE COLLEGE-LEVEL EXAMINATION PROGRAM?

The basic purpose of the College-Level Examination Program is to enable individuals who have acquired their education in nontraditional ways to demonstrate their academic achievement. It is also intended for use by those in higher education, business, industry, government, and other fields who need a reliable method of assessing a person's educational level.

Recognizing that the real issue is not how a person has acquired his education but what education he has, the College Level Examination Program has been designed to serve a variety of purposes. The basic purpose, as listed above, is to enable those who have reached the college level of education in nontraditional ways to assess the level of their achievement and to use the test results in seeking college credit or placement.

In addition, scores on the tests can be used to validate educational experience obtained at a nonaccredited institution or through noncredit college courses.

Some colleges and universities may use the tests to measure the level of educational achievement of their students, and for various institutional research purposes.

Other colleges and universities may wish to use the tests in the admission, placement, and guidance of students who wish to transfer from one institution to another.

Businesses, industries, governmental agencies, and professional groups now accept the results of these tests as a basis for advancement, eligibility for further training, or professional or semi-professional certification.

Many people are interested in the examination simply to assess their own educational progress and attainment.

The college, university, business, industry, or government agency that adopts the tests in the College-Level Examination Program makes its own decision about how it will use and interpret the test scores. The College Board will provide the tests, score them, and report the results either to the individuals who took the tests or the college or agency that administered them. It does NOT, and cannot, award college credit, certify college equivalency, or make recommendations regarding the standards these institutions should establish for the use of the test results.

Therefore, if you are taking the tests to secure credit from an institution, you should FIRST ascertain whether the college or agency involved will accept the scores. Each institution determines which CLEP tests it will accept for credit and the amount of credit it will award. If you want to take tests for college credit, first call, write, or visit the college you wish to attend to inquire about its policy on CLEP scores, as well as its other admission requirements.

The services of the program are also available to people who have been requested to take the tests by an employer, a professional licensing agency, a certifying agency, or by other groups that recognize college equivalency on the basis of satisfactory CLEP scores. You may, of course, take the tests SOLELY for your own information. If you do, your scores will be reported only to you.

While neither CLEP nor the College Board can evaluate previous credentials or award college credit, you will receive, with your scores, basic information to help you interpret your performance on the tests you have taken.

3. WHAT ARE THE COLLEGE-LEVEL EXAMINATIONS?

In order to meet different kinds of curricular organization and testing needs at colleges and universities, the College-Level Examination Program offers 35 different subject tests falling under five separate general categories: Composition and Literature, Foreign Languages, History and Social Sciences, Science and Mathematics, and Business.

4. WHAT ARE THE SUBJECT EXAMINATIONS?

The 35 CLEP tests offered by the College Board are listed below:

COMPOSITION AND LITERATURE:
- American Literature
- Analyzing and Interpreting Literature
- English Composition
- English Composition with Essay
- English Literature
- Freshman College Composition
- Humanities

FOREIGN LANGUAGES
- French
- German
- Spanish

HISTORY AND SOCIAL SCIENCES
- American Government
- Introduction to Educational Psychology
- History of the United States I: Early Colonization to 1877
- History of the United States II: 1865 to the Present
- Human Growth and Development
- Principles of Macroeconomics
- Principles of Microeconomics
- Introductory Psychology
- Social Sciences and History
- Introductory Sociology
- Western Civilization I: Ancient Near East to 1648
- Western Civilization II: 1648 to the Present

SCIENCE AND MATHEMATICS
- College Algebra
- College Algebra-Trigonometry
- Biology
- Calculus
- Chemistry
- College Mathematics
- Natural Sciences
- Trigonometry
- Precalculus

BUSINESS
- Financial Accounting
- Introductory Business Law
- Information Systems and Computer Applications
- Principles of Management
- Principles of Marketing

CLEP Examinations cover material taught in courses that most students take as requirements in the first two years of college. A college usually grants the same amount of credit to students earning satisfactory scores on the CLEP examination as it grants to students successfully completing the equivalent course.

Many examinations are designed to correspond to one-semester courses; some, however, correspond to full-year or two-year courses.

Each exam is 90 minutes long and, except for English Composition with Essay, is made up primarily of multiple-choice questions. Some tests have several other types of questions besides multiple choice. To see a more detailed description of a particular CLEP exam, visit www.collegeboard.com/clep.

The English Composition with Essay exam is the only exam that includes a required essay. This essay is scored by college English faculty designated by CLEP and does not require an additional fee. However, other Composition and Literature tests offer optional essays, which some college and universities require and some do not. These essays are graded by faculty at the individual institutions that require them and require an additional $10 fee. Contact the particular institution to ask about essay requirements, and check with your test center for further details.

All 35 CLEP examinations are administered on computer. If you are unfamiliar with taking a test on a computer, consult the CLEP Sampler online at www.collegeboard.com/clep. The Sampler contains the same tutorials as the actual exams and helps familiarize you with navigation and how to answer different types of questions.

Points are not deducted for wrong or skipped answers – you receive one point for every correct answer. Therefore it is best that an answer is supplied for each exam question, whether it is a guess or not. The number of correct answers is then converted to a formula score. This formula, or "scaled," score is determined by a statistical process called *equating*, which adjusts for slight differences in difficulty between test forms and ensures that your score does not depend on the specific test form you took or how well others did on the same form. The scaled scores range from 20 to 80 – this is the number that will appear on your score report.

To ensure that you complete all questions in the time allotted, you would probably be wise to skip the more difficult or perplexing questions and return to them later. Although the multiple-choice items in these tests are carefully designed so as not to be tricky, misleading, or ambiguous, on the other hand, they are not all direct questions of factual information. They attempt, in their way, to elicit a response that indicates your knowledge or lack of knowledge of the material in question or your ability or inability to use or interpret a fact or idea. Thus, you should concentrate on answering the questions as they appear to be without attempting to out-guess the testmakers.

5. WHAT ARE THE FEES?

The fee for all CLEP examinations is $55. Optional essays required by some institutions are an additional $10.

6. WHEN ARE THE TESTS GIVEN?

CLEP tests are administered year-round. Consult the CLEP website (www.collegeboard.com/clep) and individual test centers for specific information.

7. WHERE ARE THE TESTS GIVEN?

More than 1,300 test centers are located on college and university campuses throughout the country, and additional centers are being established to meet increased needs. Any accredited collegiate institution with an explicit and publicly available policy of credit by examination can become a CLEP test center. To obtain a list of these centers, visit the CLEP website at www.collegeboard.com/clep.

8. HOW DO I REGISTER FOR THE COLLEGE-LEVEL EXAMINATION PROGRAM?

Contact an individual test center for information regarding registration, scheduling and fees. Registration/admission forms can also be obtained on the CLEP website.

9. MAY I REPEAT THE COLLEGE-LEVEL EXAMINATIONS?

You may repeat any examination providing at least six months have passed since you were last administered this test. If you repeat a test within a period of time less than six months, your scores will be cancelled and your fees forfeited. To repeat a test, check the appropriate space on the registration form.

10. WHEN MAY I EXPECT MY SCORE REPORTS?

With the exception of the English Composition with Essay exam, you should receive your score report instantly once the test is complete.

11. HOW SHOULD I PREPARE FOR THE COLLEGE-LEVEL EXAMINATIONS?

This book has been specifically designed to prepare candidates for these examinations. It will help you to consider, study, and review important content, principles, practices, procedures, problems, and techniques in the form of varied and concrete applications.

12. QUESTIONS AND ANSWERS APPEARING IN THIS PUBLICATION

The College-Level Examinations are offered by the College Board. Since copies of past examinations have not been made available, we have used equivalent materials, including questions and answers, which are highly recommended by us as an appropriate means of preparing for these examinations.

If you need additional information about CLEP Examinations, visit www.collegeboard.com/clep.

THE COLLEGE-LEVEL EXAMINATION PROGRAM

How The Program Works

CLEP examinations are administered at many colleges and universities across the country, and most institutions award college credit to those who do well on them. The examinations provide people who have acquired knowledge outside the usual educational settings the opportunity to show that they have learned college-level material without taking certain college courses.

The CLEP examinations cover material that is taught in introductory-level courses at many colleges and universities. Faculties at individual colleges review the tests to ensure that they cover the important material taught in their courses. Colleges differ in the examinations they accept; some colleges accept only two or three of the examinations while others accept nearly all of them.

Although CLEP is sponsored by the College Board and the examinations are scored by Educational Testing Service (ETS), neither of these organizations can award college credit. Only accredited colleges may grant credit toward a degree. When you take a CLEP examination, you may request that a copy of your score report be sent to the college you are attending or plan to attend. After evaluating your scores, the college will decide whether or not to award you credit for a certain course or courses, or to exempt you from them. If the college gives you credit, it will record the number of credits on your permanent record, thereby indicating that you have completed work equivalent to a course in that subject. If the college decides to grant exemption without giving you credit for a course, you will be permitted to omit a course that would normally be required of you and to take a course of your choice instead.

What the Examinations Are Like

The examinations consist mostly of multiple-choice questions to be answered within a 90-minute time limit. Additional information about each CLEP examination is given in the examination guide and on the CLEP website.

Where To Take the Examinations

CLEP examinations are administered throughout the year at the test centers of approximately 1,300 colleges and universities. On the CLEP website, you will find a list of institutions that award credit for satisfactory scores on CLEP examinations. Some colleges administer CLEP examinations to their own students only. Other institutions administer the tests to anyone who registers to take them. If your college does not administer the tests, contact the test centers in your area for information about its testing schedule.

Once you have been tested, your score report will be available instantly. CLEP scores are kept on file at ETS for 20 years; and during this period, for a small fee, you may have your transcript sent to another college or to anyone else you specify. (Your scores will never be sent to anyone without your approval.)

APPROACHING A COLLEGE ABOUT CLEP

The following sections provide a step-by-step approach to learning about the CLEP policy at a particular college or university. The person or office that can best assist students desiring CLEP credit may have a different title at each institution, but the following guidelines will lead you to information about CLEP at any institution.

Adults returning to college often benefit from special assistance when they approach a college. Opportunities for adults to return to formal learning in the classroom are now widespread, and colleges and universities have worked hard to make this a smooth process for older students. Many colleges have established special service offices that are staffed with trained professionals who understand the kinds of problems facing adults returning to college. If you think you might benefit from such assistance, be sure to find out whether these services are available at your college.

How to Apply for College Credit

STEP 1. Obtain the General Information Catalog and a copy of the CLEP policy from the colleges you are considering. If you have not yet applied for admission, ask for an admissions application form too.

Information about admissions and CLEP policies can be obtained by contacting college admissions offices or finding admissions information on the school websites. Tell the admissions officer that you are a prospective student and that you are interested in applying for admission and CLEP credit. Ask for a copy of the publication in which the college's complete CLEP policy is explained. Also get the name and the telephone number of the person to contact in case you have further questions about CLEP.

At this step, you may wish to obtain information from external degree colleges. Many adults find that such colleges suit their needs exceptionally well.

STEP 2. If you have not already been admitted to the college you are considering, look at its admission requirements for undergraduate students to see if you can qualify.

This is an important step because if you can't get into college, you can't get college credit for CLEP. Nearly all colleges require students to be admitted and to enroll in one or more courses before granting the students CLEP credit.

Virtually all public community colleges and a number of four-year state colleges have open admission policies for in-state students. This usually means that they admit anyone who has graduated from high school or has earned a high school equivalency diploma.

If you think you do not meet the admission requirements, contact the admissions office for an interview with a counselor. Colleges do sometimes make exceptions, particularly for adult applicants. State why you want the interview and ask what documents you should bring with you or send in advance. (These materials may include a high school transcript, transcript of previous college work, completed application for admission, etc.) Make an extra effort to have all the information requested in time for the interview.

During the interview, relax and be yourself. Be prepared to state honestly why you think you are ready and able to do college work. If you have already taken CLEP examinations and scored high enough to earn credit, you have shown that you are able to do college work. Mention this achievement to the admissions counselor because it may increase your chances of being accepted. If you have not taken a CLEP examination, you can still improve your chances of being accepted by describing how your job training or independent study has helped prepare you for college-level work. Tell the counselor what you have learned from your work and personal experiences.

STEP 3. Evaluate the college's CLEP policy.

Typically, a college lists all its academic policies, including CLEP policies, in its general catalog. You will probably find the CLEP policy statement under a heading such as Credit-by-Examination, Advanced Standing, Advanced Placement, or External Degree Program. These sections can usually be found in the front of the catalog.

Many colleges publish their credit-by-examination policies in a separate brochure, which is distributed through the campus testing office, counseling center, admissions office, or registrar's office. If you find a very general policy statement in the college catalog, seek clarification from one of these offices.

Review the material in the section of this guide entitled Questions to Ask About a College's CLEP Policy. Use these guidelines to evaluate the college's CLEP policy. If you have not yet taken a CLEP examination, this evaluation will help you decide which examinations to take and whether or not to take the free-response or essay portion. Because individual colleges have different CLEP policies, a review of several policies may help you decide which college to attend.

STEP 4. If you have not yet applied for admission, do so early.

Most colleges expect you to apply for admission several months before you enroll, and it is essential that you meet the published application deadlines. It takes time to process your application for admission; and if you have yet to take a CLEP examination, it will be some time before the college receives and reviews your score report. You will probably want to take some, if not all, of the CLEP examinations you are interested in before you enroll so you know which courses you need not register for. In fact, some colleges require that all CLEP scores be submitted before a student registers.

Complete all forms and include all documents requested with your application(s) for admission. Normally, an admissions decision cannot be reached until all documents have been submitted and evaluated. Unless told to do so, do not send your CLEP scores until you have been officially admitted.

STEP 5. Arrange to take CLEP examination(s) or to submit your CLEP score(s).

You may want to wait to take your CLEP examinations until you know definitely which college you will be attending. Then you can make sure you are taking tests your college will accept for credit. You will also be able to request that your scores be sent to the college, free of charge, when you take the tests.

If you have already taken CLEP examinations, but did not have a copy of your score report sent to your college, you may request the College Board to send an official transcript at any time for a small fee. Use the Transcript Request Form that was sent to you with your score report. If you do not have the form, you may find it online at www.collegeboard.com/clep.

Your CLEP scores will be evaluated, probably by someone in the admissions office, and sent to the registrar's office to be posted on your permanent record once you are enrolled. Procedures vary from college to college, but the process usually begins in the admissions office.

STEP 6. Ask to receive a written notice of the credit you receive for your CLEP score(s).

A written notice may save you problems later, when you submit your degree plan or file for graduation. In the event that there is a question about whether or not you earned CLEP credit, you will have an official record of what credit was awarded. You may also need this verification of course credit if you go for academic counseling before the credit is posted on your permanent record.

STEP 7. Before you register for courses, seek academic counseling.

A discussion with your academic advisor can prevent you from taking unnecessary courses and can tell you specifically what your CLEP credit will mean to you. This step may be accomplished at the time you enroll. Most colleges have orientation sessions for new students prior to each enrollment period. During orientation, students are usually assigned an academic advisor who then gives them individual help in developing long-range plans and a course schedule for the next semester. In conjunction with this counseling, you may be asked to take some additional tests so that you can be placed at the proper course level.

External Degree Programs

If you have acquired a considerable amount of college-level knowledge through job experience, reading, or noncredit courses, if you have accumulated college credits at a variety of colleges over a period of years, or if you prefer studying on your own rather than in a classroom setting, you may want to investigate the possibility of enrolling in an external degree program. Many colleges offer external degree programs that allow you to earn a degree by passing examinations (including CLEP), transferring credit from other colleges, and demonstrating in other ways that you have satisfied the educational requirements. No classroom attendance is required, and the programs are open to out-of-state candidates as well as residents. Thomas A. Edison State College in New Jersey and Charter Oaks College in Connecticut are fully accredited independent state colleges; the New York program is part of the state university system and is also fully accredited. If you are interested in exploring an external degree, you can write for more information to:

Charter Oak College
The Exchange, Suite 171
270 Farmington Avenue
Farmington, CT 06032-1909

Regents External Degree Program
Cultural Education Center
Empire State Plaza
Albany, New York 12230

Thomas A. Edison State College
101 West State Street
Trenton, New Jersey 08608

Many other colleges also have external degree or weekend programs. While they often require that a number of courses be taken on campus, the external degree programs tend to be more flexible in transferring credit, granting credit-by-examination, and allowing independent study than other traditional programs. When applying to a college, you may wish to ask whether it has an external degree or weekend program.

Questions to Ask About a College's CLEP Policy

Before taking CLEP examinations for the purpose of earning college credit, try to find the answers to these questions:

1. Which CLEP examinations are accepted by this college?

A college may accept some CLEP examinations for credit and not others - possibly not the one you are considering. The English faculty may decide to grant college English credit based on the CLEP English Composition examination, but not on the Freshman College Composition examination. Or, the mathematics faculty may decide to grant credit based on the College Mathematics to non-mathematics majors only, requiring majors to take an examination in algebra, trigonometry, or calculus to earn credit. For these reasons, it is important that you know the specific CLEP tests for which you can receive credit.

2. Does the college require the optional free-response (essay) section as well as the objective portion of the CLEP examination you are considering?

Knowing the answer to this question ahead of time will permit you to schedule the optional essay examination when you register to take your CLEP examination.

3. Is credit granted for specific courses? If so, which ones?

You are likely to find that credit will be granted for specific courses and the course titles will be designated in the college's CLEP policy. It is not necessary, however, that credit be granted for a specific course in order for you to benefit from your CLEP credit. For instance, at many liberal arts colleges, all students must take certain types of courses; these courses may be labeled the core curriculum, general education requirements, distribution requirements, or liberal arts requirements. The requirements are often expressed in terms of credit hours. For example, all students may be required to take at least six hours of humanities, six hours of English, three hours of mathematics, six hours of natural science, and six hours of social science, with no particular courses in these disciplines specified. In these instances, CLEP credit may be given as 6 hrs. English credit or 3 hrs. Math credit without specifying for which English or mathematics courses credit has been awarded. In order to avoid possible disappointment, you should know before taking a CLEP examination what type of credit you can receive and whether you will only be exempted from a required course but receive no credit.

4. How much credit is granted for each examination you are considering, and does the college place a limit on the total amount of CLEP credit you can earn toward your degree?

Not all colleges that grant CLEP credit award the same amount for individual tests. Furthermore, some colleges place a limit on the total amount of credit you can earn through CLEP or other examinations. Other colleges may grant you exemption but no credit toward your degree. Knowing several colleges' policies concerning these issues may help you decide which college you will attend. If you think you are capable of passing a number of CLEP examinations, you may want to attend a college that will allow you to earn credit for all or most of them. For example, the state external degree programs grant credit for most CLEP examinations (and other tests as well).

5. What is the required score for earning CLEP credit for each test you are considering?

Most colleges publish the required scores or percentile ranks for earning CLEP credit in their general catalog or in a brochure. The required score may vary from test to test, so find out the required score for each test you are considering.

6. What is the college's policy regarding prior course work in the subject in which you are considering taking a CLEP test?

Some colleges will not grant credit for a CLEP test if the student has already attempted a college-level course closely aligned with that test. For example, if you successfully completed English 101 or a comparable course on another campus, you will probably not be permitted to receive CLEP credit in that subject, too. Some colleges will not permit you to earn CLEP credit for a course that you failed.

7. Does the college make additional stipulations before credit will be granted?

It is common practice for colleges to award CLEP credit only to their enrolled students. There are other stipulations, however, that vary from college to college. For example, does the college require you to formally apply for or accept CLEP credit by completing and signing a form? Or does the college require you to validate your CLEP score by successfully completing a more advanced course in the subject? Answers to these and other questions will help to smooth the process of earning college credit through CLEP.

The above questions and the discussions that follow them indicate some of the ways in which colleges' CLEP policies can vary. Find out as much as possible about the CLEP policies at the colleges you are interested in so you can choose a college with a policy that is compatible with your educational goals. Once you have selected the college you will attend, you can find out which CLEP examinations your college recognizes and the requirements for earning CLEP credit.

DECIDING WHICH EXAMINATIONS TO TAKE

If You're Taking the Examinations for College Credit or Career Advancement:

Most people who take CLEP examinations do so in order to earn credit for college courses. Others take the examinations in order to qualify for job promotions or for professional certification or licensing. It is vital to most candidates who are taking the tests for any of these reasons that they be well prepared for the tests they are taking so that they can advance as rapidly as possible toward their educational or career goals.

It is usually advisable that those who have limited knowledge in the subjects covered by the tests they are considering enroll in the college courses in which that material is taught. Those who are uncertain about whether or not they know enough about a subject to do well on a particular CLEP test will find the following guidelines helpful.

There is no way to predict if you will pass a particular CLEP examination, but answers to the questions under the seven headings below should give you an indication of whether or not you are likely to succeed.

1. Test Descriptions

Read the description of the test provided. Are you familiar with most of the topics and terminology in the outline?

2. Textbooks

Examine the suggested textbooks and other resource materials following the test descriptions in this guide. Have you recently read one or more of these books, or have you read similar college-level books on this subject? If you have not, read through one or more of the textbooks listed, or through the textbook used for this course at your college. Are you familiar with most of the topics and terminology in the book?

3. Sample Questions

The sample questions provided are intended to be typical of the content and difficulty of the questions on the test. Although they are not an exact miniature of the test, the proportion of the sample questions you can answer correctly should be a rough estimate of the proportion of questions you will be able to answer correctly on the test.

Answer as many of the sample questions for this test as you can. Check your answers against the correct answers. Did you answer more than half the questions correctly?

Because of variations in course content at different institutions, and because questions on CLEP tests vary from easy to difficult - with most being of moderate difficulty - the average student who passes a course in a subject can usually answer correctly about half the questions on the corresponding CLEP examination. Most colleges set their passing scores near this level, but some set them higher. If your college has set its required score above the level required by most colleges, you may need to answer a larger proportion of questions on the test correctly.

4. Previous Study

Have you taken noncredit courses in this subject offered by an adult school or a private school, through correspondence, or in connection with your job? Did you do exceptionally well in this subject in high school, or did you take an honors course in this subject?

5. Experience

Have you learned or used the knowledge or skills included in this test in your job or life experience? For example, if you lived in a Spanish-speaking country and spoke the language for a year or more, you might consider taking the Spanish examination. Or, if you have worked at a job in which you used accounting and finance skills, Principles of Accounting would be a likely test for you to take. Or, if you have read a considerable amount of literature and attended many art exhibits, concerts, and plays, you might expect to do well on the Humanities exam.

6. Other Examinations

Have you done well on other standardized tests in subjects related to the one you want to take? For example, did you score well above average on a portion of a college entrance examination covering similar skills, or did you obtain an exceptionally high score on a high school equivalency test or a licensing examination in this subject? Although such tests do not cover exactly the same material as the CLEP examinations and may be easier, persons who do well on these tests often do well on CLEP examinations, too.

7. Advice

Has a college counselor, professor, or some other professional person familiar with your ability advised you to take a CLEP examination?

If your answer was yes to questions under several of the above headings, you probably have a good chance of passing the CLEP examination you are considering. It is unlikely that you would have acquired sufficient background from experience alone. Learning gained through reading and study is essential, and you will probably find some additional study helpful before taking a CLEP examination.

If You're Taking the Examinations to Prepare for College

Many people entering college, particularly adults returning to college after several years away from formal education, are uncertain about their ability to compete with other college students. They wonder whether they have sufficient background for college study, and those who have been away from formal study for some time wonder whether they have forgotten how to study, how to take tests, and how to write papers. Such people may wish to improve their test-taking and study skills prior to enrolling in courses.

One way to assess your ability to perform at the college level and to improve your test-taking and study skills at the same time is to prepare for and take one or more CLEP examinations. You need not be enrolled in a college to take a CLEP examination, and you may have your scores sent only to yourself and later request that a transcript be sent to a college if you then decide to apply for credit. By reviewing the test descriptions and sample questions, you may find one or several subject areas in which you think you have substantial knowledge. Select one examination, or more if you like, and carefully read at least one of the textbooks listed in the bibliography for the test. By doing this, you will get a better idea of how much you know of what is usually taught in a college-level course in that subject. Study as much material as you can, until you think you have a good grasp of the subject matter. Then take the test at a college in your area. It will be several weeks before you receive your results, and you may wish to begin reviewing for another test in the meantime.

To find out if you are eligible for credit for your CLEP score, you must compare your score with the score required by the college you plan to attend. If you are not yet sure which college you will attend, or whether you will enroll in college at all, you should begin to follow the steps outlined. It is best that you do this before taking a CLEP test, but if you are taking the test only for the experience and to familiarize yourself with college-level material and requirements, you might take the test before you approach a college. Even if the college you decide to attend does not accept the test you took, the experience of taking such a test will enable you to meet with greater confidence the requirements of courses you will take.

You will find information about how to interpret your scores in WHAT YOUR SCORES MEAN, which you will receive with your score report, and which can also be found online at the CLEP website. Many colleges follow the recommendations of the American Council on Education (ACE) for setting their required scores, so you can use this information as a guide in determining how well you did. The ACE recommendations are included in the booklet.

If you do not do well enough on the test to earn college credit, don't be discouraged. Usually, it is the best college students who are exempted from courses or receive credit-by-examination. The fact that you cannot get credit for your score means that you should probably enroll in a college course to learn the material. However, if your score was close to the required score, or if you feel you could do better on a second try or after some additional study, you may retake the test after six months. Do not take it sooner or your score will not be reported and your fee will be forfeited.

If you do earn the score required to earn credit, you will have demonstrated that you already have some college-level knowledge. You will also have a better idea whether you should take additional CLEP examinations. And, what is most important, you can enroll in college with confidence, knowing that you do have the ability to succeed.

PREPARING TO TAKE CLEP EXAMINATIONS

Having made the decision to take one or more CLEP examinations, most people then want to know if it is worthwhile to prepare for them - how much, how long, when, and how should they go about it? The precise answers to these questions vary greatly from individual to individual. However, most candidates find that some type of test preparation is helpful.

Most people who take CLEP examinations do so to show that they have already learned the important material that is taught in a college course. Many of them need only a quick review to assure themselves that they have not forgotten some of what they once studied, and to fill in some of the gaps in their knowledge of the subject. Others feel that they need a thorough review and spend several weeks studying for a test. A few wish to take a CLEP examination as a kind of final examination for independent study of a subject instead of the college course. This last group requires significantly more study than those who only need to review, and they may need some guidance from professors of the subjects they are studying.

The key to how you prepare for CLEP examinations often lies in locating those skills and areas of prior learning in which you are strong and deciding where to focus your energies. Some people may know a great deal about a certain subject area, but may not test well. These individuals would probably be just as concerned about strengthening their test-taking skills as they are about studying for a specific test. Many mental and physical skills are used in preparing for a test. It is important not only to review or study for the examinations, but to make certain that you are alert, relatively free of anxiety, and aware of how to approach standardized tests. Suggestions on developing test-taking skills and preparing psychologically and physically for a test are given. The following section suggests ways of assessing your knowledge of the content of a test and then reviewing and studying the material.

Using This Study Guide

Begin by carefully reading the test description and outline of knowledge and skills required for the examination, if given. As you read through the topics listed there, ask yourself how much you know about each one. Also note the terms, names, and symbols that are mentioned, and ask yourself whether you are familiar with them. This will give you a quick overview of how much you know about the subject. If you are familiar with nearly all the material, you will probably need a minimum of review; however, if less than half of it is familiar, you will probably require substantial study to do well on the test.

If, after reviewing the test description, you find that you need extensive review, delay answering the sample question until you have done some reading in the subject. If you complete them before reviewing the material, you will probably look for the answers as you study, and then they will not be a good assessment of your ability at a later date.

If you think you are familiar with most of the test material, try to answer the sample questions.

Apply the test-taking strategies given. Keeping within the time limit suggested will give you a rough idea of how quickly you should work in order to complete the actual test.

Check your answers against the answer key. If you answered nearly all the questions correctly, you probably do not need to study the subject extensively. If you got about half the questions correct, you ought o review at least one textbook or other suggested materials on the subject. If you answered less than half the questions correctly, you will probably benefit from more extensive reading in the subject and thorough study of one or more textbooks. The textbooks listed are used at many colleges but they are not the only good texts. You will find helpful almost any standard text available to you., such as the textbook used at your college, or earlier editions of texts listed. For some examinations, topic outlines and textbooks may not be available. Take the sample tests in this book and check your answers at the end of each test. Check wrong answers.

Suggestions for Studying

The following suggestions have been gathered from people who have prepared for CLEP examinations or other college-level tests.

1. Define your goals and locate study materials

First, determine your study goals. Set aside a block of time to review the material provided in this book, and then decide which test(s) you will take. Using the suggestions, locate suitable resource materials. If a preparation course is offered by an adult school or college in your area, you might find it helpful to enroll.

2. Find a good place to study

To determine what kind of place you need for studying, ask yourself questions such as: Do I need a quiet place? Does the telephone distract me? Do objects I see in this place remind me of things I should do? Is it too warm? Is it well lit? Am I too comfortable here? Do I have space to spread out my materials? You may find the library more conducive to studying than your home. If you decide to study at home, you might prevent interruptions by other household members by putting a sign on the door of your study room to indicate when you will be available.

3. Schedule time to study

To help you determine where studying best fits into your schedule, try this exercise: Make a list of your daily activities (for example, sleeping, working, and eating) and estimate how many hours per day you spend on each activity. Now, rate all the activities on your list in order of their importance and evaluate your use of time. Often people are astonished at how an average day appears from this perspective. They may discover that they were unaware how large portions of time are spent, or they learn their time can be scheduled in alternative ways. For example, they can remove the least important activities from their day and devote that time to studying or another important activity.

4. Establish a study routine and a set of goals

In order to study effectively, you should establish specific goals and a schedule for accomplishing them. Some people find it helpful to write out a weekly schedule and cross out each study period when it is completed. Others maintain their concentration better by writing down the time when they expect to complete a study task. Most people find short periods of intense study more productive than long stretches of time. For example, they may follow a regular schedule of several 20- or 30-minute study periods with short breaks between them. Some people like to allow themselves rewards as they complete each study goal. It is not essential that you accomplish every goal exactly within your schedule; the point is to be committed to your task.

5. Learn how to take an active role in studying.

If you have not done much studying for some time, you may find it difficult to concentrate at first. Try a method of studying, such as the one outlined below, that will help you concentrate on and remember what you read.

    a. First, read the chapter summary and the introduction. Then you will know what to look for in your reading.

    b. Next, convert the section or paragraph headlines into questions. For example, if you are reading a section entitled, The Causes of the American Revolution, ask yourself: *What were the causes of the American Revolution?* Compose the answer as you read the paragraph. Reading and answering questions aloud will help you understand and remember the material.

    c. Take notes on key ideas or concepts as you read. Writing will also help you fix concepts more firmly in your mind. Underlining key ideas or writing notes in your book can be helpful and will be useful for review. Underline only important points. If you underline more than a third of each paragraph, you are probably underlining too much.

    d. If there are questions or problems at the end of a chapter, answer or solve them on paper as if you were asked to do them for homework. Mathematics textbooks (and some other books) sometimes include answers to some or all of the exercises. If you have such a book, write your answers before looking at the ones given. When problem-solving is involved, work enough problems to master the required methods and concepts. If you have difficulty with problems, review any sample problems or explanations in the chapter.

    e. To retain knowledge, most people have to review the material periodically. If you are preparing for a test over an extended period of time, review key concepts and notes each week or so. Do not wait for weeks to review the material or you will need to relearn much of it.

Psychological and Physical Preparation

Most people feel at least some nervousness before taking a test. Adults who are returning to college may not have taken a test in many years or they may have had little experience with standardized tests. Some younger students, as well, are uncomfortable with testing situations. People who received their education in countries outside the United States may find that many tests given in this country are quite different from the ones they are accustomed to taking.

Not only might candidates find the types of tests and the kinds of questions on them unfamiliar, but other aspects of the testing environment may be strange as well. The physical and mental stress that results from meeting this new experience can hinder a candidate's ability to demonstrate his or her true degree of knowledge in the subject area being tested. For this reason, it is important to go to the test center well prepared, both mentally and physically, for taking the test. You may find the following suggestions helpful.

1. Familiarize yourself, as much as possible, with the test and the test situation before the day of the examination. It will be helpful for you to know ahead of time:

    a. How much time will be allowed for the test and whether there are timed subsections.

    b. What types of questions and directions appear on the examination.

    c. How your test score will be computed.

    d. How to properly answer the questions on the computer (See the CLEP Sample on the CLEP website)

e. In which building and room the examination will be administered. If you don't know where the building is, locate it or get directions ahead of time.

f. The time of the test administration. You might wish to confirm this information a day or two before the examination and find out what time the building and room will be open so that you can plan to arrive early.

g. Where to park your car or, if you wish to take public transportation, which bus or train to take and the location of the nearest stop.

h. Whether smoking will be permitted during the test.

i. Whether there will be a break between examinations (if you will be taking more than one on the same day), and whether there is a place nearby where you can get something to eat or drink.

2. Go to the test situation relaxed and alert. In order to prepare for the test:

a. Get a good night's sleep. Last minute cramming, particularly late the night before, is usually counterproductive.

b. Eat normally. It is usually not wise to skip breakfast or lunch on the day of the test or to eat a big meal just before the test.

c. Avoid tranquilizers and stimulants. If you follow the other directions in this book, you won't need artificial aids. It's better to be a little tense than to be drowsy, but stimulants such as coffee and cola can make you nervous and interfere with your concentration.

d. Don't drink a lot of liquids before the test. Having to leave the room during the test will disturb your concentration and take valuable time away from the test.

e. If you are inclined to be nervous or tense, learn some relaxation exercises and use them before and perhaps during the test.

3. Arrive for the test early and prepared. Be sure to:

a. Arrive early enough so that you can find a parking place, locate the test center, and get settled comfortably before testing begins. Allow some extra time in case you are delayed unexpectedly.

b. Take the following with you:

- Your completed Registration/Admission Form
- Two forms of identification – one being a government-issued photo ID with signature, such as a driver's license or passport
- Non-mechanical pencil
- A watch so that you can time your progress (digital watches are prohibited)
- Your glasses if you need them for reading or seeing the chalkboard or wall clock

      c. Leave all books, papers, and notes outside the test center. You will not be permitted to use your own scratch paper; it will be provided. Also prohibited are calculators, cell phones, beepers, pagers, photo/copy devices, radios, headphones, food, beverages, and several other items.

      d. Be prepared for any temperature in the testing room. Wear layers of clothing that can be removed if the room is too hot but will keep you warm if it is too cold.

4. When you enter the test room:

      a. Sit in a seat that provides a maximum of comfort and freedom from distraction.

      b. Read directions carefully, and listen to all instructions given by the test administrator. If you don't understand the directions, ask for help before test timing begins. If you must ask a question after the test has begun, raise your hand and a proctor will assist you. The proctor can answer certain kinds of questions but cannot help you with the test.

      c. Know your rights as a test taker. You can expect to be given the full working time allowed for the test(s) and a reasonably quiet and comfortable place in which to work. If a poor test situation is preventing you from doing your best, ask if the situation can be remedied. If bad test conditions cannot be remedied, ask the person in charge to report the problem in the Irregularity Report that will be sent to ETS with the answer sheets. You may also wish to contact CLEP. Describe the exact circumstances as completely as you can. Be sure to include the test date and name(s) of the test(s) you took. ETS will investigate the problem to make sure it does not happen again, and, if the problem is serious enough, may arrange for you to retake the test without charge.

TAKING THE EXAMINATIONS

A person may know a great deal about the subject being tested, but not do as well as he or she is capable of on the test. Knowing how to approach a test is an important part of the testing process. While a command of test-taking skills cannot substitute for knowledge of the subject matter, it can be a significant factor in successful testing.

Test-taking skills enable a person to use all available information to earn a score that truly reflects his or her ability. There are different strategies for approaching different kinds of test questions. For example, free-response questions require a very different tack than do multiple-choice questions. Other factors, such as how the test will be graded, may also influence your approach to the test and your use of test time. Thus, your preparation for a test should include finding out all you can about the test so that you can use the most effective test-taking strategies.

Before taking a test, you should know approximately how many questions are on the test, how much time you will be allowed, how the test will be scored or graded, what types of questions and directions are on the test, and how you will be required to record your answers.

Taking Multiple-Choice Tests

1. Listen carefully to the instructions given by the test administrator and read carefully all directions before you begin to answer the questions.

2. Note the time that the test administrator starts timing the test. As you proceed, make sure that you are not working too slowly. You should have answered at least half the questions in a section when half the time for that section has passed. If you have not reached that point in the section, speed up your pace on the remaining questions.

3. Before answering a question, read the entire question, including all the answer choices. Don't think that because the first or second answer choice looks good to you, it isn't necessary to read the remaining options. Instructions usually tell you to select the best answer. Sometimes one answer choice is partially correct, but another option is better; therefore, it is usually a good idea to read all the answers before you choose one.

4. Read and consider every question. Questions that look complicated at first glance may not actually be so difficult once you have read them carefully.

5. Do not puzzle too long over any one question. If you don't know the answer after you've considered it briefly, go on to the next question. Make sure you return to the question later.

6. Make sure you record your response properly.

7. In trying to determine the correct answer, you may find it helpful to cross out those options that you know are incorrect, and to make marks next to those you think might be correct. If you decide to skip the question and come back to it later, you will save yourself the time of reconsidering all the options.

8. Watch for the following key words in test questions:

all	generally	never	perhaps
always	however	none	rarely
but	may	not	seldom
except	must	often	sometimes
every	necessary	only	usually

When a question or answer option contains words such as always, every, only, never, and none, there can be no exceptions to the answer you choose. Use of words such as often, rarely, sometimes, and generally indicates that there may be some exceptions to the answer.

9. Do not waste your time looking for clues to right answers based on flaws in question wording or patterns in correct answers. Professionals at the College Board and ETS put

a great deal of effort into developing valid, reliable, fair tests. CLEP test development committees are composed of college faculty who are experts in the subject covered by the test and are appointed by the College Board to write test questions and to scrutinize each question that is included on a CLEP test. Committee members make every effort to ensure that the questions are not ambiguous, that they have only one correct answer, and that they cover college-level topics. These committees do not intentionally include trick questions. If you think a question is flawed, ask the test administrator to report it, or contact CLEP immediately.

Taking Free-Response or Essay Tests

If your college requires the optional free-response or essay portion of a CLEP Composition and Literature exams, you should do some additional preparation for your CLEP test. Taking an essay test is very different from taking a multiple-choice test, so you will need to use some other strategies.

The essay written as part of the English Composition and Essay exam is graded by English professors from a variety of colleges and universities. A process called holistic scoring is used to rate your writing ability.

The optional free-response essays, on the other hand, are graded by the faculty of the college you designate as a score recipient. Guidelines and criteria for grading essays are not specified by the College Board or ETS. You may find it helpful, therefore, to talk with someone at your college to find out what criteria will be used to determine whether you will get credit. If the test requires essay responses, ask how much emphasis will be placed on your writing ability and your ability to organize your thoughts as opposed to your knowledge of subject matter. Find out how much weight will be given to your multiple-choice test score in comparison with your free-response grade in determining whether you will get credit. This will give you an idea where you should expend the greatest effort in preparing for and taking the test.

Here are some strategies you will find useful in taking any essay test:

1. Before you begin to write, read all questions carefully and take a few minutes to jot down some ideas you might include in each answer.

2. If you are given a choice of questions to answer, choose the questions you think you can answer most clearly and knowledgeably.

3. Determine in what order you will answer the questions. Answer those you find the easiest first so that any extra time can be spent on the more difficult questions.

4. When you know which questions you will answer and in what order, determine how much testing time remains and estimate how many minutes you will devote to each question. Unless suggested times are given for the questions or one question appears to require more or less time than the others, allot an equal amount of time to each question.

5. Before answering each question, indicate the number of the question as it is given in the test book. You need not copy the entire question from the question sheet, but it will be helpful to you and to the person grading your test if you indicate briefly the topic you are addressing – particularly if you are not answering the questions in the order in which they appear on the test.

6. Before answering each question, read it again carefully to make sure you are interpreting it correctly. Underline key words, such as those listed below, that often appear in free-response questions. Be sure you know the exact meaning of these words before taking the test.

analyze	demonstrate	enumerate	list
apply	derive	explain	outline
assess	describe	generalize	prove
compare	determine	illustrate	rank
contrast	discuss	interpret	show
define	distinguish	justify	summarize

If a question asks you to outline, define, or summarize, do not write a detailed explanation; if a question asks you to analyze, explain, illustrate, interpret, or show, you must do more than briefly describe the topic.

For a current listing of CLEP Colleges

where you can get credit and be tested, write:

CLEP, P.O. Box 6600, Princeton, NJ 08541-6600

Or e-mail: clep@ets.org, or call: (609) 771-7865

AMERICAN HISTORY I

EARLY COLONIZATIONS TO 1877

DESCRIPTION OF THE TEST

The Subject Examination in American History I: Early Colonization's to 1877 covers material that is usually taught in the first semester of what is often a two-semester course in American history. The examination covers the period of American history from the Spanish and French colonization's to the end of Reconstruction, with the majority of questions on the period of nationhood. In the seventeenth and eighteenth centuries, stress is placed on the English colonies.

There are approximately 120 multiple-choice questions on the 90-minute test, to be answered in two separately timed 45-minute sections.

KNOWLEDGE AND SKILLS REQUIRED

The major topics covered by the examination are:

Approximate Percent of Examination

- 50% Political institutions and behavior and public policy
- 20% Social and economic change
- 20% Cultural and intellectual developments
- 10% Diplomacy and international relations

About one-third of the questions deal with the period from 1500 to 1789, and about two-thirds are on the period from 1790 to 1877. The following are among the specific topics tested:

The character of Colonial society
British relations with the Atlantic colonies in North America
The motivations and character of American expansionism
The content of the Constitution and its amendments, and their interpretation by the Supreme Court
The growth of political parties
The changing role of government in American life
The intellectual and political expressions of nationalism Agrarianism, abolitionism, and other such movements
Long-term demographic trends
The process of economic growth and development
The origins and nature of Black slavery in America
Immigration and the history of racial and ethnic minorities
The causes and impacts of major wars in American history
Major movements and individual figures in the history of American arts and letters

Questions on the test require candidates to demonstrate the following abilities, which generally require knowledge of history before they can be exercised. Some questions may require more than one of the abilities.

- Identification and description of historical phenomena (about 45 percent of the examination)
- Characterization and classification of historical phenomena (about 15 percent of the examination)
- Analysis and interpretation of historical phenomena (about 10 percent of the examination)
- Comparison and contrast of historical phenomena (about 10 percent of the examination)
- Explanation and evaluation of historical phenomena (about 20 percent of the examination)

SAMPLE QUESTIONS

The 25 sample questions given here are similar to questions on the American History I examination, but they do not actually appear on the examination.

Before attempting to answer the sample questions, read all the information about the American History I examination given above.

Try to answer correctly as many of the questions as possible within 20 minutes. Then compare your answers with the correct answers on the last page.

Directions: Each of the questions or incomplete statements below is followed by five suggested answers or completions. Select the one that is BEST in each case.

1. The Louisiana Purchase was significant because it
   A. eliminated Spain from the North American continent
   B. gave the United States control of the Mississippi River
   C. eased tensions between Western settlers and Native Americans (Indians)
   D. forced the British to evacuate their posts in the Northwest
   E. reduced sectional conflict over the slavery issue

2. The presidential election of 1840 is often considered the first *modern* election because
   A. the slavery issue was first raised in this campaign
   B. there was a very low turnout of eligible voters
   C. voting patterns were similar to those later established in the 1890's
   D. both parties for the first time widely campaigned among all the eligible voters
   E. a second era of good feeling had just come to a close, marking a new departure in politics

3. In a sermon given aboard ship on the way to America, John Winthrop told the Puritans that their society would be regarded as *a city upon a hill* and that therefore they should be bonded together by love. But first he explained that there would always be inequalities of wealth and power, that some people would always be in positions of authority while others would be dependent.
   His statements BEST illustrate the Puritans'
   A. reaction to unsuccessful socialist experiments in the Low Countries
   B. acceptance of the traditional belief that order depended on a system of ranks
   C. intention to vest political power exclusively in the ministers
   D. desire to better themselves economically through means that included the institution of slavery
   E. inability to take clear stands on social issues

4. The issue of constitutionality figures MOST prominently in the consideration of which of the following?   4.____
    A. Tariff of 1789
    B. First Bank of the United States
    C. Funding of the national debt
    D. Assumption of state debts
    E. Excise tax on whiskey

5. If a man who had visited the United States in the 1830's had written, *unmarried women in America were unusually emancipated*, you would probably give the MOST credence to his judgment about American women if you also found that   5.____
    A. modern social psychologists contend that America is a *feminine* culture
    B. middle—class women in the 1830's were increasingly attracted to the cult of true womanhood
    C. other travelers in the 1830's who came from many different nations had come to the same conclusion as the author
    D. other travelers in the 1830's who came from the same nation as the author had come to the same conclusion
    E. the first suffragist newspaper had been founded in the 1830's

6. The idea of Manifest Destiny included all of the following EXCEPT the belief that   6.____
    A. commerce and industry would decline as the nation expanded its agriculture base
    B. the use of land for settled agriculture was preferable to its use for nomadic hunting
    C. westward expansion was both inevitable and beneficial
    D. God selected America as a chosen land
    E. the ultimate extent of the American domain was to be from the tropics to the Arctic

7. At the end of the Civil War, the vast majority of freed slaves found work as   7.____
    A. factory workers
    B. railroad employees
    C. independent craftsmen
    D. tenant farmers
    E. domestic servants

8. England defeated a major rival prior to England's successful effort to colonize the New World. England also defeated another major rival just prior to losing many of its colonies in the New World.
England's rivals were FIRST   8.____
    A. France, then the United States
    B. Spain; then France
    C. France, then Holland
    D. France, then Spain
    E. Portugal, then Spain

VOLUME OF AMERICAN COLONIES' EXPORTS TO ENGLAND AND IMPORTS FROM ENGLAND (VALUE IN POUNDS STERLING)

Year	New England		New York		Pennsylvania		Virginia and Maryland		Carolina	
	Exports	Imports	Exports	Imports	Exports	Imports	Exports	Imports	Exports	Imports
1743	63,185	172,461	15,067	135,487	9,596	79,340	557,821	328,195	235,136	111,499
1742	53,166	148,899	13,536	167,591	8,527	75,295	427,769	264,186	154,607	127,063
1741	60,052	198.147	21,142	140,430	17,158	91,010	577,109	248,582	236,830	204,770
1740	72,389	171,081	21,498	118,777	15,048	56,751	341,997	281,428	266,560	181,821

9. According to eighteenth-century theories of mercantilism, and in light of England's pattern of trade with America as shown in the chart above, England's MOST valuable colony or group of colonies was which of the following?
    A. New England
    B. New York
    C. Pennsylvania
    D. Virginia and Maryland
    E. Carolina

10. Under the Articles of Confederation, which of the following was TRUE about the national government? It
    A. had the power to conduct foreign affairs
    B. had the power to regulate commerce
    C. had the power to tax
    D. included a President
    E. included a federal judiciary

11. Henry Clay's *American System* was a plan to
    A. compromise the issue of extending slavery to new United States territories
    B. foster the economic integration of the North, West, and South
    C. export American political and economic values to oppressed peoples
    D. maintain American noninvolvement in the internal affairs of Europe
    E. assert the right of states to nullify decisions of the national government

12. Which of the following represents William Lloyd Garrison's attitude toward slavery?
    A. Immediate emancipation with compensation for owners
    B. Immediate emancipation and resettlement in the Southwest
    C. Gradual emancipation without compensation for owners
    D. Immediate emancipation and resettlement in Liberia
    E. Immediate emancipation without compensation for owners

13. Which of the following was NOT an element of the Compromise of 1850?
    A. A stronger fugitive slave law
    B. Abolition of the slave trade in Washington, D.C.
    C. Admittance of California as a free state
    D. Organization of the Kansas Territory without slavery
    E. Adjustment of the Texas-New Mexico boundary

14. The 1850's have been called the *American Renaissance* because of the important literary works that appeared in that decade.
    Included among these works are all of the following EXCEPT
    A. Herman Melville's MOBY DICK
    B. Nathaniel Hawthorne's THE SCARLET LETTER
    C. Mark Twain's HUCKLEBERRY FINN
    D. Walt Whitman's LEAVES OF GRASS
    E. Henry David Thoreau's WALDEN

Questions 15-16 refer to the following cartoon.

15. According to the cartoon above, allowing the Southern states to leave the Union would cause
    A. the North to be threatened by internal dissension
    B. the Democratic party to collapse
    C. the Southern states to be dominated by European powers
    D. the Confederacy to expand into Latin America
    E. President Buchanan to be impeached and removed

16. The BEST evidence that Hickory (Jackson) would have acted whereas Buck (Buchanan) would not consists PRIMARILY of Jackson's reaction to the
    A. election of John Quincy Adams to the presidency
    B. Spanish and Native American (Indian) border attacks on Florida
    C. South Carolina Nullification Ordinance
    D. requests for annexation of Texas
    E. Maysville Road Bill

17. The Great Awakening in the American colonies in the mid-eighteenth century had all of the following consequences EXCEPT
    A. separatism and secession from established churches, due to the democratizing effect of more accessible forms of piety
    B. the renewed persecution of witches, because of the heightened interest in the supernatural
    C. the growth of institutions of higher learning to fulfill the need for more ministers to spread the gospel
    D. a flourishing of the missionary spirit as an outgrowth of more intensive religious devotion and assurance
    E. the lessening of doctrinal rigor and a concomitant appreciation for the more direct experiences of faith

18. The Embargo Act of 1807 had which of the following effects on the United States? It
    A. improved the balance of trade
    B. enriched many cotton plantation owners
    C. ruined American shipping
    D. was ruinous to subsistence farmers
    E. had little economic impact

    18.____

19. Of the following, the MOST important foreign affairs issue that faced the United States between the enunciation of the Monroe Doctrine (1823) and the Civil War (1861) was
    A. the problem of the Canadian fisheries
    B. reopening the British West Indies to direct trade with the United States
    C. securing international recognition
    D. defining the nation's northern and southern boundaries
    E. Cuban independence

    19.____

20. *Upon these considerations, it is the opinion of the court that the act of Congress which prohibited a citizen from holding and owning property of this kind in the territory of the United States north of the line therein mentioned, is not warranted by the Constitution, and is therefore void; and that neither the plaintiff himself, nor any of his family, were made free by being carried into this territory; even if they had been carried there by the owner, who intended to become a permanent resident.*
    The congressional act referred to in the passage was the
    A. Kansas-Nebraska Act
    B. Missouri Compromise
    C. Northwest Ordinance
    D. Compromise of 1850
    E. Fugitive Slave Act

    20.____

21. Abraham Lincoln delayed making any commitment about emancipation of the slaves after his inauguration as President because he
    A. basically had no sympathy with those who wanted to end slavery
    B. was concerned that foreign governments might be critical of a proclamation freeing slaves
    C. did not feel bound by the 1860 Republican party platform
    D. did not feel he had the constitutional right to make such a commitment in regard to slavery in the territories
    E. hoped to keep as many slave states as possible in the Union

    21.____

22. Liberty of conscience was defended by Roger Williams on the ground that
    A. all religions were equal in the eyes of God
    B. the institutions of political democracy would be jeopardized without it
    C. Puritan ideas about sin and salvation were outmoded
    D. theological truths would emerge from the clash of ideas
    E. the state was an improper and ineffectual agency in matters of the spirit

    22.____

Questions 23-24 refer to the following statement:

The present King of Great Britain...has combined with others to subject us to a jurisdiction foreign to our constitution, and unacknowledged by our laws...

23. The *constitution* referred to in the quotation above from the Declaration of Independence was
    A. the principles common to all of the colonial charters
    B. the Articles of Confederation
    C. a constitution for the colonies written by Sir William Blackstone
    D. the laws passed concurrently by the several colonial legislatures
    E. the principles the colonists believed had traditionally regulated English government

24. The protest that the king had *combined with others to subject us to a jurisdiction foreign to our constitution* referred to George III's
    A. alliance with the king of France
    B. use of Hessian mercenaries
    C. reliance upon his representatives in the colonies
    D. approval of parliamentary laws impinging on colonial self-government
    E. intention to place a German prince on the throne of British America

25. *There is an opinion that parties in free countries are useful checks upon the administration of the government and serve to keep alive the spirit of liberty. This within certain limits is probably true, and in governments of a monarchical cast patriotism may look with indulgence, if not with favor, upon the spirit of party. But in those of the popular character, in governments purely elective, it is a spirit not to be encouraged.*
    Which of the following was MOST likely to have made these remarks while President?
    A. Thomas Jefferson
    B. James Madison
    C. George Washington
    D. Andrew Jackson
    E. Abraham Lincoln

KEY (CORRECT ANSWERS)

1. B	11. B
2. D	12. E
3. B	13. D
4. B	14. C
5. C	15. C
6. A	16. C
7. D	17. B
8. B	18. C
9. D	19. D
10. A	20. B

21. E
22. E
23. E
24. D
25. C

AMERICAN HISTORY II

1865 TO THE PRESENT

DESCRIPTION OF THE TEST

The Subject Examination in American History II: 1865 to the Present covers material that is usually taught in the second semester of what is often a two-semester course in American history. The examination covers the period of American history from the end of the Civil War to the present, with the majority of questions on the twentieth century.

The examination is composed of approximately 120 multiple-choice questions to be answered in two separately timed 45-minute sections.

KNOWLEDGE AND SKILLS REQUIRED
The major topics covered by the examination are: Approximate Percent of Examination
50%   Political institutions and behavior and public policy
15%   Social and economic change
15%   Cultural and intellectual development
20%   Diplomacy and international relations

About one-third of the questions deal with the period from 1865 to 1914, and about two-thirds are on the period from 1915 to the present. The following are among the specific topics tested:

The motivations and character of American expansionism
The content of constitutional amendments and their interpretations by the Supreme Court
The development of American political parties
The emergence of regulatory and welfare-state legislation
The intellectual and political expressions of liberalism, conservatism, and other such movements
Long-term demographic trends
The process of economic growth and development
The changing occupational structure, nature of work, and labor organization
Immigration and the history of racial and ethnic minorities
Urbanization
The causes and impacts of major wars in American history
Major movements and individual figures in the history of American
arts and letters

Questions on the test require candidates to demonstrate the following abilities, which generally require knowledge of history before they can be exercised. Some questions may require more than one of the abilities.

- Identification and description of historical phenomena (about 45 percent of the examination)
- Characterization and classification of historical phenomena (about 15 percent of the examination)
- Analysis and interpretation of historical phenomena (about 10 percent of the examination)
- Comparison and contrast of historical phenomena (about 10 percent of the examination)
- Explanation and evaluation of historical phenomena (about 20 percent of the examination)

SAMPLE QUESTIONS
   The 25 sample questions given here are similar to questions on the American History II examination, but they do not actually appear on the examination.

Before attempting to answer the sample questions, read all the information about the
American History II   examination given above.

   Try to answer correctly as many of the questions as possible within 20 minutes. Then compare your answers with the correct answers on the last page.

Directions: Each of the questions or incomplete statements below is followed by five suggested answers or completions. Select the one that is BEST in each case.

1. Brown v. Board of Education of Topeka was a Supreme Court decision that   1._____
    A. was a forerunner of the Kansas-Nebraska Act
    B. established free public colleges in the United States
    C. outlawed racially segregated public schools
    D. established free public elementary and secondary schools in the United States
    E. provided for federal support of parochial schools

2. For which of the following was Franklin D. Roosevelt LEAST successful in securing   2._____
   congressional support?
    A. Negotiation of tariff agreements by the executive department
    B. Reduction of the gold content of the dollar
    C. Removal of the restraints of the antitrust acts to permit voluntary trade associations
    D. The levying of processing taxes on agricultural products
    E. Reform of the judiciary to permit the enlargement of the Supreme Court

3. Which of the following is a CORRECT statement about the United States at the close of   3._____
   the First World War?
    A. It joined the League of Nations.
    B. It emerged as the world's leading creditor nation.
    C. It accorded diplomatic recognition to the Soviet Union.
    D. It repealed the prohibition amendment to the Constitution.
    E. It received large reparations payments from Germany.

4. The American Federation of Labor under the leadership of Samuel Gompers organized   4._____
    A. skilled workers in craft unions in order to achieve economic gains
    B. all industrial and agricultural workers in one big union
    C. unskilled workers along industrial lines
    D. workers and intellectuals into a labor party for political action
    E. workers into a fraternal organization to provide unemployment and old-age benefits

5. Between 1890 and 1914, most immigrants to the United States came from   5._____
    A. Southern and Eastern Europe
    B. Northern and Western Europe
    C. Latin America
    D. Southeast Asia
    E. Canada

6. In the summer of 1933, a nice old gentleman wearing a silk hat fell off the end of a pier. He was unable to swim. A friend ran down the pier, dived overboard, and pulled him out; but the silk hat floated off with the tide. After the old gentleman had been revived, he was effusive in his thanks. He praised his friend for saving his life. Today, three years later, the old gentleman is berating his friend because the silk hat was lost.
   The old gentleman and the friend in this story told by Franklin D. Roosevelt to a Democratic party convention in 1936 were meant to refer to
   A. farmers and crop acreage controls
   B. laborers and wage-hour controls
   C. businessmen and industrial regulations
   D. consumers and fixed prices
   E. the unemployed and relief-roll stipulations

7. Which of the following was the LEAST important consideration in the United States' decision to drop the atomic bomb on Japan in August, 1945?
   A. Dropping the bomb would give a new and powerful
   B. argument to the peace faction in the Japanese government.
   C. Dropping the bomb would presumably shorten the war and therefore save the lives of American soldiers that would be lost in an invasion of the Japanese homeland.
   D. Scientists could propose no acceptable technical demonstration of the bomb likely to convince Japan that further fighting was futile.
   E. Scientists wished to demonstrate to Congress that the $2 billion spent, after long debate, on the six-year Manhattan Project had not been wasted.
   F. The President and the State Department hoped to end the war in the Far East without Soviet assistance.

8. All of the following were among Wilson's Fourteen Points EXCEPT
   A. a general association of nations
   B. freedom to navigate the high seas in peace and war
   C. an independent Poland
   D. a partitioned Germany
   E. abolition of secret diplomacy

9. In his interpretation of the historical development of the United States, Frederick Jackson Turner focused on the importance of
   A. the traditions of Western European culture
   B. the absence of a feudal aristocracy
   C. Black people and Black slavery
   D. the conflict between capitalists and workers
   E. the existence of cheap unsettled land

10. The rule of reason, handed down by the Supreme Court, held that the Sherman Antitrust Act forbade only unreasonable combinations or contracts in restraint of trade. This interpretation MOST closely parallels the ideas of
    A. William McKinley
    B. Robert M. LaFollette
    C. Theodore Roosevelt
    D. Woodrow Wilson
    E. Louis D. Brandeis

11.

EDITOR   CAPITALIST   POLITICIAN   MINISTER
HAVING THEIR FLING

Reform activity during the Progressive era was similar to that of the 1960's in all of the "following ways EXCEPT:
A. Civil rights for Black Americans were supported by the federal government
B. Reform activity was encouraged by strong and active Presidents
C. Reform in the area of women's rights was advocated by feminists
D. Governmental reform initiatives were curtailed by war
E. Reform occurred despite the absence of severe economic depression

12. All of the following are characteristics of the cartoon shown on the preceding page which help to identify it as a socialist view of the First World War. EXCEPT the
A. expression of an antiwar viewpoint
B. inclusion of a capitalist among the figures portrayed
C. cynicism about the role of organized religion
D. placement of the figures symbolically from left to right
E. ridicule of Wilsonian rhetoric

13. During the closing decades of the nineteenth century, farmers complained about all of the following EXCEPT
A. rising commodity prices
B. high interest charges
C. high freight rates
D. high storage costs
E. large middleman profits

14. Which of the following sources would be useful in studying social mobility and stratification?
   I. Manuscript census returns
   II. Election returns
   III. The President's executive orders
   IV. City directories
   V. Tax records

The CORRECT answer is:
A. I, IV   B. I, IV, V   C. II, III, V   D. II, III, IV, V
E. I, II, III, IV, V

15. Many Mexicans migrated to the United States during the First World War because
    A. revolution in Mexico had caused social upheaval and dislocation
    B. immigration quotas for Europeans went unfilled as a result of the war
    C. the war in Europe had disrupted the Mexican economy
    D. American Progressives generally held liberal views on the issue of racial assimilation
    E. the United States government recruited Mexican workers to accelerate the
    F. settlement of the Southwest

15._____

16. Which of the following was the GREATEST source of tension between the United States and the Soviet Union during the Second World War?
    A. The Soviet refusal to fight Japan
    B. The delay on the part of the United States in opening a second front in Europe
    C. Lend-Lease allocations
    D. The United States refusal to share atomic secrets
    E. The Soviet massacre of Polish officers at Katyn Forest

16._____

17. *Modern Republicanism*, as reflected in the policies of President Eisenhower, encompassed which of the following?
    A. A moderate extension of some of the New Deal and Fair Deal programs
    B. Support for the United Nations
    C. Military aid for United States allies
    D. Economic aid for developing countries
    The CORRECT answer is:
    A. III *only*
    B. I, II
    C. I, II, III
    D. II, III, IV
    E. I, II, III IV

17._____

18. Which of the following is TRUE of the forced relocation of Japanese-Americans from the West Coast during the Second World War?
    A. President Roosevelt claimed that military necessity justified the action.
    B. The Supreme Court declared the action unconstitutional.
    C. Widespread Japanese-American disloyalty and sabotage preceded the action.
    D. The Japanese-Americans received the same treatment as that accorded the German-Americans and Italian-Americans.
    E. Few of those relocated were actually United States citizens.

18._____

19. A number of changes took place in the intellectual life of college-educated Americans between about 1880 and 1930. Which of the following changes is LEAST characteristic of this group in this period?
    A. Growth in influence of religious fundamentalism
    B. Rise of pluralistic and relativistic world views
    C. Accelerated professionalization of intellectual roles
    D. Expanded popularity of nonrational explanations for human behavior
    E. Increased attention to the methods and outlook of the sciences

19._____

20. Reformers of the Progressive era proposed all of the following changes in city government and politics at the turn of the century EXCEPT
    A. a large city council elected by wards
    B. civil service
    C. home rule for cities
    D. city manager and commission governments
    E. nonpartisan elections

20._____

21. *United States foreign policy is often formulated in the belief that an earlier policy was mistaken.*
    All of the following pairs of events support this statement EXCEPT the
    A. passage of the Embargo Act of 1807 and the declaration of war against Great Britain in 1812
    B. announcement of the Open Door policy in 1900 and the refusal to recognize Japan's control over Manchuria in 1932
    C. promulgation of President Wilson's neutrality policy in the period 1914-1917 and the passage of the Neutrality Acts of the mid-1930's
    D. rejection of the Treaty of Versailles in 1919 and 1920 and the ratification of the United Nations Charter in 1945
    E. acquiescence in the Munich Agreement in 1938 and the decision to intervene in South Korea in 1950

21._____

22. Which of the following constitutes a significant change in the treatment of Native Americans (Indians) during the last half of the nineteenth century? The
    A. beginnings of negotiation with individual tribes
    B. start of a removal policy
    C. abandonment of the reservation system
    D. admission of Native Americans (Indians) to United States citizenship
    E. division of the tribal lands among individual members

22._____

23. *This, then, is held to be the duty of the man of wealth: to consider all surplus revenues which come to him simply as trust funds, which he is called upon to administer and strictly bound as a matter of duty to administer in the manner which, in his judgment, is best calculated to produce the most beneficial results for the community - the man of wealth thus becoming the mere agent and trustee for his poorer brethren.*
    These sentiments are MOST characteristic of
    A. transcendentalism
    B. pragmatism
    C. the Gospel of Wealth
    D. the Social Gospel
    E. Reform Darwinism

23._____

24. *The reasons for the failures of the Chinese National Government appear in some detail in the attached record. They do not stem from any inadequacy of American aid. Our military observers on the spot have reported that Nationalist armies did not lose a single battle during the crucial year 1948 through Zack of arms or ammunition. The fact was that the decay which our observers had detected in Chungking early in the war had fatally sapped the powers of resistance of the Kuomintang.*
    The 1949 Department of State White Paper, from which the excerpt above is taken, had which of the following effects?
    A. It led to a closer relationship between the United States and the Union of Soviet Socialist Republics.
    B. It led to friendly relations between the Union of Soviet Socialist Republics and the People's Republic Of China.
    C. It convinced the *China Lobby* that the downfall of Nationalist China had been inevitable.
    D. It temporarily quieted the charges of Senator Joseph McCarthy that there were Communists in the Department of State.
    E. It augmented bitter domestic controversy about the Far Eastern policy of the United States.

24._____

25. The so-called lost generation after the First World-War was
    A. represented by Ernest Hemingway in the figures of Jake Barnes and Brett Ashley
    B. depicted in John Steinbeck's THE GRAPES OF WRATH
    C. C.- glorified by T.S. Eliot in THE LOVE SONG OF J. ALFRED PRUFROCK
    D. portrayed as the principal subject of Sinclair Lewis' BABBITT
    E. portrayed as the principal subject of Theodore Dreiser's AN AMERICAN TRAGEDY

KEY (CORRECT ANSWERS)

1.	C	6.	C	11.	A	16.	B	21.	B
2.	E	7.	D	12.	D	17.	E	22.	E
3.	B	8.	D	13.	A	18.	A	23.	C
4.	A	9.	E	14.	B	19.	A	24.	E
5.	A	10.	C	15.	A	20.	A	25.	A

HOW TO TAKE A TEST

You have studied long, hard and conscientiously.

With your official admission card in hand, and your heart pounding, you have been admitted to the examination room.

You note that there are several hundred other applicants in the examination room waiting to take the same test.

They all appear to be equally well prepared.

You know that nothing but your best effort will suffice. The "moment of truth" is at hand: you now have to demonstrate objectively, in writing, your knowledge of content and your understanding of subject matter.

You are fighting the most important battle of your life—to pass and/or score high on an examination which will determine your career and provide the economic basis for your livelihood.

What extra, special things should you know and should you do in taking the examination?

I. YOU MUST PASS AN EXAMINATION

A. WHAT EVERY CANDIDATE SHOULD KNOW
Examination applicants often ask us for help in preparing for the written test. What can I study in advance? What kinds of questions will be asked? How will the test be given? How will the papers be graded?

B. HOW ARE EXAMS DEVELOPED?
Examinations are carefully written by trained technicians who are specialists in the field known as "psychological measurement," in consultation with recognized authorities in the field of work that the test will cover. These experts recommend the subject matter areas or skills to be tested; only those knowledges or skills important to your success on the job are included. The most reliable books and source materials available are used as references. Together, the experts and technicians judge the difficulty level of the questions.
Test technicians know how to phrase questions so that the problem is clearly stated. Their ethics do not permit "trick" or "catch" questions. Questions may have been tried out on sample groups, or subjected to statistical analysis, to determine their usefulness.
Written tests are often used in combination with performance tests, ratings of training and experience, and oral interviews. All of these measures combine to form the best-known means of finding the right person for the right job.

II. HOW TO PASS THE WRITTEN TEST

A. BASIC STEPS

1) Study the announcement

How, then, can you know what subjects to study? Our best answer is: "Learn as much as possible about the class of positions for which you've applied." The exam will test the knowledge, skills and abilities needed to do the work.

Your most valuable source of information about the position you want is the official exam announcement. This announcement lists the training and experience qualifications. Check these standards and apply only if you come reasonably close to meeting them. Many jurisdictions preview the written test in the exam announcement by including a section called "Knowledge and Abilities Required," "Scope of the Examination," or some similar heading. Here you will find out specifically what fields will be tested.

2) Choose appropriate study materials

If the position for which you are applying is technical or advanced, you will read more advanced, specialized material. If you are already familiar with the basic principles of your field, elementary textbooks would waste your time. Concentrate on advanced textbooks and technical periodicals. Think through the concepts and review difficult problems in your field.

These are all general sources. You can get more ideas on your own initiative, following these leads. For example, training manuals and publications of the government agency which employs workers in your field can be useful, particularly for technical and professional positions. A letter or visit to the government department involved may result in more specific study suggestions, and certainly will provide you with a more definite idea of the exact nature of the position you are seeking.

3) Study this book!

III. KINDS OF TESTS

Tests are used for purposes other than measuring knowledge and ability to perform specified duties. For some positions, it is equally important to test ability to make adjustments to new situations or to profit from training. In others, basic mental abilities not dependent on information are essential. Questions which test these things may not appear as pertinent to the duties of the position as those which test for knowledge and information. Yet they are often highly important parts of a fair examination. For very general questions, it is almost impossible to help you direct your study efforts. What we can do is to point out some of the more common of these general abilities needed in public service positions and describe some typical questions.

1) General information

Broad, general information has been found useful for predicting job success in some kinds of work. This is tested in a variety of ways, from vocabulary lists to questions about current events. Basic background in some field of work, such as sociology or economics, may be sampled in a group of questions. Often these are principles which have become familiar to most persons through exposure rather than through formal training. It is difficult to advise you how to study for these questions; being alert to the world around you is our best suggestion.

2) Verbal ability

An example of an ability needed in many positions is verbal or language ability. Verbal ability is, in brief, the ability to use and understand words. Vocabulary and grammar tests are typical measures of this ability. Reading comprehension or paragraph interpretation questions are common in many kinds of civil service tests. You are given a paragraph of written material and asked to find its central meaning.

IV. KINDS OF QUESTIONS

1. Multiple-choice Questions

Most popular of the short-answer questions is the "multiple choice" or "best answer" question. It can be used, for example, to test for factual knowledge, ability to solve problems or judgment in meeting situations found at work.

A multiple-choice question is normally one of three types:
- It can begin with an incomplete statement followed by several possible endings. You are to find the one ending which best completes the statement, although some of the others may not be entirely wrong.
- It can also be a complete statement in the form of a question which is answered by choosing one of the statements listed.
- It can be in the form of a problem – again you select the best answer.

Here is an example of a multiple-choice question with a discussion which should give you some clues as to the method for choosing the right answer:

When an employee has a complaint about his assignment, the action which will best help him overcome his difficulty is to
- A. discuss his difficulty with his coworkers
- B. take the problem to the head of the organization
- C. take the problem to the person who gave him the assignment
- D. say nothing to anyone about his complaint

In answering this question, you should study each of the choices to find which is best. Consider choice "A" – Certainly an employee may discuss his complaint with fellow employees, but no change or improvement can result, and the complaint remains unresolved. Choice "B" is a poor choice since the head of the organization probably does not know what assignment you have been given, and taking your problem to him is known as "going over the head" of the supervisor. The supervisor, or person who made the assignment, is the person who can clarify it or correct any injustice. Choice "C" is, therefore, correct. To say nothing, as in choice "D," is unwise. Supervisors have and interest in knowing the problems employees are facing, and the employee is seeking a solution to his problem.

2. True/False

3. Matching Questions

Matching an answer from a column of choices within another column.

V. RECORDING YOUR ANSWERS

Computer terminals are used more and more today for many different kinds of exams.

For an examination with very few applicants, you may be told to record your answers in the test booklet itself. Separate answer sheets are much more common. If this separate answer sheet is to be scored by machine – and this is often the case – it is highly important that you mark your answers correctly in order to get credit.

VI. BEFORE THE TEST

YOUR PHYSICAL CONDITION IS IMPORTANT

If you are not well, you can't do your best work on tests. If you are half asleep, you can't do your best either. Here are some tips:

1) Get about the same amount of sleep you usually get. Don't stay up all night before the test, either partying or worrying—DON'T DO IT!
2) If you wear glasses, be sure to wear them when you go to take the test. This goes for hearing aids, too.
3) If you have any physical problems that may keep you from doing your best, be sure to tell the person giving the test. If you are sick or in poor health, you relay cannot do your best on any test. You can always come back and take the test some other time.

Common sense will help you find procedures to follow to get ready for an examination. Too many of us, however, overlook these sensible measures. Indeed, nervousness and fatigue have been found to be the most serious reasons why applicants fail to do their best on civil service tests. Here is a list of reminders:

- Begin your preparation early – Don't wait until the last minute to go scurrying around for books and materials or to find out what the position is all about.
- Prepare continuously – An hour a night for a week is better than an all-night cram session. This has been definitely established. What is more, a night a week for a month will return better dividends than crowding your study into a shorter period of time.
- Locate the place of the exam – You have been sent a notice telling you when and where to report for the examination. If the location is in a different town or otherwise unfamiliar to you, it would be well to inquire the best route and learn something about the building.
- Relax the night before the test – Allow your mind to rest. Do not study at all that night. Plan some mild recreation or diversion; then go to bed early and get a good night's sleep.
- Get up early enough to make a leisurely trip to the place for the test – This way unforeseen events, traffic snarls, unfamiliar buildings, etc. will not upset you.
- Dress comfortably – A written test is not a fashion show. You will be known by number and not by name, so wear something comfortable.
- Leave excess paraphernalia at home – Shopping bags and odd bundles will get in your way. You need bring only the items mentioned in the official notice you received; usually everything you need is provided. Do not bring reference books to the exam. They will only confuse those last minutes and be taken away from you when in the test room.

- Arrive somewhat ahead of time – If because of transportation schedules you must get there very early, bring a newspaper or magazine to take your mind off yourself while waiting.
- Locate the examination room – When you have found the proper room, you will be directed to the seat or part of the room where you will sit. Sometimes you are given a sheet of instructions to read while you are waiting. Do not fill out any forms until you are told to do so; just read them and be prepared.
- Relax and prepare to listen to the instructions
- If you have any physical problem that may keep you from doing your best, be sure to tell the test administrator. If you are sick or in poor health, you really cannot do your best on the exam. You can come back and take the test some other time.

VII. AT THE TEST

The day of the test is here and you have the test booklet in your hand. The temptation to get going is very strong. Caution! There is more to success than knowing the right answers. You must know how to identify your papers and understand variations in the type of short-answer question used in this particular examination. Follow these suggestions for maximum results from your efforts:

1) Cooperate with the monitor

The test administrator has a duty to create a situation in which you can be as much at ease as possible. He will give instructions, tell you when to begin, check to see that you are marking your answer sheet correctly, and so on. He is not there to guard you, although he will see that your competitors do not take unfair advantage. He wants to help you do your best.

2) Listen to all instructions

Don't jump the gun! Wait until you understand all directions. In most civil service tests you get more time than you need to answer the questions. So don't be in a hurry. Read each word of instructions until you clearly understand the meaning. Study the examples, listen to all announcements and follow directions. Ask questions if you do not understand what to do.

3) Identify your papers

Civil service exams are usually identified by number only. You will be assigned a number; you must not put your name on your test papers. Be sure to copy your number correctly. Since more than one exam may be given, copy your exact examination title.

4) Plan your time

Unless you are told that a test is a "speed" or "rate of work" test, speed itself is usually not important. Time enough to answer all the questions will be provided, but this does not mean that you have all day. An overall time limit has been set. Divide the total time (in minutes) by the number of questions to determine the approximate time you have for each question.

5) Do not linger over difficult questions

If you come across a difficult question, mark it with a paper clip (useful to have along) and come back to it when you have been through the booklet. One caution if you do this – be sure to skip a number on your answer sheet as well. Check often to be sure that you have not lost your place and that you are marking in the row numbered the same as the question you are answering.

6) Read the questions

Be sure you know what the question asks! Many capable people are unsuccessful because they failed to read the questions correctly.

7) Answer all questions

Unless you have been instructed that a penalty will be deducted for incorrect answers, it is better to guess than to omit a question.

8) Speed tests

It is often better NOT to guess on speed tests. It has been found that on timed tests people are tempted to spend the last few seconds before time is called in marking answers at random – without even reading them – in the hope of picking up a few extra points. To discourage this practice, the instructions may warn you that your score will be "corrected" for guessing. That is, a penalty will be applied. The incorrect answers will be deducted from the correct ones, or some other penalty formula will be used.

9) Review your answers

If you finish before time is called, go back to the questions you guessed or omitted to give them further thought. Review other answers if you have time.

10) Return your test materials

If you are ready to leave before others have finished or time is called, take ALL your materials to the monitor and leave quietly. Never take any test material with you. The monitor can discover whose papers are not complete, and taking a test booklet may be grounds for disqualification.

VIII. EXAMINATION TECHNIQUES

1) Read the general instructions carefully. These are usually printed on the first page of the exam booklet. As a rule, these instructions refer to the timing of the examination; the fact that you should not start work until the signal and must stop work at a signal, etc. If there are any special instructions, such as a choice of questions to be answered, make sure that you note this instruction carefully.

2) When you are ready to start work on the examination, that is as soon as the signal has been given, read the instructions to each question booklet, underline any key words or phrases, such as least, best, outline, describe and the like. In this way you will tend to answer as requested rather than discover on reviewing your paper that you listed without describing, that you selected the worst choice rather than the best choice, etc.

3) If the examination is of the objective or multiple-choice type – that is, each question will also give a series of possible answers: A, B, C or D, and you are called upon to select the best answer and write the letter next to that answer on your answer paper – it is advisable to start answering each question in turn. There may be anywhere from 50 to 100 such questions in the three or four hours allotted and you can see how much time would be taken if you read through all the questions before beginning to answer any. Furthermore, if you

come across a question or group of questions which you know would be difficult to answer, it would undoubtedly affect your handling of all the other questions.

4) If the examination is of the essay type and contains but a few questions, it is a moot point as to whether you should read all the questions before starting to answer any one. Of course, if you are given a choice – say five out of seven and the like – then it is essential to read all the questions so you can eliminate the two that are most difficult. If, however, you are asked to answer all the questions, there may be danger in trying to answer the easiest one first because you may find that you will spend too much time on it. The best technique is to answer the first question, then proceed to the second, etc.

5) Time your answers. Before the exam begins, write down the time it started, then add the time allowed for the examination and write down the time it must be completed, then divide the time available somewhat as follows:
    - If 3-1/2 hours are allowed, that would be 210 minutes. If you have 80 objective-type questions, that would be an average of 2-1/2 minutes per question. Allow yourself no more than 2 minutes per question, or a total of 160 minutes, which will permit about 50 minutes to review.
    - If for the time allotment of 210 minutes there are 7 essay questions to answer, that would average about 30 minutes a question. Give yourself only 25 minutes per question so that you have about 35 minutes to review.

6) The most important instruction is to read each question and make sure you know what is wanted. The second most important instruction is to time yourself properly so that you answer every question. The third most important instruction is to answer every question. Guess if you have to but include something for each question. Remember that you will receive no credit for a blank and will probably receive some credit if you write something in answer to an essay question. If you guess a letter – say "B" for a multiple-choice question – you may have guessed right. If you leave a blank as an answer to a multiple-choice question, the examiners may respect your feelings but it will not add a point to your score. Some exams may penalize you for wrong answers, so in such cases only, you may not want to guess unless you have some basis for your answer.

7) Suggestions
    a. Objective-type questions
        1. Examine the question booklet for proper sequence of pages and questions
        2. Read all instructions carefully
        3. Skip any question which seems too difficult; return to it after all other questions have been answered
        4. Apportion your time properly; do not spend too much time on any single question or group of questions
        5. Note and underline key words – all, most, fewest, least, best, worst, same, opposite, etc.
        6. Pay particular attention to negatives
        7. Note unusual option, e.g., unduly long, short, complex, different or similar in content to the body of the question
        8. Observe the use of "hedging" words – probably, may, most likely, etc.

9. Make sure that your answer is put next to the same number as the question
10. Do not second-guess unless you have good reason to believe the second answer is definitely more correct
11. Cross out original answer if you decide another answer is more accurate; do not erase until you are ready to hand your paper in
12. Answer all questions; guess unless instructed otherwise
13. Leave time for review

b. Essay questions
1. Read each question carefully
2. Determine exactly what is wanted. Underline key words or phrases.
3. Decide on outline or paragraph answer
4. Include many different points and elements unless asked to develop any one or two points or elements
5. Show impartiality by giving pros and cons unless directed to select one side only
6. Make and write down any assumptions you find necessary to answer the questions
7. Watch your English, grammar, punctuation and choice of words
8. Time your answers; don't crowd material

8) Answering the essay question

Most essay questions can be answered by framing the specific response around several key words or ideas. Here are a few such key words or ideas:

M's: manpower, materials, methods, money, management
P's: purpose, program, policy, plan, procedure, practice, problems, pitfalls, personnel, public relations

a. Six basic steps in handling problems:
1. Preliminary plan and background development
2. Collect information, data and facts
3. Analyze and interpret information, data and facts
4. Analyze and develop solutions as well as make recommendations
5. Prepare report and sell recommendations
6. Install recommendations and follow up effectiveness

b. Pitfalls to avoid
1. Taking things for granted – A statement of the situation does not necessarily imply that each of the elements is necessarily true; for example, a complaint may be invalid and biased so that all that can be taken for granted is that a complaint has been registered
2. Considering only one side of a situation – Wherever possible, indicate several alternatives and then point out the reasons you selected the best one
3. Failing to indicate follow up – Whenever your answer indicates action on your part, make certain that you will take proper follow-up action to see how successful your recommendations, procedures or actions turn out to be
4. Taking too long in answering any single question – Remember to time your answers properly

EXAMINATION SECTION

EXAMINATION SECTION
TEST 1

DIRECTIONS: Each question or incomplete statement is followed by several suggested answers or completions. Select the one that BEST answers the question or completes the statement. *PRINT THE LETTER OF THE CORRECT ANSWER IN THE SPACE AT THE RIGHT.*

1. The doctrine of predestination, the belief in the salvation of *the elect,* was MOST closely associated with the theology of the   1.____

   A. Anglicans   B. Mormons   C. Puritans   D. Quakers

2. The French and Indian War is significant in the history of America because it   2.____

   A. led to the French subjugation of the Indians in Canada
   B. left only France and England as colonial powers on the North American continent
   C. eliminated Spanish claims to Florida
   D. opened the area west of the Appalachians to settlement by the English rather than by the French

3. Which one of the following is NOT true of British relations with the American colonies before 1763?   3.____

   A. The American, as well as the British, merchant marine benefited from the exclusion of the Dutch and others from the imperial trade.
   B. Generous bounties were given to producers of colonial goods such as naval stores.
   C. Colonial smugglers violated the Navigation Laws.
   D. Parliament facilitated the export of English coin to the colonies to permit the latter to meet unfavorable trade balances.

4. The Quebec Act of 1774 can be considered a contributory cause of the American Revolution because it   4.____

   A. encouraged land speculation west of the Alleghenies
   B. closed the port of Boston to ships coming from Canada
   C. extended the boundaries of the Province of Quebec to the Ohio River
   D. deprived the French Canadians of all privileges of self-government

5. The MAJOR issue in the trial of John Peter Zenger in New York in 1735 was whether   5.____

   A. Zenger was responsible for the publication of the article in question
   B. Zenger was entitled to the same rights as Englishmen in England were under their libel laws
   C. the Royal Governor, as the representative of the King of England in the colonies, was above the law to the same degree as the King of England
   D. a jury should take into consideration the truth or falsity of a printed statement in reaching a decision in a libel case

6. Which one of the following MOST accurately describes the effect of the American Revolution on the system of land-holding in the United States?   6.____

A. Inauguration of a free-homestead policy in the Northwest Territory
B. Abolition of entails and primogeniture in many states
C. Transfer of control of western territory to individual states
D. Introduction of a system of quitrents

7. Which one of the following statements concerning the government under the Articles of Confederation is CORRECT?

   A. There was no executive branch.
   B. Congress could control foreign but not interstate commerce.
   C. Any amendment of the Articles required at least a two-thirds vote.
   D. States were represented in Congress according to the size of their population.

8. A president and vice president from different parties were elected in the United States in the election of

   A. 1796   B. 1800   C. 1828   D. 1860

9. Which one of the following BEST expresses Jefferson's views?

   A. To be effective, democracy must depend on an agrarian base.
   B. A system of checks and balances is incompatible with a democratic system.
   C. Democracy can best be safeguarded by eliminating propertied classes.
   D. Democracy can best be safeguarded by universal suffrage.

10. Jefferson's Administration demonstrated its disagreement with the Hamiltonian system by

    A. abolishing the excise tax
    B. sharply reducing the tariff on imports
    C. abolishing the Bank of the United States
    D. repealing the Alien and Sedition Laws

11. Which one of the following was achieved within the twenty years following the adoption of our Constitution?

    A. Settling the Maine boundary
    B. Gaining recognition of our rights as a neutral nation
    C. Gaining control of the Mississippi River
    D. Avoiding involvements with European countries

12. By the Treaty of Ghent (1814), the United States

    A. gained important Great Lakes forts
    B. gained New Orleans
    C. gained territory along the St. Lawrence River
    D. neither gained nor lost any territory

13. During the period from 1812 to 1828, the CENTRAL fact in national politics in the United States was the

    A. strengthening of the two-party system based on broad differences over public policy
    B. decreasing popular interest in politics as a result of more stringent qualifications for voting

C. consolidation of the political powers of the bureaucratic office holders
D. virtual disappearance of the two-party system and the resulting emphasis on personal, local, and sectional conflicts

14. In which one of the following respects did the First Bank of the United States differ from the Second Bank of the United States?
It

    A. was chartered despite the opposition of the Jeffer-sonians
    B. served as a depository of United States government funds
    C. issued paper notes which circulated as currency
    D. was owned in part by the United States government

14.____

15. In connection with which one of the following did John Marshall assert the right of the Supreme Court to review decisions of state courts in cases which involve the powers of the federal government?

    A. Cohens vs. Virginia
    B. Dartmouth College vs. Woodward
    C. Gibbons vs. Ogden
    D. McCulloch vs. Maryland

15.____

16. All of the following are correctly paired with authors who wrote outstanding biographies about them EXCEPT

    A. Benjamin Franklin - Carl Van Doren
    B. Andrew Jackson - Marquis James
    C. Thomas Jefferson - Allan Nevins
    D. Abraham Lincoln - Carl Sandburg

16.____

17. Which one of the following lived during the period which is the MAIN theme of Van Wyck Brooks' THE FLOWERING OF NEW ENGLAND?

    A. Jonathan Edwards   B. Nathaniel Hawthorne
    C. John P. Marquand   D. Cotton Mather

17.____

18. Which one of the following decades was the golden age of the American merchant marine?

    A. 1790's   B. 1820's   C. 1850's   D. 1880's

18.____

19. Which one of the following statements is CORRECT concerning the positions of Calhoun and Webster on the tariffs of 1816 and 1828?

    A. Both men were in favor of both tariffs.
    B. Calhoun favored both tariffs; Webster opposed both tariffs.
    C. Calhoun opposed both tariffs; Webster favored both tariffs.
    D. Each changed his position between 1816 and 1828.

19.____

20. When South Carolina nullified the Tariff Act of 1832,

    A. the provisions of her Nullification Act were implemented promptly
    B. several of her sister Southern states took similar action

20.____

C. nullification was never put into effect because of the prompt measures taken by Jackson and the United States Congress
D. nullification was never put into effect because of the Supreme Court's quick decision declaring such action unconstitutional

21. Calhoun's principle of the *concurrent majority* is, in effect, currently in operation

    A. among the members of the General Assembly of the United Nations
    B. in the Congress of the United States
    C. in the case of the British Commonwealth
    D. in the Security Council of the United Nations with reference to the Big Five

22. Jackson attacked the Second Bank of the United States on all of the following grounds EXCEPT that it

    A. was a threat to the stability of the currency
    B. was monopolistic
    C. enriched capitalists in the Northeast at the expense of the West and South
    D. was unconstitutional

23. During the second quarter of the 19th century, state laws in the United States had enacted reforms in each of the following areas EXCEPT the

    A. limitation on the use of injunctions in trade disputes
    B. extension of free public education
    C. introduction of mechanics' lien laws
    D. abolition of imprisonment for debt

24. In the Dred Scott decision, the Supreme Court held that Congress was powerless to

    A. give citizenship to Negro slaves
    B. keep slavery out of the territories
    C. pass a fugitive slave law
    D. ban slavery in the District of Columbia

25. Hinton R. Helper's THE IMPENDING CRISIS OF THE SOUTH attempted to prove that in the South slavery had the WORST effect on

    A. families of wealthy slave owners
    B. owners of fewer than ten slaves
    C. the middle class
    D. non-slaveholding whites

KEY (CORRECT ANSWERS)

1. C
2. D
3. D
4. C
5. D

6. B
7. A
8. A
9. A
10. A

11. C
12. D
13. D
14. A
15. A

16. C
17. B
18. C
19. D
20. C

21. D
22. A
23. A
24. B
25. D

TEST 2

DIRECTIONS: Each question or incomplete statement is followed by several suggested answers or completions. Select the one that BEST answers the question or completes the statement. *PRINT THE LETTER OF THE CORRECT ANSWER IN THE SPACE AT THE RIGHT.*

1. Which one of the following statements applies to the South during the Reconstruction Era?   1._____

    A. Control of the southern economy by the plantation aristocracy was shattered.
    B. The Democratic Party maintained control of the Senate despite Radical Republican control in the House of Representatives.
    C. The Ku Klux Klan dominated southern state legislatures.
    D. The *black codes* were enacted to protect the voting rights of Negroes.

2. Which one of the following was a BASIC reason for the passage of the Fifteenth Amendment?   2._____
    The

    A. Supreme Court's decision that the Civil Rights Act of 1866 was unconstitutional
    B. desire to assure the Negro's permanent status as a free man by replacing the Emancipation Proclamation with an amendment
    C. conviction of many Radical Republicans that penalties provided by the Fourteenth Amendment for disfranchising the Negro were inadequate
    D. general feeling throughout the nation that Negro advances warranted such a step

3. Which one of the following events MOST immediately preceded the end of the Reconstruction period in the South?   3._____
    The

    A. second inauguration of Ulysses S. Grant as President
    B. adoption of the Fourteenth Amendment
    C. election of Rutherford B. Hayes as President
    D. impeachment of Andrew Johnson

4. The demand for *resumption* in the 1870's was a demand that the United States government restore the   4._____

    A. gold standard
    B. unlimited coinage of silver
    C. issuance of greenbacks
    D. redemption of paper currency with metallic money on demand

5. What is the correct chronological order of the following events in the monetary history of the United States?   5._____
    I. Demonetization of silver
    II. Panic of 1893
    III. *Cross of Gold* speech
    IV. Sherman Silver Purchase Act
    The CORRECT answer is:

    A. I, II, III, IV   B. II, III, IV, I
    C. I, IV, II, III   D. IV, I, II, III

6. Which one of the following was the MAJOR reason for the disappearance of free silver as an important political issue?

   A. The United States adopted bimetallism as its official monetary standard.
   B. The Republican Party won the election of 1900.
   C. Large gold deposits were discovered in South Africa and in the Yukon.
   D. The National Bank Act was rescinded.

7. The issue over which the Republican and Democratic parties differed MOST sharply in the three decades after the Civil War was

   A. tariff
   B. imperialism
   C. railroad regulation
   D. banking reform

8. In the 1880's, *Stalwarts* and *Half-Breeds* were factions within

   A. the Republican Party
   B. the Democratic Party
   C. both Democratic and Republican Parties
   D. the Populist Party

9. Which one of the following changes was NOT made by the Pendleton Act of 1883? It

   A. established a Civil Service Commission to administer open competitive examinations
   B. removed the filling of posts in the federal government from political control
   C. recognized the principle of appointment to office on the basis of aptitude
   D. prohibited financial assessments on office holders

10. Which one of the following Supreme Court decisions made it imperative for Congress to take action in connection with interstate railroads?

    A. Munn vs. Illinois
    B. Peik vs. Chicago and Northwestern Railroad
    C. Stone vs. Farmers' Loan and Trust Co.
    D. Wabash vs. Illinois

11. In which one of the following situations did a President of the United States send troops to the scene despite the objections of the Governor of the state? The

    A. railroad strikes of 1877
    B. Haymarket riot of 1886
    C. Pullman strike of 1894
    D. steel strike of 1894

12. The year 1890 is often selected to mark the *end of the frontier* in the United States because

    A. the Homestead Act expired in 1890
    B. after 1890 little land was taken up under the Homestead Act
    C. the Census Bureau declared there was no longer a discernible frontier
    D. the forty-eighth state was admitted into the Union in 1890

13. In order to alleviate a monetary crisis in 1895, President Cleveland

    A. inaugurated a program of banking reform
    B. recommended a higher protective tariff
    C. borrowed gold from private banking interests
    D. signed the Gold Standard Act

14. Thomas B. Reed, Speaker of the House of Representatives in the 1890's, changed House rules so that

    A. the Speaker could appoint the Rules Committee
    B. the Speaker was excluded from the Rules Committee
    C. quorums were more difficult to obtain in the House of Representatives
    D. minorities could not readily obstruct legislation in the House of Representatives

15. In what respect was the situation of the American farmer in the 1920's different from that of the American farmer in the period 1865-1900?
    He

    A. faced foreign competition because of the expansion of agricultural production in Canada, Latin America, Australia, and Europe
    B. faced a decline in American exports of food and other farm products
    C. had inadequate credit facilities and high interest charges
    D. bought supplies and equipment in a protected market and sold his crops in a competitive world market

16. Secretary of State Olney brought the United States to the brink of war in 1895-96, which was a result of a dispute with

    A. Chile over the death of American sailors in Valparaiso
    B. Germany over rights in the Samoan Islands
    C. Great Britain over seal fishing in the Bering Sea
    D. Great Britain over the boundary of Venezuela

17. Which one of the following groups includes ONLY those who had been opposed to the United States going to war with Spain in 1898?

    A. Theodore Roosevelt - Whitelaw Reid - American sugar planters in Cuba
    B. William McKinley - *Wall Street* - American sugar planters in Cuba
    C. Henry Cabot Lodge - Nelson W. Aldrich - *Wall Street*
    D. Theodore Roosevelt - Henry Cabot Lodge - American sugar planters in Cuba

18. Marcus Hanna was the personification of

    A. the lunatic fringe of the free-silverites
    B. the corrupt boss of the local political machine
    C. big business in politics
    D. the clergyman in politics

19. The Chisholm Trail gained fame from its association with the

    A. *Long Drive* of cattle from Texas to Kansas
    B. movement of covered wagons to Pike's Peak

C. route to the Comstock Lode
D. rush of *Forty-Niners* to California

20. Helen Hunt Jackson's A CENTURY OF DISHONOR aroused the national conscience in regard to our

    A. Latin-American policy
    B. treatment of the Indians
    C. failure to give equal rights to women
    D. exploitation of immigrants

20.____

21. Which one of the following was NOT a stimulus to immigration into the United States in the last quarter of the nineteenth century?

    A. Persecution of Jews, Poles, and Czechs in Europe
    B. Advertising of railroads and steamship companies
    C. Need of American industry for cheap labor
    D. Pressure from the ranks of labor for a liberal immigration policy

21.____

22. Which one of the following groups sent the LARGEST number of immigrants to the United States during the period 1890-1920?

    A. Italy, Austria, Hungary, Russia
    B. Italy, Austria, Hungary, Scandinavian countries
    C. Italy, Russia, Scandinavian countries
    D. Italy, Russia, Canada

22.____

23. During which one of the following periods did emigration from the United States EXCEED immigration into the United States?

    A. 1911-1915
    B. 1921-1925
    C. 1931-1935
    D. 1941-1945

23.____

24. During which one of the following decades was there the LEAST resistance to Negro participation in government by the existing state governments in the South?

    A. 1855-1865
    B. 1865-1875
    C. 1900-1910
    D. 1950-1960

24.____

25. Which one of the following represents a tariff philosophy that is opposed to that of the others?

    _____ Tariff

    A. Dingley
    B. Morrill
    C. Payne-Aldrich
    D. Underwood-Simmons

25.____

KEY (CORRECT ANSWERS)

1. A
2. C
3. C
4. D
5. C

6. C
7. A
8. A
9. B
10. D

11. C
12. C
13. C
14. D
15. B

16. D
17. B
18. C
19. A
20. B

21. D
22. A
23. C
24. B
25. D

TEST 3

DIRECTIONS: Each question or incomplete statement is followed by several suggested answers or completions. Select the one that BEST answers the question or completes the statement. *PRINT THE LETTER OF THE CORRECT ANSWER IN THE SPACE AT THE RIGHT.*

1. Which one of the following is the MOST accurate characterization of the status of organized labor in the United States by 1900? 1.____

    A. The right of unions to bargain collectively was legally recognized.
    B. The American Federation of Labor had replaced the Knights of Labor as the largest single labor organization.
    C. Unions had won a significant victory in the Homestead strike.
    D. Organized labor had made significant advances as a result of the Sherman Anti-Trust Law of 1890.

2. The policy of bolstering farm prices by government purchases of farm surpluses had its origin in the 2.____

    A. Federal Farm Loan Act of 1916
    B. Agricultural Marketing Act of 1929
    C. Agricultural Adjustment Act of 1933
    D. Agricultural Adjustment Act of 1938

3. During which one of the following decades did the United States sharply reduce its national debt? 3.____

    A. 1910-1920   B. 1920-1930
    C. 1930-1940   D. 1950-1960

4. Which one of the following laws, as interpreted by the courts, proved MOST disappointing to labor? 4.____

    A. The labor provisions of the Clayton Act
    B. Fair Labor Standards Act (Wages and Hours Act)
    C. The National Labor Relations Act (Wagner Act)
    D. The Norris-LaGuardia Anti-Injunction Act

5. Current *right-to-work* laws stem from the provisions of the Taft-Hartley Act which 5.____

    A. outlaw featherbedding
    B. permit states to outlaw the union shop
    C. outlaw excessive union initiation fees
    D. authorize the President of the United States to postpone strikes for eighty days

6. Which one of the following authors was LEAST concerned with social criticism of the American scene? 6.____

    A. Theodore Dreiser   B. Henry James
    C. Frank Norris   D. Booth Tarkington

7. Which one of the following statements is BEST identified with the legal philosophy of Justice Oliver Wendell Holmes? 7.____

A. The life of the law has been experience, not logic.
B. The Constitution, except for the amendments, is the same now as it was in 1787.
C. Law, like chemistry, follows a pattern of inexorable principles.
D. The law is a body of moral principles, not susceptible of scientific study.

8. At the turn of the century, which one of the following states served as an outstanding experimental laboratory in economic and social democracy? 8.____

   A. California
   B. Connecticut
   C. Pennsylvania
   D. Wisconsin

9. Which one of the following third-party leaders is INCORRECTLY paired with the presidential election in which he was a candidate? 9.____

   A. Eugene V. Debs, Socialist Party - election of 1920
   B. Robert M. LaFollette, Progressive Party - election of 1924
   C. Henry A. Wallace, Progressive Party - election of 1944
   D. James B. Weaver, Populist Party - election of 1892

10. Which one of the following statements BEST describes a significant characteristic of Theodore Roosevelt's New Nationalism? 10.____
    It

    A. emphasized the need for the decentralization of federal services
    B. placed the national need before sectional or personal advantage
    C. regarded the increasing growth of executive power as dangerous to the public welfare
    D. disregarded the concept of federalism

11. Which one of the following statements BEST explains Theodore Roosevelt's reasons for helping to bring the Russo-Japanese War to an end? 11.____
    He wanted to

    A. prevent an upset in the balance of power in the Far East
    B. thwart the ambitions of Great Britain in the Far East
    C. help Japan continue her westernization
    D. repay a debt of gratitude to Russia, for having sold Alaska to the United States

12. Theodore Roosevelt supported a revolution in Panama after the 12.____

    A. Colombian government prevented the completion of a canal by a French company
    B. Colombian Senate unanimously rejected a treaty permitting the United States to build a canal
    C. Colombian government took steps to give Great Britain permission to build a canal
    D. Nicaraguan government refused to allow a canal built on its territory

13. In which one of the following areas was Woodrow Wilson MOST successful during his first administration? 13.____

    A. Maintaining good relations with England
    B. Bringing dollar diplomacy to an end
    C. Bringing about the repeal of anti-Japanese legislation in California
    D. Avoiding United States interference in Latin America

14. Which one of the following statements MOST correctly describes our military position in 1917?

    A. Modern equipment compensated for the small size of our army and navy.
    B. While our army was strong, our navy was weak.
    C. Both our army and navy were weak.
    D. Our navy was relatively stronger than our army.

15. In 1919, Senator Lodge, Chairman of the Senate Committee on Foreign Relations, urged that the Treaty of Versailles be

    A. rejected and a new treaty drawn up
    B. ratified with reservations
    C. ratified without the League Covenant
    D. rewritten by the Senate Committee on Foreign Relations

16. Which one of the following BEST describes the Kellogg-Briand Pact of 1928?
    It

    A. was popularly known as the Locarno Pact
    B. contributed materially to international peace
    C. outlawed all wars, regardless of cause
    D. permitted war for purposes of defense

17. Which one of the following statements is TRUE of both the Agricultural Adjustment Act and the National Industrial Recovery Act of Franklin D. Roosevelt's first hundred days? Both

    A. embodied the idea of recovery through the creation of scarcities
    B. relied on the export of surpluses
    C. rested on the principle of non-interference in private industry by government agencies
    D. were based on the theory that credit was most likely to expand by deflation of the currency

18. Which one of the following statements about the United States neutrality legislation of 1935-37 is NOT true?
    It

    A. prohibited loans or credits to belligerents
    B. placed a mandatory embargo upon direct or indirect shipments of arms and implements of war to belligerents
    C. was vigorously supported by President Roosevelt
    D. permitted American citizens to travel on ships of belligerents

19. Which one of the following statements is NOT true of the election campaign of 1940?

    A. Both major candidates favored *all-out* aid to Great Britain *short of war.*
    B. Both major candidates advocated a conscription law.
    C. Roosevelt favored, and Wilkie opposed, a program of full preparedness.
    D. Both major candidates promised not to send American forces overseas.

20. Which one of the following was the MOST direct cause for the promulgation of the Truman Doctrine?
    The

    A. decision of Great Britain to withdraw its forces from Greece
    B. demands made on the United States during the Korean War
    C. need to strengthen the Marshall Plan
    D. decision to build up the military strength of NATO

21. In June 1950, the Security Council of the United Nations was able to act quickly to brand North Korea the aggressor because the

    A. General Assembly happened to be in session
    B. Soviet Union was boycotting its meetings
    C. veto does not apply in the case of armed conflict
    D. President of the United States had already ordered American armed forces to support South Korea

22. Which one of the following statements is TRUE of both Theodore Roosevelt and Harry S. Truman?
    He

    A. was elected to the Presidency for two successive terms
    B. was succeeded by a Democratic President
    C. sponsored a reactionary program in domestic affairs
    D. was much concerned with foreign affairs

23. The Caribbean policy of the United States in the twentieth century has had as a continuing cardinal objective the

    A. economic domination of the region by the United States
    B. preservation of stable political regimes
    C. extension of American political influence
    D. security of the Panama Canal Zone

24. Which one of the following groups consists of foreign visitors who wrote books delineating the character of American society?

    A. Mary Antin, Andrew Carnegie, Allan Nevins
    B. James Bryce, Alexis de Tocqueville, Frances Trollope
    C. Hamlin Garland, Marquis James, Jacob Riis
    D. Edward Bok, Merle Curti, Carl C. Jensen

25. Which one of the following is paired CORRECTLY with a book which he wrote?

    A. Theodore Dreiser - BABBITT
    B. Jack London - THEORY OF THE LEISURE CLASS
    C. O.E. Rolvaag - SON OF THE MIDDLE BORDER
    D. Lincoln Steffens - THE SHAME OF THE CITIES

KEY (CORRECT ANSWERS)

1.	B	11.	A
2.	B	12.	B
3.	B	13.	A
4.	A	14.	D
5.	B	15.	B
6.	B	16.	D
7.	A	17.	A
8.	D	18.	D
9.	C	19.	C
10.	B	20.	A

21. B
22. D
23. D
24. B
25. D

TEST 4

DIRECTIONS: Each question or incomplete statement is followed by several suggested answers or completions. Select the one that BEST answers the question or completes the statement. *PRINT THE LETTER OF THE CORRECT ANSWER IN THE SPACE AT THE RIGHT.*

1. During the 17th and 18th centuries, MOST colonial powers believed that a nation should   1.____

   A. import more than it exported
   B. export more than it imported
   C. balance exports and imports
   D. not engage in foreign trade

2. In which one of the following areas were the colonial interests of France and England in GREATEST conflict at the outbreak of the French and Indian War?   2.____
   The _____ Valley.

   A. St. Lawrence   B. Mississippi
   C. Hudson   D. Ohio

3. Which one of the following was MOST unlike the other three in his attitude toward separation of Church and State?   3.____

   A. William Bradford   B. Roger Williams
   C. John Winthrop   D. John Endicott

4. Which one of the following practices was MOST typical of education during the colonial period?   4.____

   A. Elementary education for all
   B. Higher education for leaders
   C. Vocational education for interested persons
   D. Identical educational opportunities for all

5. The trend in colonial governments from their founding to the American Revolution was toward   5.____

   A. proprietary governments
   B. self-governing colonies
   C. royal provinces
   D. remaining as originally organized

6. Which one of the following had the SAME relationship to the American Revolution as UNCLE TOM'S CABIN had to the Civil War?   6.____

   A. The Declaration of Independence
   B. The Declaration of the Rights of Man
   C. Social Contract
   D. Common Sense

7. The Northwest Ordinance of 1787 is one of the great creative contributions of the United States because it   7.____

A. solved the frictions over conflicting claims to the territory
B. established the principle of using the national domain as a source of revenue
C. peopled the territory with those committed to the doctrine of *manifest destiny*
D. laid the permanent foundations for the American territorial system and colonial policy

8. Which one of the following groups contains the names of men, ALL of whom played an influential role in the Constitutional Convention of 1787?

    A. James Madison, Alexander Hamilton, Benjamin Franklin, John Adams
    B. James Madison, Benjamin Franklin, William Patterson, Alexander Hamilton
    C. George Washington, Thomas Jefferson, Alexander Hamilton, Benjamin Franklin
    D. George Washington, Thomas Jefferson, Edmund Randolph, John Jay

9. Which of the following United States Presidents resorted to the prohibition of American exports as a means of maintaining United States neutrality?

    A. George Washington
    B. John Adams
    C. Thomas Jefferson
    D. James Monroe

10. The War of 1812 was similar to the American Revolution in that, in both,

    A. naval warfare played a minor role
    B. the Atlantic seaboard was controlled by the British
    C. the British were fighting both France and America
    D. the British forces were not as well supplied as the American

11. Which one of the following was different from the others in its interpretation of the nature of the Federal Union?

    A. The Virginia and Kentucky Resolutions
    B. The Hartford Convention
    C. The Exposition and Protest
    D. Webster's Reply to Hayne

12. During Jackson's administration, rapid settlement of the West was stimulated by

    A. the building of transcontinental railroads subsidized by federal grants
    B. the adoption of a program of internal improvements at federal expense
    C. moving Indian tribes from Georgia to lands west of the Mississippi River
    D. grants of free land to homesteaders who settled west of the Mississippi River

13. Which one of the following statements is NOT true of Jackson's spoils system? It

    A. increased the power of the chief executive
    B. provided greater equality of opportunity in office holding
    C. strengthened the political machine
    D. provided security of tenure

14. What is the CORRECT order of acquisition by the United States of the following territories?

    I. Florida
    II. Oregon Territory
    III. Mexican Cession
    IV. Louisiana Territory

    The CORRECT answer is:

    A. I, II, III, IV
    B. III, IV, I, II
    C. II, III, IV, I
    D. IV, I, II, III

15. In which one of the following respects was the period between 1850 and 1860 in the United States MOST different from the period between 1840 and 1850?

    A. Emphasis on the establishment of a national banking system
    B. Concern over federal regulation of interstate commerce
    C. Recurring crises over sectional issues
    D. Desire to abandon the policy of isolation

16. During the pre-Civil War period, MOST immigrants settled in the North and West because

    A. the South discouraged them by discriminatory legislation
    B. they preferred small farms rather than the large plantation holdings of the South
    C. they could not compete with the slave labor of the South
    D. they encountered no discrimination in these regions

17. The Republican Party platform in 1860 contained a plank on slavery which advocated the

    A. abolition of slavery in all states and territories of the union
    B. prohibition of expansion of slavery into the territories
    C. emancipation of the slaves in areas where it existed with just compensation to owners
    D. emancipation of all slaves with provision for economic assistance to the freed slaves

18. The history of mankind is a history of repeated injuries and usurpations on the part of men toward women.
    This statement was part of a declaration adopted by the

    A. Populist Party Convention of 1892
    B. Progressive Party Convention of 1912
    C. Seneca Falls Convention of 1848
    D. Communist International in 1919

19. Which one of the following was the LAST to attract public support in the United States? Interest in

    A. humanitarian and social reform
    B. international political organizations
    C. overseas expansion
    D. conservation of natural resources

20. Which group was MOST likely to win the sympathy of Southerners during the middle decades of the nineteenth century?　20.____

    A. Copperheads
    B. Carpetbaggers
    C. Liberal Party
    D. Scalawags

21. The MOST popular method of travel in the United States from the east coast to the west coast during the period 1849-1869 was　21.____

    A. transcontinental railroad
    B. ship and wagon train via the isthmus of Panama
    C. ship around Cape Horn
    D. wagon train across the country

22. Though Congress had levied a tax on personal incomes during the Civil War, the Supreme Court FIRST declared such a tax unconstitutional during President Cleveland's administration because the　22.____

    A. Civil War income tax law had been upheld as a war measure
    B. Civil War income tax law was never tested in the Supreme Court before it was repealed in 1873
    C. passage of an income tax law over President Cleveland's veto made a Supreme Court test obligatory
    D. Supreme Court was ineffectual during the Civil War and the years that followed

23. In the Teller Amendment of 1898, Congress　23.____

    A. relinquished all claims to territories taken from Spain
    B. asserted the right to govern Puerto Rico
    C. set up a commission to rehabilitate Cuba
    D. disclaimed any intention of exercising permanent control over Cuba

24. In the United States, during the latter part of the nineteenth century, the bimetallist movement　24.____

    A. had a special appeal to workmen engaged in mining precious metals of all kinds
    B. had a special appeal for government employees
    C. looked to international action as the method of establishing a bimetallic standard
    D. expected that the United States would act unilaterally to maintain the price of silver

25. The FIRST American university that was founded PRIMARILY for the purpose of fostering graduate study and research was　25.____

    A. Oberlin
    B. Swarthmore
    C. Johns Hopkins
    D. Chicago

KEY (CORRECT ANSWERS)

1. B
2. D
3. B
4. B
5. C

6. D
7. D
8. B
9. C
10. C

11. D
12. C
13. D
14. D
15. C

16. C
17. B
18. C
19. B
20. A

21. C
22. B
23. D
24. D
25. C

TEST 5

DIRECTIONS: Each question or incomplete statement is followed by several suggested answers or completions. Select the one that BEST answers the question or completes the statement. *PRINT THE LETTER OF THE CORRECT ANSWER IN THE SPACE AT THE RIGHT.*

1. Which of the following benefits did American colonials NOT enjoy under British mercantilism?   1.____

   A. Bounties for ships and ships' stores
   B. Protection from Algerian pirates
   C. An adequate currency
   D. Monopoly of the British tobacco market

2. The Treaty of Paris (1763) resulted in an expansion of _____ colonial power in _____ at the expense of _____.   2.____

   A. British; North America; France
   B. French; North America and India; England
   C. French; North America; Spain
   D. Spanish; North America; England

3. The reaction of the colonial public to the American Revolution was   3.____

   A. one of overwhelming support of the revolutionary leaders
   B. one of overwhelming opposition to separation from England
   C. about one-third for the Revolution, one-third neutral, and one-third opposed
   D. about 50 percent for and 50 percent opposed to the Revolution

4. The revolt of the American colonies against British rule became a world-wide war after the battle of   4.____

   A. Trenton   B. Long Island
   C. Saratoga   D. Yorktown

5. An IMPORTANT result of the American Revolution was the   5.____

   A. strengthening of the executive power in state governments
   B. abolition of entail and primogeniture in most of the states
   C. disappearance of the slave trade
   D. abolition of property qualifications for voting

6. The time-honored doctrine that colonies existed for the benefit of the mother country and were politically subordinate and socially inferior to her was DEFINITELY repudiated by the   6.____

   A. Land Ordinance
   B. Constitution of the United States
   C. Bill of Rights
   D. Northwest Ordinance

7. Which one of the following American Revolutionary patriots was violently opposed to ratification of the Constitution of the United States?   7.____

   A. Patrick Henry   B. John Marshall
   C. John Hancock   D. Thomas Jefferson

21

8. The fundamental object of Hamilton's domestic and foreign policy was to strengthen the federal government by

    A. favoring a policy of free trade
    B. substituting the parliamentary system for the federal system
    C. averting entanglement in the wars of Europe
    D. favoring the interests of the propertied and monied classes

9. Which one of the following great documents in the history of American democracy appeared after the inauguration of George Washington?
   The

    A. Declaration of Independence
    B. Federal Bill of Rights
    C. Virginia Bill of Rights
    D. Northwest Ordinance

10. An IMPORTANT cause of the repudiation of the Federalist Party in the election of 1800 was the

    A. suppression of the Whiskey Rebellion
    B. adoption of a policy of tariff protection
    C. cancellation of the Franco-American alliance
    D. adoption of the Alien and Sedition Acts

11. The United States found it expedient to build a navy as a result of the

    A. Genet Affair
    B. XYZ Affair
    C. War with the Barbary pirates
    D. War of 1812

12. Which of the following periods in the tariff history of the United States was MOST clearly protectionist in policy?

    A. The Federalist Period (1789-1800)
    B. The Era of Good Feeling (1816-1823)
    C. 1824-1833
    D. 1833-1861

13. In its opposition to which one of the following did the North uphold the States' Rights Doctrine?
    The

    A. Alien and Sedition Acts   B. War of 1812
    C. Tariff of Abominations   D. Dred Scott Decision

14. The Embargo Act of 1807 provided that

    A. exports to England and France were forbidden
    B. all exports from the United States were forbidden
    C. all imports as well as exports were forbidden
    D. trade with England and France would be resumed when they ceased interfering with American shipping

15. Which of the following is TRUE with regard to the Monroe Doctrine?

    A. Canning suggested that the Americans issue it.
    B. The Cabinet was unanimous in its support of it.
    C. Russia had decided to retreat on the West Coast before it was issued.
    D. Congress made it law in 1824.

16. Henry Clay's American system was designed to

    A. strengthen the political power of the West as against the East and South
    B. compromise differences between North and South on tariff legislation
    C. facilitate expansion to the Pacific coast
    D. reduce sectional differences by creation of a unified economy

17. Which one of the following is NOT correctly grouped with the school of writers known as New England Transcendentalists?

    A. Bronson Alcott
    B. Henry Thoreau
    C. William Cullen Bryant
    D. Ralph Waldo Emerson

18. A common demand of labor organizations during the Jacksonian period was

    A. more liberal sick pay
    B. the ten-hour day
    C. seniority rights
    D. the worker's right to an individual labor contract

19. The importance of the case of Commonwealth vs. Hunt was that the decision rejected the doctrine that labor unions

    A. have a right to bargain collectively
    B. must admit employers to membership
    C. are illegal conspiracies in restraint of trade
    D. have a right to strike

20. In which one of the following treaties did the United States make NO territorial gains?

    A. Spanish Treaty of 1819
    B. Treaty of Ghent
    C. Treaty of Guadalupe Hidalgo
    D. Oregon Treaty of 1846

21. The traditional method of determining the extension of slavery into new territories by Congressional enactments that defined its limits was abandoned in the case of the

    A. Northwest Territory
    B. Louisiana Territory
    C. Mexican Cession
    D. Oregon Territory

22. Daniel Webster reversed his traditional stand in regard to states' rights in the

    A. Dartmouth College Case
    B. Webster-Hayne Debates
    C. debate on the Compromise of 1850
    D. Kansas-Nebraska Bill

23. The various government land acts passed prior to the Civil War had the effect of _____ the minimum of acres which had to be purchased and _____ the cost per acre.

    A. reducing; decreasing
    B. increasing; increasing
    C. reducing; increasing
    D. increasing; decreasing

24. In the election of 1860, Abraham Lincoln's Republican Party advocated the

    A. abolition of slavery throughout the United States
    B. abolition of slavery in the territories only
    C. prevention of the extension of slavery into the territories
    D. adoption of the principle of squatter sovereignty

25. Lincoln's Emancipation Proclamation had an important effect on Great Britain's policies toward the Confederacy because it strengthened sympathy with the North among British

    A. landowners
    B. workers
    C. exporters
    D. manufacturers

KEY (CORRECT ANSWERS)

1.	C	11.	B
2.	A	12.	C
3.	C	13.	B
4.	C	14.	B
5.	B	15.	C
6.	D	16.	D
7.	A	17.	C
8.	D	18.	B
9.	B	19.	C
10.	D	20.	B

21. C
22. C
23. A
24. C
25. B

EXAMINATION SECTION
TEST 1

DIRECTIONS: Each question or incomplete statement is followed by several suggested answers or completions. Select the one that BEST answers the question or completes the statement. *PRINT THE LETTER OF THE CORRECT ANSWER IN THE SPACE AT THE RIGHT.*

1. Which one of the following statements is CORRECT concerning economic conditions in the South from 1865 to 1900?

    A. By 1900, the South was manufacturing more woolen goods than New England.
    B. The proportion of the nation's manufacturing done in the South was much the same in 1900 as it was in 1860.
    C. There was a steady rise in the price of cotton from the close of the Civil War to 1900.
    D. Landlords and merchants to whom sharecroppers were indebted encouraged diversified farming.

    1.____

2. Which one of the following disputes between Great Britain and the United States since 1865 was settled by diplomacy rather than by arbitration?
The

    A. Bering Sea Controversy
    B. Alabama Claims
    C. Alaskan Boundary Dispute
    D. Isthmian Question

    2.____

3. In which instance was an important compromise involving the North and the South arrived at without public debate or open publication?

    A. 1820 B. 1833 C. 1850 D. 1877

    3.____

4. Which one of the following prominent Americans is associated with the following observation: *Though competitiveness may sometimes be hard for the individual, it is best for the race because it insures the survival of the fittest in every department?*

    A. Andrew Carnegie
    B. Walt Whitman
    C. Henry Adams
    D. James Russell Lowell

    4.____

5. Which statement BEST describes the major objective of the Populist movement?
It

    A. was directed against monopolistic control of western lands by large-scale entrepreneurs
    B. advocated government ownership and operation of agricultural lands
    C. sought to achieve lower railroad rates through the elimination of marginal unprofitable roads
    D. was an effort by segments of our agricultural population to restore profits in the face of unfavorable market and price conditions

    5.____

6. Historians are GENERALLY agreed that, when the U.S. declared war on Spain in 1898,

    6.____

A. there was conclusive evidence that the Spanish government had been responsible for the sinking of the Maine
B. the possibilities of settlement by measures short of war had by no means been exhausted
C. the Spanish government had refused to submit the whole question of responsibility for the sinking of the Maine to international arbitration as we had suggested
D. Spain had as yet failed to repudiate the De Lome letter or to remove the Minister from his post

7. In which of the following instances are BOTH items characteristic of the American scene during the period from January 1, 1898 to January 1, 1904? 7._____

   A. The U.S. was at peace with the world and insulated, as well, from Latin American problems.
   B. There was an upward surge in labor union membership and a great expansion of trusts.
   C. Prices declined, and there was a serious business recession.
   D. The federal government became more decentralized, and local government became less corrupt.

8. In which one of the following pairs are there two members of the same political party, both of whom were so-called *dark horses* and who were ultimately nominated for the Presidency by the national conventions of their party? 8._____

   A. Wilson in 1912 and Stevenson in 1952
   B. Harding in 1920 and Willkie in 1940
   C. Taft in 1908 and Hoover in 1928
   D. Coolidge in 1924 and Dewey in 1944

9. Which series is arranged in CORRECT chronological order? 9._____

   A. Wabash vs. Illinois; Granger Laws; Sherman Anti-Trust Law
   B. Granger Laws; Sherman Anti-Trust Act; Wabash vs. Illinois
   C. Interstate Commerce Act; Wabash vs. Illinois; Granger Laws
   D. Granger Laws; Wabash vs. Illinois; Interstate Commerce Act

10. Which was the MOST important international factor that led to agrarian depressions in the U.S. from the early 1870's to the 1890's? 10._____

    A. An almost uninterrupted international price decline
    B. Japanese rise to power in the Far East
    C. European wars
    D. European emigration to America

11. In which labor dispute did government interference, either federal or local, result in a solution generally SATISFACTORY to labor? 11._____

    A. Homestead strike of 1892
    B. Railroad strikes of 1877
    C. Pullman strike of 1894
    D. Anthracite coal strike of 1902

12. Which group contains a list of names of foreign heads of state, all of whom Theodore Roosevelt had to deal with while he occupied the office of President?

    A. Sun Yat Sen, Tsar Alexander III, Pancho Villa
    B. Emperor Mutsuhito, Emperor Francis Joseph, Joseph Pilsudski
    C. Mustapha Kemal, Yuan Shih-kai, Emperor Louis Napoleon
    D. Porfirio Diaz, Kaiser William II, Tsar Nicholas II

13. The PRIMARY concern of American foreign policy in the years between the Peace of Paris of 1898 and the outbreak of World War I was to

    A. prevent the rise of Germany as a threat to world peace
    B. restrain Japanese aggression in the Pacific
    C. consolidate our newly established position in the Caribbean and Central America
    D. unify China

14. Which BEST describes the reformist tradition of the Progressive movement of the early 1900's?
    It was

    A. chiefly concerned with a desire to democratize an economy already in sound working order
    B. chiefly concerned with managing an economy to meet the problems of collapse in such a way as to restore prosperity
    C. largely free of the type of crusading that aimed to restore government to the people through greater direct popular democracy and the defeat of political bosses
    D. strongly in favor of a change in viewpoint in foreign policy from isolationism to internationalism

15. *A peace forced upon the loser, a victor's terms imposed upon the vanquished would be accepted in humiliation, under duress, at an intolerable sacrifice, and would leave a sting, a resentment, a bitter memory upon which the terms of peace would rest...as upon quicksand.*
    This statement is part of an(the)

    A. address by Woodrow Wilson in January 1917
    B. Fourteen Points
    C. Atlantic Charter
    D. address by Franklin D. Roosevelt in January 1942

16. *Despairing of crusades and crusaders, the American voters sent to the White House a handsome, genial mediocrity who promised not heroics, but healing.*
    This statement attempts to portray President

    A. Andrew Johnson   B. William Howard Taft
    C. Warren Harding   D. Harry S. Truman

17. Which one of the following contains a list of movements in American history, all of which were ALIKE in their antagonism towards minority groups?

    A. American Protective Association, Know Nothing Party, Klu Klux Klan
    B. Populist Party, Muckrakers, Stalwarts
    C. Coxey's Army, N.A.A.C.P., Mugwumps
    D. Knights of Labor, Radical Republicans, Mormonism

18. A list of Presidents elected by a minority of the popular vote would include

    A. T. Roosevelt in 1900 and Taft in 1908
    B. Harding in 1920 and Hoover in 1928
    C. F.D. Roosevelt in 1944 and Eisenhower in 1952
    D. Cleveland in 1892 and Wilson in 1912

19. In which instance are the items listed CLOSELY associated with corruption in government?

    A. McDuffie-Tydings Act, Coxey's Army
    B. *Dollar Diplomacy,* Northern Securities Case
    C. Credit Mobilier, Teapot Dome
    D. Fair Labor Standards Act, Granger Laws

20. Which was characteristic of the depression period of the 1930's?

    A. The existence of prohibitive tariffs in western Europe and in the U.S.
    B. Successful international collaboration in currency stabilization
    C. Rising prices of raw materials and consumer goods throughout the world
    D. Restoration of the gold standard in western Europe and the U.S.

21. President Franklin D. Roosevelt's conflict with the Supreme Court stemmed LARGELY from the Court's decision in the cases involving

    A. T.V.A. and the Wages and Hours Law
    B. The Wagner Labor Relations Act and the Hatch Act
    C. Social Security and the S.E.C.
    D. The A.A.A. and the N.I.R.A.

22. The U.S. Neutrality Laws of the 1930's, in effect, constituted an abandonment of our traditional policy of

    A. Freedom of the Seas   B. The Open Door
    C. The Monroe Doctrine   D. Pan Americanism

23. Which of the following statements apply to ALL of the following: Lend Lease; The Destroyer-Naval Base Deal; Cash and Carry?
    All of these acts

    A. were made in the form of treaties that were ultimately ratified by the U.S. Senate
    B. were promulgated for the purpose of aiding England against Germany
    C. were an outgrowth of the Atlantic Charter
    D. are associated with the First World War

24. Which one of the following American writers is INCORRECTLY included as a contemporary of the others?

    A. Van Wyck Brooks   B. Vernon Louis Parrington
    C. Edward Bellamy   D. Henry L. Mencken

25. In which one of the following pairs is the person linked with a field in which he or she did NOT attain prominence? 25.____

    A. Frank Lloyd Wright - architecture
    B. Edna St. Vincent Millay - poetry
    C. Sherwood Anderson - literary criticism
    D. John Dos Passes - the novel

KEY (CORRECT ANSWERS)

1.	B	11.	D
2.	D	12.	D
3.	D	13.	C
4.	A	14.	A
5.	D	15.	A
6.	B	16.	C
7.	B	17.	A
8.	B	18.	D
9.	D	19.	C
10.	A	20.	A

21. D
22. A
23. B
24. C
25. C

TEST 2

DIRECTIONS: Each question or incomplete statement is followed by several suggested answers or completions. Select the one that BEST answers the question or completes the statement. *PRINT THE LETTER OF THE CORRECT ANSWER IN THE SPACE AT THE RIGHT.*

1. Which of the following, commonly used in Europe before the 15th century, was NEVER discovered by the American Indian?

    A. Potter's wheel
    B. Tanning of skins
    C. Smelting of minerals
    D. Dugout canoe

2. The quitrent in Colonial New York was a

    A. tax paid by landowners for the right to rent land
    B. substitute payment for feudal dues
    C. tax paid by a colonial proprietor for his right to contract the services of an indentured servant
    D. special levy to help finance the cost of the militia

3. Which one of the following is TRUE with respect to the Proclamation Line of 1763?

    A. The price of land west of the Appalachians was raised.
    B. The area between the Appalachians and the Mississippi was reserved for the Indians.
    C. Virginia's claim to land north and west of the Ohio River was nullified.
    D. The Townshend Acts were repealed.

4. Which of the following is a CORRECT statement with respect to the crises between England and the 13 colonies?

    A. It was illegal for England to have exploited the colonies for the benefit of the mother country.
    B. The colonies disputed the right of Parliament to legislate for the colonies.
    C. In most of the colonial charters, the assembly was given the right to make such laws as did not conflict with the laws of England.
    D. The King of England insisted on the right to veto acts of Parliament and of the colonial legislatures.

5. Which one of the following did NOT help the American cause during the American Revolution?

    A. Thaddeus Kosciuszko
    B. Baron Steuben
    C. Edmond Genet
    D. Baron de Kalb

6. Which one of the following measures was NOT employed to finance the American Revolution?

    A. Foreign loans
    B. Income taxes
    C. Requisitions from states
    D. Continental currency

7. Which one of the following was NOT a provision of the Northwest Ordinance of 1787?

   A. No more than three states could be formed
   B. Newly admitted states to be on an equal footing with the original thirteen states
   C. Civil liberties were guaranteed
   D. Slavery was prohibited in this territory

8. Under the Articles of Confederation, Congress lacked the power to

   A. make treaties
   B. borrow money
   C. declare war
   D. collect taxes

9. Shays' Rebellion was a protest against the

   A. Alien and Sedition Acts
   B. ratification of the Constitution
   C. tax on whiskey
   D. plight of the debtor clause

10. The only state which did NOT send delegates to the Constitutional Convention was

    A. New York
    B. Rhode Island
    C. Connecticut
    D. North Carolina

11. In which group did NEITHER individual participate in the debates of the Constitutional Convention?

    A. Alexander Hamilton, George Washington
    B. James Madison, Samuel Adams
    C. Benjamin Franklin, William Paterson
    D. John Hancock, Thomas Paine

12. Which of the following statements about the nature of the Constitutional Convention are CORRECT?
    I. Delegates to the Convention were not instructed to draw up a new Constitution.
    II. There was general agreement on the need for a strong central government.
    III. The majority of the delegates were in favor of manhood suffrage.
    IV. There was a surprising absence of sectional rivalries.

    The CORRECT answer is:

    A. I, II
    B. II, III, IV
    C. I, III
    D. I, II, IV

13. One effect of Hamilton's financial system was that it

    A. gained the support of the farmers
    B. won the support of all sections in the United States
    C. increased states' rights
    D. strengthened the central government

14. The resentment in the United States following the XYZ Affair resulted in an undeclared war with

    A. Spain   B. France   C. Canada   D. England

15. Of the following, the MOST important reason for the downfall of the Federalists was the

    A. Alien and Sedition Laws
    B. establishment of the First National Bank
    C. failure of the Federalists to pay off the national debt
    D. failure of the Federalists to remain neutral

16. Which one of the Presidents listed below defended his policy of filling vacancies in public office with members of his own party by saying, *Few government officials die and none resign.*

    A. Thomas Jefferson
    B. Theodore Roosevelt
    C. Andrew Jackson
    D. Abraham Lincoln

17. Which one of the following reasons did NOT influence the purchase of Louisiana? The

    A. desire to obtain new land for western settlement
    B. fear of France as a western neighbor of the United States
    C. report by Lewis and Clark of the discovery of abundant natural resources
    D. withdrawal of the *right of deposit* at New Orleans

18. Which of the following was NOT a cause of westward migration in the United States in the period after the War of 1812?

    A. Hard times in the East
    B. The need for more land for cotton cultivation
    C. An increasing number of immigrants
    D. The construction of transcontinental railroads

19. *The American System* was advocated in 1817 by Henry Clay and

    A. John Calhoun
    B. James Monroe
    C. James Madison
    D. John Marshall

20. Which of the following did NOT take place while Monroe was President?

    A. The purchase of Florida
    B. The agreement with Britain for the joint occupation of Oregon
    C. Settlement of the Maine boundary dispute
    D. The limitation of armaments on the Great Lakes

21. Great Britain and the United States arranged for naval disarmament on the Great Lakes by the

    A. Treaty of 1818
    B. Rush-Bagot Agreement
    C. Treaty of 1846 with England
    D. Webster-Ashburton Treaty

22. Andrew Jackson did all of the following EXCEPT

    A. threatened to use force against South Carolina for nullifying the Tariff Acts of 1828 and 1832
    B. refused to enforce a Supreme Court decision preventing Georgia from extending its authority over Indian lands within its borders

C. encouraged the spending of federal funds for roads within individual western states
D. vetoed a bill to renew the charter of the Second Bank of the United States

23. Which one of the following was NOT a result of the Jacksonian movement? 23._____
The

   A. abolition of the party caucus as a means of selecting presidential candidates
   B. widespread extension of the suffrage
   C. prevention of sectional friction over slavery
   D. increased practice of rotation in office

24. All of the following factors helped bring about the annexation of Texas in 1845 EXCEPT: 24._____

   A. Texas was becoming a center of foreign intrigue
   B. Mexican officials finally recognized Texas' independence
   C. Americans were caught up in the fever of manifest destiny
   D. Annexation was an important campaign issue in the election of 1844

25. Which one of the following may NOT be included in a list of the influences of the *frontier* 25._____
on American history? It

   A. acted as a possible *safety valve* for economic unrest
   B. retarded the development of the industrial East
   C. had a democratizing influence on the country
   D. was a spur at once to individual initiative and collective social action

KEY (CORRECT ANSWERS)

1. A
2. B
3. B
4. C
5. C

6. B
7. A
8. D
9. D
10. B

11. D
12. A
13. D
14. B
15. A

16. A
17. C
18. D
19. A
20. C

21. B
22. C
23. C
24. B
25. B

TEST 3

DIRECTIONS: Each question or incomplete statement is followed by several suggested answers or completions. Select the one that BEST answers the question or completes the statement. *PRINT THE LETTER OF THE CORRECT ANSWER IN THE SPACE AT THE RIGHT.*

1. Which one of the following men was MOST unlike the other three in his views regarding slavery?   1.____

    A. Wendell Phillips
    B. Henry Ward Beecher
    C. Daniel Webster
    D. John G. Whittier

2. The doctrine of popular sovereignty was FIRST stated in the   2.____

    A. Wilmot Proviso
    B. Compromise of 1850
    C. Kansas-Nebraska Act
    D. Missouri Compromise

3. Of the following, the TWO leading senators who made possible the passage of the Compromise of 1850 were   3.____

    A. Calhoun and Clay
    B. Clay and Webster
    C. Clay and Douglas
    D. Calhoun and Webster

4. Which one of the following was NOT a provision of the Compromise of 1850?   4.____

    A. A strict fugitive slave law
    B. Missouri to be admitted as a slave state
    C. Texas to be given ten million dollars for surrendering territory to the federal government
    D. California to be admitted as a free state

5. Which of the following did NOT represent a clash of interest between the United States and Great Britain during the Civil War?   5.____
    I. Trent Affair
    II. Monitor v. Merrimac
    III. Alabama Raids
    IV. Maximilian Affair

    The CORRECT answer is:

    A. I, IV   B. I, III   C. II, III   D. II, IV

6. Which one of the following reasons was NOT advanced by the Radical Republicans who opposed the Lincoln-Johnson plans for Reconstruction?   6.____

    A. They believed that southern leaders should be punished by being stripped of civil rights and property.
    B. They wanted to restore the balance of power between the executive and legislative branches of the government which had existed prior to the war.
    C. They feared that granting the ballot to the Negro would drive Southern whites into the Democratic Party.
    D. Southern governments set up under the Lincoln-Johnson plan were under the control of the Democratic Party.

7. Which of the following is NOT true regarding the 14th Amendment?
It

   A. provided for a proportionate reduction in representation in the House when a state denied the franchise except for participation in rebellion or other crime
   B. abrogated the *three-fifths* clause, thereby increasing Southern representation in the House of Representatives
   C. was formulated because of widespread doubt as to the constitutionality of the Civil Rights Act
   D. honored the payment of both the Union and the Confederate debt

8. Which one of the following promises was NOT made to Southern Democratic leaders in return for their support in the election of Hayes over Tilden?
The

   A. withdrawal of federal troops from the South
   B. appropriation by Congress of substantial funds for internal improvements in the South
   C. downward revision of the high post-war tariffs
   D. appointment of at least one Southerner to the Cabinet

9. Which one of the following statements is NOT true concerning the currency situation after the Civil War?

   A. At the close of the war, farmers urged that government bonds be redeemable in greenbacks.
   B. In 1875, Congress provided for the redemption of greenbacks by specie.
   C. In order to maintain purchasing power, businessmen favored continuance of greenback currency.
   D. At his inauguration, President Grant favored redemption of government bonds in gold.

10. The Populist platform in 1892 called for
    I. a continuation of silver purchases under the Sherman Act
    II. a graduated income tax
    III. postal savings banks
    IV. direct election of senators
    The CORRECT answer is:

    A. I, III
    B. I, II, III
    C. II, III, IV
    D. II, IV

11. Which one of the following was NOT a factor responsible for the rapid settlement of the Far West from 1870 to 1890?

    A. Transportation facilities
    B. Increased immigration
    C. Government soil conservation policies
    D. New methods of fencing

12. Which of the following statements does NOT describe an essential factor of the Economic Revolution (1865-1900) in the U.S.?
The

A. acquisition of a labor supply sufficiently large and cheap for the purposes of industry
B. acquisition of colonies containing many valuable raw materials
C. discovery and the exploitation of natural resources such as iron, coal, copper, oil
D. growth of a domestic market and the development of foreign markets

13. Which of the following did NOT significantly improve the lot of the United States farmer from 1900 to 1920?

    A. A larger supply of money in circulation
    B. An expanding foreign trade
    C. The encouragement of agricultural cooperatives by the United States government
    D. An easing of short- and long-term credit facilities

14. A MAJOR cause for the decrease in United States farm exports immediately after World War I was that

    A. production in the United States declined
    B. competition with other agricultural nations increased
    C. domestic demands increased
    D. Europe quickly regained her economic self-sufficiency

15. Which one of the following is NOT true concerning immigration to the United States during and after World War I?

    A. The AFL did not oppose the Displaced Persons Act.
    B. Great Britain and Germany are the two countries from which the largest number of immigrants have come to the United States since 1924.
    C. Carry-over provisions of unfilled quotas of previous years have allowed for some measure of flexibility in our quota law.
    D. A powerful deterrent to immigration was the exercising of the right to exclude all prospective immigrants likely to become public charges.

16. Which one of the following statements BEST describes the significance of the Interstate Commerce Act?

    A. The long and short haul abuse was eliminated.
    B. Rebates and pooling were declared unlawful.
    C. It set up the first federal regulatory commission in United States history.
    D. It gave the judiciary the power to fix the scope and enforceability of the measure.

17. The presidential elections of 1916 and 1940 may be compared in all of the following EXCEPT that in both campaigns

    A. the Democrats promised to keep the United States out of war, if possible
    B. the Republicans were divided between interventionists and isolationists
    C. the Democrats gave first and second place on the ticket to the men who had been serving in that office
    D. only the Republicans appealed to the isolationist vote

18. The *return to normalcy* after World War I found which of the following statements TRUE?
    I. The Federal Trade Commission issued many *cease and desist* orders because of the alarming growth of monopoly
    II. Because of a complete laissez-faire philosophy, the government decided to reverse post-Civil War practice and not grant any subsidies to industry
    III. The railroads were returned to private ownership despite the Plumb Plan, in addition to which such practices as pooling were made lega
    IV. The Federal Power Commission was authorized to grant licenses to power corporations on public lands

    The CORRECT answer is:

    A. I, II
    B. I, II, III, IV
    C. III, IV
    D. I, III, IV

19. Which one of the following would NOT be included in a list of famous American women who achieved fame as social reformers?

    A. Jane Addams
    B. Frances Willard
    C. Emily Dickinson
    D. Lillian Wald

20. Which one of the following did NOT achieve fame because of his writings on the role of the immigrant in the United States?

    A. Jacob Riis
    B. Louis Adamic
    C. Mary Antin
    D. Louis D. Brandeis

21. Which one of the following INCORRECTLY pairs a newspaper and newspaperman?

    A. NEW YORK HERALD - James Gordon Bennett
    B. NEW YORK TRIBUNE - Horace Greeley
    C. NEW YORK EVENING POST - Walt Whitman
    D. NEW YORK TIMES - Henry Raymond

22. Of the following American scientists, which one is NOT famous for his research in physical science?

    A. William C. Menninger
    B. Harold C. Urey
    C. Robert A. Millikan
    D. Arthur H. Compton

23. Which of the following developments could be observed in education in the United States during the period from 1865-1900?
    I. Educational facilities increased faster than population.
    II. Graduate studies were offered by an increasing number of universities.
    III. There was a growing interest in adult education and in library building.
    IV. The teaching profession achieved adequate standards throughout the nation.

    The CORRECT answer is:

    A. II, III, IV
    B. I, II, III, IV
    C. I, II, III
    D. I, III, IV

24. The American territorial acquisitions of 1898 differed from previous acquisitions in that   24._____
    A. the acquired lands were not desired for settlement
    B. military force was first used in 1898 as a means of acquisition
    C. agricultural interests demanded the new territories
    D. economic motives were important reasons for the new expansion

25. Which one of the following events may be considered a CAUSE of the other three?   25._____
    A. Purchase of the Danish West Indies
    B. Occupation of Haiti
    C. Building of the Panama Canal
    D. Intervention in Santo Domingo

KEY (CORRECT ANSWERS)

1. C		11. C	
2. B		12. B	
3. B		13. C	
4. B		14. B	
5. D		15. C	
6. C		16. C	
7. D		17. C	
8. C		18. C	
9. C		19. C	
10. C		20. D	

21. C
22. A
23. C
24. A
25. C

TEST 4

DIRECTIONS: Each question or incomplete statement is followed by several suggested answers or completions. Select the one that BEST answers the question or completes the statement. *PRINT THE LETTER OF THE CORRECT ANSWER IN THE SPACE AT THE RIGHT.*

1. An IMPORTANT motive for Hawaii's request for annexation was the desire of influential Hawaiian business interests for   1.____

    A. naval protection against German threats
    B. a profitable market for Hawaiian sugar
    C. unrestricted Hawaiian immigration into the United States
    D. large investments of American capital in Hawaiian agriculture

2. Which of the following did NOT contribute to the difficulties faced by Puerto Rico under American administration?   2.____

    A. Reliance on sugar and tobacco as cash crops
    B. Absentee ownership of a large proportion of the land
    C. Indifference of the U.S. government to sanitary conditions
    D. The extreme density of population of the island

3. *The public debt CANNOT occasion armed intervention nor even the actual intervention of the territory of American nations by a European nation* is a quotation from the   3.____

    A. Drago Doctrine   B. Stimson Doctrine
    C. Good Neighbor Policy   D. Teller Resolution

4. Which one of the following was NOT one of the accomplishments of Grant's administration in foreign affairs?   4.____

    A. Settlement of the Alabama claims
    B. Breaking up of the attempt of the Fenians to seize Canada
    C. Encouragement of the principle of international arbitration
    D. Purchase of Alaska

5. Theodore Roosevelt's interpretation of the presidency led him to play an important part in all but one of the following events. In which one was he NOT involved?   5.____

    A. Treaty of Portsmouth at the close of the Russo-Japanese War
    B. Morocco Crisis of 1905-1906
    C. Hague Conference of 1907
    D. The Venezuelan Boundary Dispute

6. The Gentlemen's Agreement of 1907 between the United States and Japan provided for   6.____

    A. mutual recognition of the Open Door policy in China
    B. Japanese restriction of Japanese emigration to the United States
    C. restrictions on the naval armaments of the two nations
    D. United States restrictions on Japanese immigration

7. Which of the following would be MOST likely to appear on a list of examples of international cooperation on the part of the United States between World War I and World War II?
    I. Washington Arms Conference
    II. Fordney-McCumber Tariff
    III. Stimson Doctrine
    IV. Kellogg-Briand Pact
   The CORRECT answer is:

   A. I, II, IV
   C. I, III, IV
   B. I, II, III
   D. II, III, IV

8. In which of the following items is an American statesman INCORRECTLY associated with a foreign policy of the United States?

   A. Henry L. Stimson - non-recognition of Manchukuo
   B. Cordell Hull - reciprocal trade agreements
   C. William Jennings Bryan - strict interpretation of American neutral rights
   D. Charles Evans Hughes - naval disarmament

9. The problem of war debts was largely avoided in World War II through the operation of the

   A. Johnson Act
   B. Lend-Lease Act
   C. World War Foreign Debt Commission
   D. Office of War Mobilization

10. The Atlantic Charter was reminiscent of Wilson's Fourteen Points, but differed from the latter in that it

    A. did not advocate self-determination of peoples
    B. omitted reference to disarmament
    C. did not emphasize economic advancement
    D. was stated in general rather than specific terms

11. Which of the following statements regarding the provisions of the Clayton Act of 1914 are TRUE?
    It
    I. established the FTC to enforce the rule that *unfair competition* was illegal
    II. did not regard labor unions and farm organizations as conspiracies in restraint of trade
    III. declared illegal *tying clauses* if the result was to prevent competition
    IV. permitted the purchase of stock in another company solely for investment purposes
    The CORRECT answer is:

    A. I, II, III, IV
    C. I, III, IV
    B. II, III, IV
    D. I, II, IV

12. Which of the following statements are TRUE regarding the 1957 decision of the Supreme Court against the E.I. DuPont de Nemours and Company?
    I. The court applied the original Clayton Act to vertical combinations.
    II. DuPont was ordered to sell its General Motors shares by January 1, 1958.
    III. Stock acquisition gave an illegal competitive advantage in the sale to General Motors of DuPont fabrics and paints.
    IV. Justice Clark disqualified himself because he had been an attorney for the DuPont Company.
    The CORRECT answer is:

    A. II, IV   B. I, III   C. I, II   D. III, IV

13. The Pullman Strike of 1894 is significant because

    A. it was the first strike in American history that was fomented by a radical political party
    B. the federal government cooperated with a state government in breaking a strike
    C. it resulted in the passage of laws against anarcho-syndicalist unions
    D. the Sherman Anti-Trust Law was used against a labor union

14. Which one of the following was NOT advocated by the American farmer between 1870-1890 in his attempt to solve his problems?

    A. Cooperative marketing of produce
    B. Government regulation of interstate carriers
    C. Contraction of the currency to raise prices
    D. Political action through the formation of third parties

15. The *Tide Lands Oil Controversy* resulted in

    A. federal government ownership and control over offshore oil and other resources up to the three mile limit
    B. complete state ownership and control over off-shore soil and other resources up to the three mile limit
    C. co-ownership and control by the states and federal government
    D. ownership and control by private interests over offshore oil and other resources up to the three mile limit

16. The Populists of the 1890's revered Jefferson and Jackson because these Presidents had

    A. championed local government and limitations on the federal power
    B. espoused the cause of the farmer and opposed monopoly
    C. advocated cheap money
    D. upheld the majesty of the United States in its dealings with foreign nations

17. Which group of states created from territories acquired before the Civil War was admitted to the Union after 1900?

    A. Oklahoma, New Mexico, Arizona
    B. Minnesota, Michigan, Wisconsin
    C. Washington, Oregon, Utah
    D. Nevada, Wyoming, Idaho

18. By which one of the following United States tariff laws were tariff rates GENERALLY lowered?   18.____

    A. Dingley   B. Underwood-Simmons
    C. Morrill   D. Payne-Aldrich

19. An act which placed restrictions on the use of injunctions in labor disputes was the _____ Act.   19.____

    A. Norris-LaGuardia   B. Wagner-Connery
    C. Fair Labor Standards   D. Keating-Owen

20. The Hapburn Act, the Elkins Act, and the Mann-Elkins Act ALL helped to strengthen the power of the   20.____

    A. Federal Trade Commission
    B. Interstate Commerce Commission
    C. Federal Reserve Bank
    D. Federal Communications Commission

21. The impetus for the formation of the C.I.O. came from   21.____

    A. employees of the railways
    B. employees of mass production industries
    C. workers in skilled trades
    D. construction workers

22. Which one of the following is INCORRECTLY paired?   22.____

    A. John Peter Altgeld - Pullman Strike
    B. Terence V. Powderly - Knights of Labor
    C. Samuel Gompers - American Federation of Labor
    D. William Green - National Labor Union

23. The IMMEDIATE occasion for the issuance of the Roosevelt Corollary to the Monroe Doctrine was a controversy involving   23.____

    A. the Dominican Republic   B. Venezuela
    C. Haiti   D. Colombia

24. Which term BEST describes the foreign policy views, in 1898, of Theodore Roosevelt, Henry Cabot Lodge, and Alfred T. Mahan?   24.____

    A. Expansionist   B. Isolationist
    C. Anti-imperialist   D. Pacifist

25. Which document lists specific territorial changes sought as an outcome of war?   25.____

    A. Wilson's War Message to Congress in April 1917
    B. The Fourteen Points
    C. The Atlantic Charter
    D. Franklin D. Roosevelt's War Message to Congress in December 1941

KEY (CORRECT ANSWERS)

1. B
2. C
3. A
4. D
5. D

6. B
7. C
8. C
9. B
10. D

11. B
12. B
13. D
14. C
15. B

16. B
17. A
18. B
19. A
20. B

21. B
22. D
23. A
24. A
25. B

TEST 5

DIRECTIONS: Each question or incomplete statement is followed by several suggested answers or completions. Select the one that BEST answers the question or completes the statement. *PRINT THE LETTER OF THE CORRECT ANSWER IN THE SPACE AT THE RIGHT.*

1. Which one of the following was the OLDEST Indian culture in Mexico? 1.____

   A. Aztec   B. Inca   C. Toltec   D. Mayan

2. With respect to the Spanish conquest in America, all of the following statements are correct EXCEPT: 2.____

   A. In one generation, the Spaniards acquired more new territory than Rome conquered in five centuries
   B. Spaniards organized and administered all they conquered, brought in the arts and letters of Europe, and converted millions to their faith
   C. The conquests of the Spaniards were motivated mainly by their desire to spread Christianity
   D. For the most part, the Spaniards treated the Indians with great cruelty

3. Society in colonial America was characterized by 3.____

   A. aristocratic ancestry of colonial settlers
   B. social equality within the colonies
   C. a large wage-earning class of citizens
   D. fluidity of classes

4. The MAIN influence on the law and government of the United States today may be traced back to the 4.____

   A. Celts   B. Anglo-Saxons
   C. Romans   D. Greeks

5. The New England Confederation was formed PRIMARILY to 5.____

   A. protest more effectively against oppressive taxes levied by England
   B. prevent revocation of colonial charters
   C. organize colonial defenses against possible Indian attacks
   D. foster increased trade among the colonies along the North Atlantic seaboard

6. Which one of the following statements is CORRECT according to modern scholarship? 6.____

   A. The Boston Massacre was an unprovoked attack upon the citizenry.
   B. Samuel and John Adams were alike in their radical views.
   C. New England merchants were generally less concerned with possibilities of uninterrupted trade than with questions of Parliamentary supremacy.
   D. The passage of the Intolerable Acts switched the colonial grievances from basically economic to political ones.

7. All of the following are embodied in the Declaration of Independence EXCEPT: 7.____

   A. Governments derive their just power from the consent of the governed
   B. A petition to King George III for redress of colonial grievances

C. All men are created equal and have certain inalienable rights
D. People have a right to alter or abolish their government

8. One of the BASIC weaknesses in the Articles of Confederation was the failure to grant Congress the power to

   A. borrow money
   B. regulate commerce
   C. regulate coinage and the postal system
   D. declare war and make peace

9. Which of the following statements applies to the government of the United States under the Articles of Confederation?
   I. The central government had control of admiralty cases arising on the high seas.
   II. The President had complete charge of all executive functions.
   III. Congress had the power to fix tariff rates.
   IV. Congress had the right to make treaties.
   V. Congress could raise money through the sale of public lands.

   The CORRECT answer is:

   A. III, IV, V   B. I, II, III
   C. II, III, IV   D. I, IV, V

10. The significance of the Ordinance of 1787 lay in the establishment of the principle that

    A. territories were politically subordinate to the mother country
    B. new states would be admitted to the Union on the basis of the number of free inhabitants only
    C. territorial self-government was subject to the approval of Congress
    D. territories were entitled, as a right, to all the benefits of equality with the original 13 states

11. An IMPORTANT leader in the Constitutional Convention of 1787 was

    A. Alexander Hamilton   B. Henry Clay
    C. Thomas Jefferson   D. Patrick Henry

12. Which one of the following statements concerning the Constitutional Convention of 1787 is LEAST accurate?

    A. James Madison kept a journal of the proceedings.
    B. Thomas Jefferson and Patrick Henry supported the Virginia Plan.
    C. The delegates generally favored a stronger central government.
    D. There were many major compromises.

13. Which of the following arguments were advanced in the Federalist Papers?
    I. Action is necessary in view of the failure of the Articles of Confederation.
    II. A sovereign, unitary state is urgently needed.
    III. Justice takes precedence over the wishes of the majority.
    IV. A republican form of government can best control a large area of land on which live people of widely divergent interests.

    The CORRECT answer is:

A. I, III		B. I, II, IV	
C. II, III, IV		D. I, II, III, IV	

14. The MOST probable reason for our early foreign policy as expressed in Washington's Farewell Address was the

    A. importance of the United States in European affairs
    B. need for European aid to the United States
    C. youth and weakness of the new republic
    D. influence of political parties

15. Of the following, which was LEAST influential in causing the decline of the Federalist Party?
    The

    A. Alien and Sedition Acts
    B. undeclared naval war with France following the *XYZ* Affair
    C. growth of the West and of democratic ideas
    D. Hartford Convention

16. Which of the following statesmen are INCORRECTLY paired in view of their philosophies of government?

    A. Alexander Hamilton - Daniel Webster
    B. Thomas Jefferson - John Marshall
    C. Woodrow Wilson - Franklin D. Roosevelt
    D. James G. Blaine - Mark Hanna

17. Which one of the following Supreme Court cases is NOT associated with Chief Justice John Marshall?

    A. Gibbons vs. Ogden   B. Munn vs. Illinois
    C. Fletcher vs. Peck   D. Cohens vs. Virginia

18. The Monroe Doctrine was all of the following EXCEPT a

    A. policy supported by England for trade reasons
    B. reversal of our early policy of isolation
    C. warning to European aggressors to stay away from this hemisphere
    D. Presidential message to Congress on foreign policy

19. The purpose of Henry Clay's *American System* was to

    A. prevent the dissolution of the Union over the slavery issue
    B. isolate the United States from foreign entanglements
    C. unify the sections of the country by having the federal government meet their economic needs
    D. win the South from its allegiance to John Calhoun

20. John Calhoun's EXPOSITION AND PROTEST concerned his

    A. expressed belief that a protective tariff was unconstitutional
    B. resignation from the Vice Presidency following his breach with President Jackson

C. opposition to the dissolution of the Second Bank of the United States
D. opposition to the Force Act, which was passed as a means of enforcing federal laws in South Carolina

21. The elections of 1800 and 1824 were similar because, in

    A. each, the victorious candidate received a majority of the electoral votes but not of the popular votes
    B. each, the victorious candidate received an overwhelming majority of the popular votes
    C. neither, did the most popular candidate win
    D. each, the election was decided by the House of Representatives

21._____

22. Which one of the following elections was MOST expressive of sectional differences? The election of

    A. 1840   B. 1824   C. 1828   D. 1820

22._____

23. An evidence of increasing popular control in governmental matters in the period from 1800-1828 in the United States was the

    A. introduction of the spoils system
    B. substitution of popular vote in the selection of presidential electors
    C. establishment of the principle of squatter sovereignty for settling the question of slavery in the western territories
    D. introduction of the caucus method for selecting candidates for the Presidency

23._____

24. Which of the following factors did NOT contribute to the election of Andrew Jackson?

    A. Jackson's support of the states' rights doctrine
    B. Reduction of property qualifications for voting
    C. Popular election of electors
    D. Votes of the workingmen in the East

24._____

25. In Jackson's administrations, which of the following disputes did NOT involve constitutional questions?

    A. Use of the Spoils System
    B. The Cherokee Indian Affair
    C. The Maysville Road Bill
    D. The tariff controversy

25._____

KEY (CORRECT ANSWERS)

1. D
2. C
3. D
4. B
5. C

6. D
7. A
8. A
9. D
10. D

11. A
12. B
13. D
14. C
15. B

16. B
17. B
18. B
19. C
20. A

21. D
22. B
23. B
24. A
25. A

EXAMINATION SECTION
TEST 1

DIRECTIONS: Each question or incomplete statement is followed by several suggested answers or completions. Select the one that BEST answers the question or completes the statement. *PRINT THE LETTER OF THE CORRECT ANSWER IN THE SPACE AT THE RIGHT.*

1. Which one of the following was NOT an important factor in bringing about the Panic of 1837 and subsequent depression?

    A. The establishment of the Independent Treasury System
    B. Overspeculation in western lands
    C. Too rapid building of canals and other means of transportation
    D. The previous financial policies of President Jackson

    1.____

2. The dispute between Great Britain and the United States over the Maine-New Brunswick boundary was settled by the

    A. Clayton-Bulwer Treaty
    B. Oregon settlement
    C. Webster-Ashburton Treaty
    D. Rush-Bagot Agreement

    2.____

3. The revival of American foreign commerce in the 1840's was helped by the
    I. building of speedy Yankee clipper ships
    II. low tariff policy ushered in by the Walker tariff
    III. demand for American manufactured products in Europe
    IV. lowering of English tariffs in 1846

    The CORRECT answer is:

    A. I, III, IV
    B. I, II, III
    C. II, III, IV
    D. I, II, IV

    3.____

4. Which one of the following was NOT a provision of the Omnibus Bill of 1850?

    A. A stricter fugitive slave law was to be enacted
    B. Adjustment of the Texas-New Mexico boundary
    C. Slavery was to be prohibited in the District of Columbia
    D. California was to be admitted as a free state

    4.____

5. Which one of the following was NOT part of the platform of the Republican Party in the Presidential Campaign of 1860?

    A. Support of local option with regard to the question of slavery in the territories
    B. No interference with slavery in the states
    C. Support of the protective tariff
    D. Promise of free public land to settlers

    5.____

6. Which one of the following statements is NOT true of the *New South* after the Civil War?

    A. The agricultural revolution touched the South less than any other section of the country.
    B. Though farms were smaller, farm tenancy was more widespread.
    C. The most striking difference between the *New South* and the *Old South* was the rise of industry and manufacturers.
    D. Since immigration avoided the South, there was a severe shortage of cheap labor.

    6.____

7. Which one of the following statements would NOT correctly apply to the West after the Civil War?

    A. The generation after the Civil War witnessed the most extensive movement of population in our history.
    B. Many new states with a taste for social and political experiments arose in the West.
    C. The region of the Great Plains was one in which Eastern farming methods could best be applied.
    D. The Plains environment necessitated a modification of social attitudes and of political and legal institutions.

8. Which of the following statements would NOT appear in a chapter in a textbook on American history entitled, *The Economic Revolution - 1865-1900?*

    A. It was the dream of Jefferson that his country was to be a great agrarian democracy.
    B. The U.S. was progressing in the direction of a diversified, self-sufficing nation, as advocated by Hamilton.
    C. Spokesmen of big business were appealing for Hamilton's interpretation of the Constitution as against Jefferson's.
    D. Within two generations of Jefferson's death, the value of American manufactured products was almost triple that of the agricultural.

9. Which of the following was NOT a reason for the general expansion of U.S. agriculture after 1860?

    A. Lack of competition in world markets from other countries
    B. Opening up of new agricultural land
    C. Growth of population
    D. Improved transportation facilities

10. Which of the following methods was NOT included in the states' attempts to regulate railroads in the 1870's?

    A. Regulation of rates and services
    B. Prohibition of further state aid
    C. Prohibition of specific abuses
    D. State operation of railroads

11. In the following series of items, which one does NOT contain a contrasting pair?

    A. Bland-Allison Act - Gold Standard Act
    B. <u>Square Deal</u> - <u>New Freedom</u>
    C. Doctrine of <u>continuous voyage</u> - Doctrine of <u>freedom of the seas</u>
    D. 18th Amendment - 21st Amendment

12. Which one of the following distinguished American immigrants is INCORRECTLY associated with the field in which he won distinction?

    A. John Peter Altgeld - politics
    B. James Gordon Bennett - science
    C. Walter Damrosch - music
    D. Jacob Riis - social reform

13. The Credit Mobilier Scandal, the Salary Grab, and the Whiskey Ring Scandal ALL occurred during the administration of

    A. Grant   B. Hayes   C. Garfield   D. Arthur

    13.____

14. Among the demands of the Populist Party during the 1890's were

    A. a graduated income tax, removal of restrictions on immigration, public ownership, and operation of railroads
    B. direct election of senators, prohibition of alcoholic liquors, eight-hour day for labor
    C. public ownership and operation of railroads, a graduated income tax, direct election of senators
    D. eight-hour day for labor, postal savings banks, a minimum wage

    14.____

15. Which one of the following would NOT be grouped with the other three as a leader of the new progressivism in the two decades 1900-1920?

    A. Robert M. LaFollette   B. Woodrow Wilson
    C. Theodore Roosevelt   D. William Howard Taft

    15.____

16. Which of the statements about the reform movement of 1901-1917 are TRUE?
    I. The progressive movement differed from Populism as it had urban as well as agrarian leadership.
    II. Reforms were made in city and state governments.
    III. Changes in state constitutions tended to increase the executive power.
    IV. Progressives adopted the Socialist demand for public ownership of the means of production and distribution.
    V. <u>Muckrakers</u> were praised by Theodore Roosevelt for spearheading the reform movement.

    The CORRECT answer is:

    A. II, III, V   B. I, II, IV, V
    C. I, II, III, IV   D. I, II, III

    16.____

17. Which one of the following statements would NOT be true concerning Theodore Roosevelt?

    A. He denounced <u>malefactors of great wealth</u> and vigorously advocated income and inheritance taxes.
    B. He dramatized popular issues and avoided dangerous ones such as tariff and banking reform.
    C. He advocated <u>trust-busting</u>, but made a distinction between <u>good</u> and <u>bad</u> trusts.
    D. He demanded a <u>square deal</u> for labor but denounced bitterly pro-labor men such as Altgeld and Debs.

    17.____

18. About which one of the labor organizations listed below could it be said that membership in it was open to ALL workers regardless of sex, color, skill, or occupation? The

    A. Knights of St. Crispin
    B. Noble Order of the Knights of Labor
    C. American Federation of Labor
    D. International Workers of the World

    18.____

19. The C.I.O. originally split off from the American Federation of Labor because of differences over

    A. the National Labor Relations Act
    B. the sit-down strike policy
    C. industrial versus craft unionism
    D. political activity on behalf of the Roosevelt administration

20. The person whose major field of interest was DIFFERENT from that of the other three was

    A. Lucretia Mott
    B. Elizabeth Cady Stanton
    C. Lillian Wald
    D. Susan B. Anthony

21. Which one of the following was NOT a famous American newspaper editor of the 19th century?

    A. William Dean Howells
    B. Henry J. Raymond
    C. William Cullen Bryant
    D. James Gordon Bennett

22. Which one of the following was NOT a famous American architect?

    A. Henry H. Richardson
    B. Louis Sullivan
    C. Augustus St. Gaudens
    D. Frank Lloyd Wright

23. President Eisenhower's position on the development of federal power resources is BEST described by the following statement:

    A. The federal government should build dams wherever the project would service areas in more than one state
    B. Private companies should build power projects wherever they are able to provide the financial and technical resources
    C. State governments should finance the building of projects which are completely intra-state
    D. The federal government should give financial assistance to those states desiring to build intra-state projects

24. Which of the following American statesmen did NOT favor expansion of the United States beyond its natural borders?

    A. Franklin Pierce
    B. James G. Blaine
    C. William E. Seward
    D. William Jennings Bryan

25. Which one of the following could NOT be considered an important factor in the emergence of the United States as a world power at the close of the 19th century?

    A. Acquisition of control of Pago Pago in the Samoan Islands by the United States
    B. Extension of the idea of <u>manifest destiny</u> to the Pacific by President Cleveland
    C. Naval writings of Captain A. T. Mahan of the U.S. Navy
    D. Editorial writings of William Randolph Hearst

5 (#1)

KEY (CORRECT ANSWERS)

1. A   11. B
2. C   12. B
3. D   13. A
4. C   14. C
5. A   15. D

6. D   16. D
7. C   17. A
8. C   18. B
9. A   19. C
10. D   20. C

21. A
22. C
23. B
24. D
25. B

TEST 2

DIRECTIONS: Each question or incomplete statement is followed by several suggested answers or completions. Select the one that BEST answers the question or completes the statement. *PRINT THE LETTER OF THE CORRECT ANSWER IN THE SPACE AT THE RIGHT.*

1. Which one of the following statements does NOT reflect the dilemma in which the United States found itself in preparing to make the peace treaty ending the Spanish-American War?

    A. Aguinaldo's attempt to set up an independent republic in the Philippines
    B. Spain's refusal to grant Cuba her independence
    C. McKinley's statement of 1897 that *forcible annexation... cannot be thought of. That ... would be criminal aggression*
    D. The fear that Germany or Japan might annex the Philippines if we were to *haul down the flag*

1.____

2. Which of the following reflects the decision of the United States Supreme Court in the Insular Cases?

    A. The inhabitants of our overseas unincorporated territories were not entitled to fundamental rights.
    B. The inhabitants of unincorporated territories were entitled to all the rights and privileges of American citizens
    C. The overseas territories must be guaranteed a republican form of government
    D. Congress could apply special duties on imports from Puerto Rico and the Philippines

2.____

3. All of the following statements regarding the official attitude of the United States toward independence for the Philippines are true EXCEPT:

    A. The Jones Act was designed to prepare the Filipinos for self-government
    B. In 1920, President Wilson urged Congress to grant the Philippines their independence
    C. The Thompson report of 1926 discouraged large land-holding estates and advocated immediate independence
    D. The Tydings-McDuffie Act established a Philippine Commonwealth under an American High Commissioner

3.____

4. One characteristic of the territorial form of government as it was established in Alaska and Hawaii was that the governor of the territory was

    A. appointed by the President of the United States
    B. elected by the people of the territory
    C. chosen by the territorial legislature
    D. chosen by the Congress of the United States

4.____

5. Which of the following was NOT a reason for the Senate's rejection of the League of Nations?

    A. The right to declare war is reserved to the Congress.
    B. The League might interfere with domestic questions.
    C. The League had inadequate authority to enforce peace.
    D. Membership would reverse our historic foreign policy.

5.____

54

6. Which one of the following did F.D. Roosevelt NOT foster in the spirit of the Good Neighbor Policy?

    A. He entered into a treaty with Cuba abrogating the Platt Amendment.
    B. He dropped the United States' demand for compensation to American owners of agricultural lands expropriated by the Mexican government since 1927.
    C. He ended the American customs receivership in the Dominican Republic.
    D. At a Pan-American Conference at Montevideo in 1933, the United States and other American republics pledged not to intervene in the external or internal affairs of one another.

7. Which was NOT among the provisions of the Atlantic Charter?

    A. The sea should be free to all in time of peace.
    B. All people should be allowed to choose their own form of government.
    C. All nations should have access to the trade and raw materials of the world.
    D. An international court of arbitration should be formed to resolve international disputes.

8. The North Atlantic Pact includes

    A. a commitment for greater United States international cooperation
    B. a pledge on the part of the United States to participate in any war in defense of the signatory nations
    C. a provision for military assistance by the United States to the pact nations.
    D. the signatures of all members of the U.N., except the U.S.S.R. and its satellites

9. In January 1949, President Truman proposed his *Point Four* program PRIMARILY to

    A. furnish technical aid to undeveloped areas so that they might make better use of their own resources
    B. provide immediate relief for the starving and sick in undeveloped areas
    C. disseminate information about the democratic way of life to people in backward areas
    D. provide military aid to undeveloped areas which were threatened by communist neighbors

10. Which of the following statements is NOT correct regarding Korea?

    A. The United States government opposed the Portsmouth Treaty's clause on Korea as a violation of the *Open Door.*
    B. Korea was a protectorate from 1904-1910.
    C. President Theodore Roosevelt, in return for a Japanese disavowal of aggressive designs on the Philippines, approved a free hand for Japan in Korea.
    D. By making a treaty with Korea as an independent state in the 19th century, the United States helped later Japanese expansionism.

11. The history of the United States is told by means of pictures and other graphic material in all of the following EXCEPT:

    A. R.H. Gabriel (Editor) - THE PAGEANT OF AMERICA
    B. Roger Butterfield - THE AMERICAN PAST
    C. Louis M. Hacker - THE SHAPING OF THE AMERICAN TRADITION
    D. Marshall Davidson - LIFE IN AMERICA

12. Separation of Church and State in the English colonies in America FIRST appeared in

    A. Maryland
    B. Plymouth
    C. Rhode Island
    D. Pennsylvania

13. Which one of the following statements characterized the British administration of the American colonies before 1750?

    A. Every colony was required to maintain a uniform land policy, Indian policy, and administrative system.
    B. The Navigation Acts disregarded the principles of the mercantilist theory.
    C. Control of the colonies was lodged in a single bureau to formulate and coordinate colonial policy.
    D. The colonies benefited from preferential customs rates, bounties on naval stores, and subsidies to the shipbuilding industry.

14. Which is the CORRECT chronological sequence of the following?
    I.   Albany Congress
    II. First Continental Congress
    III. Grenville Program
    IV. Townshend Duties

    The CORRECT answer is:

    A. I, II, IV, III
    B. I, III, IV, II
    C. II, I, III, IV
    D. IV, III, II, I

15. Which pairs of men are associated with similar attitudes toward governmental powers?
    I.   Nathaniel Bacon - Daniel Shays
    II. James Madison - Richard Henry Lee
    III. Thomas Jefferson - John Locke
    IV. Samuel Adams - Patrick Henry

    The CORRECT answer is:

    A. I, II, III
    B. I, II, IV
    C. II, III, IV
    D. I, III, IV

16. Under the Articles of Confederation, the government had the power to
    I.   make treaties
    II. levy taxes
    III. raise an army
    IV. set up national courts

    The CORRECT answer is:

    A. I, II, IV
    B. I, III
    C. I, II, III
    D. II, III, IV

17. The state constitutions adopted after the Revolution GENERALLY

    A. reflected the theories of Montesquieu
    B. eliminated restrictions on the right to vote
    C. gave the governors the right of veto
    D. did not contain any *Bill of Rights*

18. An important result of the Revolution on American life is evidenced by the fact that 18.____

   A. the system of primogeniture and entail was recognized as protected by state constitutions
   B. a majority of the states showed a marked tendency to increase the power of the popularly elected legislatures while reducing the authority of the executive
   C. all the states abolished established churches and introduced complete religious freedom
   D. the states adopted uniform regulations for office-holding and voting

19. The Virginia and Kentucky Resolutions and those of the Hartford Convention 19.____

   A. declared for secession
   B. demanded impartial umpires for disputes
   C. upheld the compact theory of government
   D. demanded the right of nullification

20. Laws passed under Hamilton's leadership and those passed in 1816 BOTH resulted in the 20.____

   A. assumption of state debts
   B. establishment of a national bank
   C. levying of a whiskey tax
   D. financing of internal improvements

21. The policy which was consistent with John Marshall's decisions concerning the nature of the Constitution and federalism was 21.____

   A. Thomas Jefferson's acquisition of Louisiana
   B. Andrew Jackson's attitude toward the recharter of the United States bank
   C. Georgia's cancellation of the treaty rights of the Cherokee Indians
   D. James Madison's veto of Calhoun's Bonus Bill

22. The relations between the United States and France were improved by the 22.____

   A. XYZ Affair   B. Convention of 1800
   C. Genet Affair   D. Berlin and Milan Decrees

23. Thomas Jefferson's administration adhered to its campaign promises in 23.____

   A. purchasing Louisiana
   B. removing the *midnight judges*
   C. repealing the excise tax
   D. vetoing the bill to recharter the Bank

24. In which one of the following pairs was the first item unaffected by the second? 24.____

   A. French Alliance - Proclamation of Neutrality (1793)
   B. Neutrality Laws - Lend-Lease
   C. Monroe Doctrine - NATO
   D. Alabama-Claims - Kellogg-Briand Pact

25. The Rule of War of 1756 enunciated the doctrine of   25. ____
   A. free ships make free goods
   B. freedom of the seas
   C. illegality of paper blockades
   D. continuous voyage

KEY (CORRECT ANSWERS)

1. B
2. D
3. C
4. A
5. C

6. B
7. D
8. A
9. A
10. A

11. C
12. C
13. D
14. B
15. D

16. B
17. A
18. B
19. C
20. B

21. A
22. B
23. C
24. D
25. D

TEST 3

DIRECTIONS: Each question or incomplete statement is followed by several suggested answers or completions. Select the one that BEST answers the question or completes the statement. *PRINT THE LETTER OF THE CORRECT ANSWER IN THE SPACE AT THE RIGHT.*

1. The War of 1812 has been called the second War of Independence because　　　　　1.____

    A. it was followed by an era in which the American people devoted their major energies to domestic rather than foreign problems
    B. the American merchant marine and navy had practically destroyed the British navy by 1814
    C. it won the support and cooperation of the commercial Northeast and the agrarian West and South
    D. England agreed to respect the neutral rights of the United States

2. Which one of the following statements applies to BOTH the election of 1800 and the election of 1824?　　　　　2.____
    The

    A. successful candidates for President and Vice President represented different parties
    B. method of choosing the President and Vice President was changed by constitutional amendment
    C. President was chosen by the House of Representatives
    D. man who received the largest number of electoral votes became President

3. Which one of the following statements concerning the Monroe Doctrine is CORRECT?　　　　　3.____

    A. Former Presidents Jefferson and Madison opposed a joint declaration and alliance with Great Britain
    B. Secretary of State John Quincy Adams favored an independent course of action by the United States
    C. Subsequent treaties with Great Britain guaranteed that the British fleet would be used to enforce the Doctrine
    D. European governments that violated the Doctrine were to be deprived of their existing colonies or dependencies

4. Which one of the following results may CORRECTLY be attributed to the actions of Andrew Jackson as President?　　　　　4.____

    A. A system of direct election of presidential electors replaced the selection of state legislatures.
    B. Religious and property barriers to manhood suffrage were removed.
    C. The spoils system and rotation in office were institutionalized and justified as practices of political parties.
    D. The caucus system for presidential nominations was replaced by party conventions.

5. The reformers who had a profound effect on the American Utopian movement during the first half of the nineteenth century were　　　　　5.____

A. Dorothea L. Dix and Henry David Thoreau
B. Robert Owen and Charles Fourier
C. Horace Mann and Henry Barnard
D. William Lloyd Garrison and James Russell Lowell

6. Which one of the following American historians is INCORRECTLY paired with the field of interest mentioned?

    A. Prescott - Mexico
    B. Washington Irving - Spain
    C. Parkman - Canada
    D. Motley - Germany

7. In the 1840's, two MAIN routes from Independence, Missouri to the West were the

    A. Genesee Road and Oregon Trail
    B. Oregon Trail and Santa Fe Trail
    C. Cumberland Gap Road and Santa Fe Trail
    D. National Road and Lewis and Clark Trail

8. Western migration was encouraged in all of the following EXCEPT

    A. Jay Treaty
    B. Pinckney Treaty
    C. Homestead Act
    D. Proclamation of 1763

9. Which one of the following statements is NOT in accord with the basic teachings of Frederick Jackson Turner?

    A. Eastern labor and reform groups contributed the dynamic elements of Jacksonian democracy at least as much as did the West.
    B. The frontier became distinctly American only after it reached the Appalachians.
    C. The lure of cheap land was the most significant factor in the expansion of the frontier.
    D. The West promoted individualism, democracy, and freedom of opportunity.

10. Which statement CORRECTLY expresses John C. Calhoun's attitudes on sectional issues?

    A. He reversed his position on the tariff issue between 1816 and 1828.
    B. His Exposition and Protest expressed an attitude toward states' rights which was similar to that of Webster's reply to Hayne.
    C. He supported Jackson's Force Bill in 1833.
    D. In 1846, he supported the aims of the Wilmot Proviso concerning the eventual territorial settlement with Mexico.

11. Manifest Destiny is a phrase which refers to

    A. American growth of independence from Europe
    B. the inevitable elimination of slavery
    C. territorial expansion to America's natural boundaries
    D. American arrival at a balanced economy

12. Which of the following was NOT an issue on which Daniel Webster took a prominent position?
    The

    A. Compact Theory
    B. Compromise of 1850
    C. Dartmouth College Charter
    D. Yazoo land claims

13. Which one of the following pairs expressed a similar purpose or principle concerning the slavery issue?   13.____

    A. Northwest Ordinance - Compromise of 1850
    B. Missouri Compromise - Kansas-Nebraska Act
    C. Dred Scott Decision - Freeport Doctrine
    D. Free Soil Party - Republican Party (1854-1860)

14. Colorful campaign slogans have been attached to particular periods and particular campaigns in American history. What is the CORRECT chronological order of the slogans given below?   14.____
    I. Rum, Romanism and Rebellion
    II. Fifty-four forty or fight
    III. Free soil, free speech, free labor, free men
    IV. Tippecanoe and Tyler too

    The CORRECT answer is:

    A. IV, III, II, I   B. I, III, II, IV
    C. IV, II, III, I   D. IV, II, I, III

15. Which of the following statements BEST explains England's neutrality in the American Civil War?   15.____
    I. The effect of the Emancipation Proclamation
    II. Dependence on Northern exports of wheat
    III. The democratic attitudes in the English government
    IV. The surpluses of Egyptian cotton
    V. English war profits

    The CORRECT answer is:

    A. I, II, IV   B. III, IV, V
    C. I, IV, V   D. I, II, V

16. The pair which does NOT represent a cause and effect relationship is   16.____

    A. Tenure of Office Act - Impeachment of Andrew Johnson
    B. National Banking Acts - Establishment of the Independent Treasury System
    C. Black codes - Civil Rights Bill
    D. Ku Klux Klan - Force Acts (1870-1871)

17. Thomas Nast achieved prominence through his cartoons attacking the   17.____

    A. Tweed Ring   B. Whiskey Ring
    C. Teapot Dome Scandal D. carpetbag governments

18. By which of the following acts did the federal government promote the work of education and experimentation in the field of agriculture? _____ Act.   18.____
    I. Morrill Land Grant
    II. Homestead
    III. Hatch
    IV. McNary-Haugen

    The CORRECT answer is:

    A. I, III   B. I, IV   C. II, III   D. II, IV

19. The insurgent political group which is NOT correctly matched with the appropriate presidential incumbent or aspirant is

    A. James G. Blaine - Mugwumps
    B. Grover Cleveland - Hunkers
    C. Ulysses S. Grant - Liberal Republicans
    D. William H. Taft - Progressives (Bull Moosers)

20. The trio which includes individuals who did NOT engage in the same field of activity is

    A. George Selden - Henry Ford - Charles Duryea
    B. Henry George - Edward Bellamy - Henry Demarest Lloyd
    C. Uriah S. Stephens - Samuel Gompers - Eugene V. Debs
    D. Benjamin Cardozo - William Dean Howells - Frank Lloyd Wright

21. Which of the following may be CORRECTLY considered as contributing to the rapid development of the West between 1865 and 1900?
    I. Federal government's liberal land grants
    II. High prices offered for farm products
    III. Marked increase in migration from Europe
    IV. Protection of the farmers' market through tariff legislation

    The CORRECT answer is:

    A. I, III   B. II, IV   C. I, IV   D. II, III

22. Which one of the following statements is CORRECT with respect to the settlement of the last western frontier?

    A. The rights of native Indian tribes were respected.
    B. The first settlers were the miners.
    C. It was the last step in the unbroken westward settlement.
    D. Most of the mining wealth enabled the mining settlers to get a start in ranching or farming.

23. Which one of the following statements is FALSE concerning the Interstate Commerce Act during the first decade after its passage?
    The

    A. Interstate Commerce Commission was the first of the great regulatory commissions of the Federal government to be set up
    B. Act established the principle of federal regulation of railroads
    C. Act was weakened by adverse decisions in the federal courts
    D. Supreme Court ruled that the Interstate Commerce Commission had the power to fix rates

24. Which statement concerning the Populist Party is CORRECT?

    A. It supported the gold standard as opposed to free and unlimited coinage of silver.
    B. It favored an alliance of agrarian interests of the West with business interests of the East.
    C. Although its platform was considered radical, many of its planks were subsequently enacted into law.
    D. It opposed public ownership and operation of railroads, telegraph, and telephones.

25. The development of an effective labor movement in the United States in the 19th century was retarded because 25._____
    I. the frontier attracted discontented city workers
    II. there was a large supply of unskilled labor
    III. racial and religious antagonisms embittered relations between native and foreign-born workers
    IV. there was a strong tradition of individualism
    The CORRECT answer is:

    A. II, III, IV   B. I, III
    C. II, IV   D. I, IV

KEY (CORRECT ANSWERS)

1.	A	11.	C
2.	C	12.	D
3.	B	13.	D
4.	C	14.	C
5.	B	15.	D
6.	D	16.	B
7.	B	17.	A
8.	D	18.	A
9.	A	19.	B
10.	A	20.	D

21.	A
22.	B
23.	D
24.	C
25.	A

TEST 4

DIRECTIONS: Each question or incomplete statement is followed by several suggested answers or completions. Select the one that BEST answers the question or completes the statement. PRINT THE LETTER OF THE CORRECT ANSWER IN THE SPACE AT THE RIGHT.

1. The tariff philosophy of Woodrow Wilson's *New Freedom* was enacted into law by the _____ Tariff.

   A. Wilson-Gorman
   B. Payne Aldrich
   C. Fordney-McCumber
   D. Underwood

   1.___

2. Of the following laws, which one had objectives DIFFERENT from the objectives of the other three?
   _____ Act.

   A. Sherman
   B. Clayton
   C. Interstate Commerce
   D. National Industrial Recovery

   2.___

3. All of the following boards and commissions were established during the administration of Herbert Hoover EXCEPT the

   A. Federal Farm Board
   B. Council of Economic Advisers to the President
   C. Reconstruction Finance Corporation
   D. Wickersham Law Enforcement Commission

   3.___

4. Which one of the following statements concerning population trends in the United States is CORRECT?

   A. In 1870, one-third of the country's population was urban; in 1900, the proportion was one-fifth.
   B. Up to the 1880's, three-fourths of all the immigrants to the United States came from Southern and Eastern Europe.
   C. During the decade 1920-1930, the percentage increase of Blacks in the North exceeded the percentage increase of Blacks in the South.
   D. During the decade 1940-1950, the region that showed the largest percentage increase in population was the Northeast.

   4.___

5. The depression of the 1930's drew attention to certain faults in the American economy. Which one of the following would NOT be a correct statement of what was happening?

   A. Productive capacity was in excess of effective consumptive ability.
   B. Technological changes were increasing at a faster rate than employment opportunities.
   C. The rapid decline of savings as compared with consumption resulted in a shortage of investment money and an overabundance of funds in consumptive channels.
   D. Continued depression in agriculture reduced the purchasing power of a large sector of the American population.

   5.___

6. A factor which was NOT common to the administrations of Theodore Roosevelt and Franklin D. Roosevelt was

   A. support of the *Roosevelt corollary* to the Monroe Doctrine
   B. the promotion of conservation of our natural resources
   C. a vigorous assertion of executive leadership
   D. an increase in the supervision exercised by government over business enterprise

6.____

7. In which one of the following respects did the New Freedom and the New Deal differ?

   A. Basic philosophy of government concern for the general welfare
   B. Need for government regulation of industry and business
   C. Enactment of social security legislation
   D. Regulation of banking by the national government

7.____

8. The Supreme Court, stating that Congress had improperly delegated its power to the Executive branch, declared unconstitutional the _____ Act.

   A. National Industrial Recovery
   B. Walsh-Healey Public Contracts
   C. National Labor Relations
   D. Fair Labor Standards

8.____

9. The change in attitude of the U.S. toward Cuban revolution between the time of the 1868-78 disorders and the revolution of 1898 was due to all of the following EXCEPT:

   A. Newspaper methods had become increasingly sensational
   B. The economic interest of the U.S. in Cuba had increased greatly
   C. There was no overt action similar to the sinking of the Maine
   D. The U.S. had developed a new set of world interests

9.____

10. The Monroe Doctrine has never been invoked to prevent possible extension of control of a European nation in

    A. Mexico   B. Honduras   C. Venezuela   D. Haiti

10.____

11. Dwight W. Morrow's mission to Mexico was MAINLY concerned with

    A. interpretation of the Monroe Doctrine
    B. United States economic aid to Mexico
    C. Communist activities in Mexico
    D. Mexican land laws

11.____

12. Which sequence of events BEST indicates a trend towards isolationism in the history of American foreign policy?

    A. Jefferson's first Inaugural Address - Embargo Act - Louisiana Purchase
    B. Open Door Policy - Portsmouth Treaty - Gentlemen's Agreement
    C. Fourteen Points - Nine Power Treaty - Cash and Carry
    D. Atlantic Charter - Truman Doctrine - Point Four Program

12.____

13. Which of the following characteristics of United States policy toward Latin-America may CORRECTLY be regarded as features of the Good Neighbor Policy?
    I. Unilateral intervention to protect United States interests
    II. Hemispheric solidarity on equal basis with other American states
    III. Reciprocal trade agreements to promote economic well-being
    IV. Granting of independence to American possessions in the Caribbean
    V. Multilateral interpretation and application of the Monroe Doctrine

    The CORRECT answer is:

    A. I, II, III
    B. III, IV, V
    C. II, III, V
    D. I, II, IV

14. Of the following events,
    I. Venezuela debt controversy
    II. Venezuela boundary dispute
    III. Passage of Platt Amendment
    IV. Completion of the Panama Canal

    the CORRECT chronological order is

    A. II, III, I, IV
    B. I, III, IV, II
    C. III, II, I, IV
    D. III, II, IV, I

15. Which one of the following is a VALID argument against building a canal in Nicaragua?

    A. It would be a violation of the Monroe Doctrine.
    B. There is no treaty between the United States and Nicaragua which permits such a canal.
    C. There is persistent danger of recurring earthquakes and volcanic eruptions.
    D. The size of the American Navy would have to be doubled to protect another canal.

16. In which one of the following struggles was Franklin D. Roosevelt victorious? The

    A. attempt to increase the size of the Supreme Court
    B. effort to defeat the Smith Act
    C. effort to get the Vice Presidential nomination for Henry Wallace in 1944
    D. plea for revision of the neutrality laws which had been passed before World War II

17. In the period since the end of World War II, the United States has signed peace treaties with all of the following EXCEPT

    A. Italy
    B. Austria
    C. Bulgaria
    D. Rumania

18. The Act of Chapultepec provided that:

    A. a council of inter-American countries would take over European colonies in the Western Hemisphere in time of war
    B. common action, short of armed force, would be taken against an aggressor
    C. force would not be used to collect debts in this hemisphere
    D. consultation would precede U.N. action applicable to this hemisphere

19. All of the following were initiated during the Truman administration EXCEPT the

    A. Atlantic Charter
    B. Commission on Organization of the Executive Branch of the Government (Hoover Commission)
    C. Marshall Plan
    D. Point Four Program

20. At the Tenth Inter-American Conference at Caracas, the United States' resolution against Communist infiltration within the Western Hemisphere was supported by all countries EXCEPT

    A. Mexico, Brazil, El Salvador
    B. Guatemala, Argentina, Brazil
    C. Guatemala, Mexico, Argentina
    D. Nicaragua, Argentina, Ecuador

21. Which one of the following men is INCORRECTLY paired with the scene of his explorations?

    A. Ponce de Leon - Florida
    B. Francisco Coronado - California
    C. Bartholomew Diaz - Cape of Good Hope
    D. Hernando de Soto - Mississippi River

22. Which of the following universities was NOT founded before the American Revolution?

    A. Rutgers University
    B. Brown University
    C. University of Virginia
    D. Dartmouth University

23. Of the following pairs, which one contains the names of individuals famous for their achievements in UNRELATED fields of endeavor?

    A. Jonathan Edwards - Increase Mather
    B. Benjamin West - Gilbert Stuart
    C. Benjamin Silliman - Benjamin Franklin
    D. Andrew Hamilton - Meriwether Lewis

24. Of which religious group was William Ellery Channing a leader?

    A. Methodists   B. Quakers   C. Baptists   D. Unitarians

25. Which of the following statements is TRUE concerning the American colonies' trade in the period between 1660 and 1763?

    A. American colonists were permitted to carry on trade directly with the Orient.
    B. All colonial trade with England had to be carried by English-built or English colonial vessels.
    C. Tobacco and sugar could be exported to any European country from the American colonies.
    D. Only English-made goods could be imported into the American colonies.

KEY (CORRECT ANSWERS)

1.	D	11.	D
2.	D	12.	A
3.	B	13.	C
4.	C	14.	A
5.	C	15.	C
6.	A	16.	D
7.	C	17.	B
8.	A	18.	B
9.	C	19.	A
10.	B	20.	C

21. B
22. C
23. D
24. D
25. B

TEST 5

DIRECTIONS: Each question or incomplete statement is followed by several suggested answers or completions. Select the one that BEST answers the question or completes the statement. *PRINT THE LETTER OF THE CORRECT ANSWER IN THE SPACE AT THE RIGHT.*

1. Which one of the following was a CAUSE of the other three?

    A. Quebec Act
    B. Boston Port Act
    C. Reorganization of the government of Massachusetts
    D. Boston Tea Party

2. Which one of the following was NOT a feature of the Articles of Confederation?

    A. The states retained complete control over taxation and regulation of commerce.
    B. Congress had the power to regulate the coinage.
    C. The vote of nine states was required to amend the Articles of Confederation.
    D. No provision was made for a federal judiciary.

3. Which one of the following groups includes ONLY members of the Constitutional Convention?

    A. James Wilson, William Paterson, Patrick Henry, Benjamin Franklin
    B. Couverneur Morris, John Dickinson, James Madison, Thomas Jefferson
    C. George Washington, Edmund Randolph, Roger Sherman, George Mason
    D. John Adams, Luther Martin, Alexander Hamilton, Robert Morris

4. Which of the following statements is TRUE of the struggle over ratification of the Federal Constitution?

    A. It is probable that most of the states would have ratified the Constitution if it had been submitted to popular vote.
    B. All of the states had ratified the Constitution by the time Washington took the oath of office as President in 1789.
    C. There was generally less opposition to ratification in the small states than in those with larger populations.
    D. The Constitution was generally more popular in agricultural areas than among town inhabitants.

5. Which is the MOST accurate description of the principal cause for the breach between Jefferson and Hamilton?

    A. Personal dislike caused by a clash of personalities
    B. Disagreement concerning the location of the nation's capital city
    C. Conflict between the dominant economic interests of New England and Virginia
    D. Conflict between radicalism and conservatism

6. The review by the Supreme Court of the United States of appeals from state courts in designated types of cases was established by

    A. Article III of the Federal Constitution
    B. the adoption of the 11th Amendment
    C. the Judiciary Act of 1789
    D. John Marshall's opinion in Marbury vs. Madison

7. Which principles were included in Jefferson's plans for the University of Virginia?
    I. Separation from church control
    II. Elective system
    III. No entrance examinations
    IV. Coeducation
   The CORRECT answer is:

   A. I, II, III
   B. I, II, IV
   C. II, III, IV
   D. I, III, IV

8. Which one of the following pairs of events did NOT occur in the same presidential administration?

   A. Alien and Sedition Acts - XYZ Affair
   B. Marbury vs. Madison - Louisiana Purchase
   C. Hartford Convention - Macon's Bill No. 2
   D. Whiskey Rebellion - Virginia and Kentucky Resolutions

9. Which was a characteristic of the election of 1824?

   A. States rights was a major issue.
   B. The election went to the House of Representatives.
   C. Nominating conventions were used for the first time.
   D. The Federalist party nominated a presidential candidate for the last time.

10. Which of the following events PRECEDED the issuance of the Monroe Doctrine?
    I. Britain recognized the independence of the Latin American republics.
    II. The United States recognized the independence of the Latin American republics.
    III. Russia attempted to extend the southern boundary of Alaska to the fifty-first parallel.
    IV. Canning proposed that the United States join Britain in a joint declaration against intervention by the Holy Alliance.
    The CORRECT answer is:

    A. I, II, III
    B. II, III, IV
    C. I, II, IV
    D. I, III, IV

11. Which of the following can be CORRECTLY associated with the election of 1828?
    I. Clay-Adams coalition
    II. Jackson-Calhoun coalition
    III. Jackson's defeat in Pennsylvania and New York
    IV. Jackson's victory in Virginia and South Carolina
    The CORRECT answer is:

    A. I, II, III
    B. I, II, IV
    C. I, III, IV
    D. II, III, IV

12. Which one showed the LEAST change in his political views between 1816 and 1830?

    A. Daniel Webster
    B. John C. Calhoun
    C. John Marshall
    D. Henry Clay

13. In connection with the slavery issue, the *gag rule* was fought on the floor of Congress in the 1830's by

    A. Henry Clay
    B. William Lloyd Garrison
    C. John Quincy Adams
    D. James G. Birney

14. On which one of the following policies were Clay and Calhoun LEAST in harmony?

    A. Declaration of war on England in 1812
    B. Tariff of 1816
    C. Chartering the second Bank of the United States
    D. Election of John Quincy Adams

15. As President, which one of the following measures did Madison veto?

    A. Federal aid for internal improvements
    B. A protective tariff
    C. A charter for a Bank of the United States
    D. Requisitions for state militias in the War of 1812

16. The MOST important route to the Northwest from the eastern states prior to 1840 was

    A. steamboats up the Mississippi
    B. the Cumberland Road
    C. the Erie Canal
    D. the Baltimore and Ohio Railroad

17. Which of the following men played a part in the liberation of Latin American republics?
    I. Jose de San Martin
    II. Bernardo O'Higgins
    III. Simon de Bolivar
    IV. Oliveira Salazar

    The CORRECT answer is:

    A. I, III, IV
    B. I, II, III
    C. I, IV
    D. II, III, IV

18. The two men who were MOST in agreement in the debate on the Compromise of 1850 were

    A. Clay and Calhoun
    B. Calhoun and Webster
    C. Clay and Webster
    D. Seward and Webster

19. Which is the CORRECT chronological order of the following events?
    I. Gadsden Purchase
    II. Treaty of Guadalupe Hidalgo
    III. Wilmot Proviso
    IV. Admission of California as a state

    The CORRECT answer is:

    A. III, II, IV, I
    B. III, IV, I, II
    C. II, III, IV, I
    D. IV, III, II, I

20. Which of the following were considered by Southerners to be attacks on slavery?
    I. Tallmadge Amendment
    II. Wilmot Proviso
    III. Ostend Manifesto
    IV. *The Impending Crisis*
    The CORRECT answer is:

    A. II, III, IV
    B. I, III, IV
    C. I, II, III
    D. I, II, IV

21. What is the CORRECT chronological order of the following events?
    I. John Brown's raid
    II. Dred Scott decision
    III. Lincoln-Douglas debates
    IV. Founding of the Republican party
    The CORRECT answer is:

    A. II, IV, III, I
    B. III, II, I, IV
    C. IV, III, II, I
    D. IV, II, III, I

22. Which statement is CORRECT in regard to the Kansas-Nebraska Act? It

    A. made Kansas free and Nebraska slave
    B. repealed the Missouri Compromise
    C. admitted Kansas as a slave state
    D. repealed the Compromise of 1850

23. Which of the following is TRUE of the election of 1850?

    A. Lincoln obtained a large popular majority.
    B. Republicans were a minority in each house of Congress.
    C. Douglas lost practically all the Southern popular vote to Breckinridge.
    D. Lincoln was elected by a narrow majority of electoral votes.

24. During the American Civil War, England

    A. refrained from declaring her neutrality
    B. recognized the independence of the Confederacy
    C. recognized the Confederacy as a belligerent
    D. obtained sufficient cotton from the South to keep its factories going

25. The opponent of Lincoln in the election of 1864 was

    A. Fremont   B. McClellan   C. Greeley   D. Stanton

KEY (CORRECT ANSWERS)

1. D
2. C
3. C
4. C
5. C

6. C
7. A
8. D
9. B
10. B

11. B
12. C
13. C
14. D
15. A

16. B
17. B
18. C
19. A
20. D

21. D
22. B
23. B
24. C
25. B

EXAMINATION SECTION
TEST 1

DIRECTIONS: Each question or incomplete statement is followed by several suggested answers or completions. Select the one that BEST answers the question or completes the statement. *PRINT THE LETTER OF THE CORRECT ANSWER IN THE SPACE AT THE RIGHT.*

1. A famous case in the Civil War period in which the Supreme Court held that neither the President nor Congress could declare martial law in places where civil courts were open was

    A. Mississippi vs. Johnson
    B. ex parte Milligan
    C. Georgia vs. Stanton
    D. ex parte McCardle

    1.____

2. An excellent example of the Supreme Court's refusal to increase the power of the central government at the expense of state governments in the field of regulating business is

    A. Gibbons vs. Ogden, 1824
    B. Slaughter House cases, 1873
    C. Wabash vs. Illinois, 1886
    D. Pollock vs. Farmers Loan and Trust Company, 1895

    2.____

3. The United States vs. E.C. Knight case of the 1890's illustrates

    A. the application of the Sherman Anti-trust Act to combinations of common carriers
    B. failure in the application of the Sherman Anti-trust Act to a manufacturing combination
    C. the application of the Sherman Anti-trust Act to combinations of workers
    D. the failure of the Sherman Anti-trust Act to eliminate basing point agreements

    3.____

4. All of the following can be correctly associated with the Knights of Labor EXCEPT

    A. rise in influence after the Haymarket Affair
    B. legislation opposing contract labor
    C. leadership of Stephens and Powderly
    D. sponsorship of the eight hour day

    4.____

5. Of the following tariff acts, the one which DIFFERED in its nature from the other three was the _____ Act.

    A. Wilson-Gorman
    B. Dingley
    C. Payne-Aldrich
    D. Underwood

    5.____

6. The Pullman strike of 1894 is notable in labor history because

    A. it was the first strike settled as a result of government mediation
    B. the Sherman Anti-trust Act was applied to a labor combination
    C. the national government recognized the right of workers to bargain collectively
    D. it marked the downfall of the Knights of Labor

    6.____

7. The significance of the Northern Securities case lay in the fact that it

    A. marked the first successful prosecution under the Clayton Anti-trust Act
    B. upheld the constitutionality of the Securities Exchange Act

    7.____

C. led to the passage of the Interstate Commerce Act
D. gave a serious setback to the use of the holding company device for the consolidation of businesses

8. An important purpose of the Federal Trade Commission is to

   A. eliminate unfair methods of composition
   B. assist American merchants in securing foreign markets
   C. advise the President on such tariff changes as are necessary to equalize production costs abroad and in the U.S.
   D. supervise trading on the stock and commodity exchanges of the country

8._____

9. The MOST valuable form of aid given by the Federal government to railroads in the period after the Civil War was

   A. land grants   B. loans
   C. subsidies   D. tariff remission on rails

9._____

10. Which of the following statements about Grover Cleveland are TRUE?
    I. He believed that the high tariff encouraged both high prices and the development of trusts.
    II. His liberal policy concerning Civil War pensions was a factor in his victory in the election of 1888.
    III. He favored government regulation of railroads.
    IV. He was responsible for the annexation of Hawaii.
    The CORRECT answer is:

    A. III, IV   B. II, III   C. II, IV   D. I, III

10._____

11. Which is the proper chronological order for the creation of these Federal agencies?
    I. Civil Service Commission
    II. Federal Communications Commission
    III. Interstate Commerce Commission
    IV. Federal Trade Commission
    The CORRECT answer is:

    A. I, II, III, IV   B. I, III, IV, II
    C. II, I, III, IV   D. III, II, I, IV

11._____

12. Which of the following was NOT a popular magazine that played a great part in the muckraking movement?

    A. McClure's   B. Cosmopolitan
    C. Collier's   D. New Republic

12._____

13. Which of the following statements concerning the program of conservation of natural resources are TRUE?
    I. No federal legislation on the subject had been enacted prior to Theodore Roosevelt's administration.
    II. Theodore Roosevelt recognized that the success of a conservation program required cooperation by the states.
    III. Theodore Roosevelt's program provided for the construction of irrigation works under the supervision of the federal government.

13._____

IV. The Ballinger-Pinchot controversy indicated that Taft was hostile to Roosevelt's conservation policies.

The CORRECT answer is:

A. II, IV
B. I, II, III
C. I, IV
D. I, II, III, IV

14. Which one of the following did NOT expound the thesis that legal institutions and interpretations should conform to changing social needs?

    A. Oliver Wendell Holmes
    B. Roscoe Pound
    C. Louis D. Brandeis
    D. George Sutherland

15. Which of the following statements BEST characterizes the original Open Door Policy as enunciated by Secretary of State John Hay in 1899?
    It

    A. guaranteed China's territorial integrity
    B. was readily accepted by all the great powers
    C. recognized the right of all nations to trade with all of China
    D. applied only to leaseholds and spheres of influence established by the great powers

16. The American statesman who was MOST active in the termination of a major conflict in the Orient was

    A. John Hay
    B. Henry L. Stimson
    C. Matthew Perry
    D. Theodore Roosevelt

17. Which important position did ALL of the following men occupy during the period from 1860 to 1900: Hamilton Fish, Thomas F. Bayard, F.T. Frelinghysen, James G. Blaine?

    A. Supreme Court Justice
    B. Secretary of State
    C. Speaker of the House of Representatives
    D. Chairman, Senate Foreign Relations Committee

18. The MOST important factor contributing to the election result in 1912 was the

    A. war record of the victorious candidate
    B. schism within one of the parties
    C. strong independent vote for the victor
    D. program of social change offered by the successful candidate

19. Which one of the following may CORRECTLY be considered a result of the influence of the other three?
    The

    A. influx of large numbers of immigrants
    B. rise of big business
    C. urbanization of American life
    D. increased mechanization of agriculture

20. The abrogation of the Platt Amendment

   A. was ordered by President Truman
   B. furthered the *Good Neighbor* policy
   C. was resented by the Cubans
   D. hampered hemisphere defense

21. Which of the following statements concerning the Senate's rejection of the Treaty of Versailles are TRUE?
   I. The majority of the Republicans, who controlled the Senate, were unalterably opposed to ratification.
   II. The League of Nations was an issue in the election of 1920.
   III. Jealousy of Senatorial prerogative and personal hatred of the President were important factors in bringing about the result.
   IV. The President refused to accept a ratification coupled with reservations.
   The CORRECT answer is:

   A. III, IV
   B. II, III, IV
   C. I, II, IV
   D. I, II, III

22. Which statements relating to the Four-Power Treaty concluded at the Washington Conference are CORRECT?
   I. It provided for the reduction of naval armaments.
   II. It replaced the Anglo-Japanese Alliance.
   III. It pledged the signatories to respect China's territorial integrity.
   IV. It provided for mutual respect of the signatories' rights in the Pacific.
   The CORRECT answer is:

   A. I, III
   B. I, IV
   C. II, IV
   D. II, III

23. Which one of the following can CORRECTLY be considered a result of the other three?

   A. High mortgage indebtedness in a period of falling prices
   B. Increased production of grain in foreign countries
   C. Decline in American agricultural prosperity
   D. Passage of the Hawley-Smoot Tariff

24. Of the following federal agencies, the one which was created FIRST was the

   A. SEC
   B. FDIC
   C. HOLC
   D. RFC

25. In rendering a decision on the Agricultural Adjustment Act, the Supreme Court ruled that

   A. crop regulation by Congress infringed on the rights of the states
   B. the processing tax was valid
   C. the *due process* clause had been violated
   D. crop regulation could be undertaken only as an aspect of conservation

KEY (CORRECT ANSWERS)

1. B
2. B
3. B
4. A
5. D

6. B
7. D
8. A
9. A
10. D

11. B
12. D
13. A
14. D
15. D

16. D
17. B
18. B
19. C
20. B

21. B
22. C
23. C
24. D
25. A

TEST 2

DIRECTIONS: Each question or incomplete statement is followed by several suggested answers or completions. Select the one that BEST answers the question or completes the statement. *PRINT THE LETTER OF THE CORRECT ANSWER IN THE SPACE AT THE RIGHT.*

1. There was no serious difference of opinion in the Constitutional Convention on how to deal with the problem of

    A. the regulation of commerce by Congress
    B. laws impairing the obligation of contracts
    C. the representation of the states in Congress
    D. popular election of the branches of the central government

    1._____

2. In which one of the following New World settlements was religion NOT a significant reason for colonization?

    A. Maryland
    B. Pennsylvania
    C. New Amsterdam
    D. South Carolina

    2._____

3. The EARLIEST representative assembly in the New World was provided for by the

    A. New England town meeting
    B. Virginia House of Burgesses
    C. Mayflower Compact
    D. New Netherlands government

    3._____

4. Which one of the following was NOT an accomplishment of the American government under the Articles of Confederation?
   The

    A. negotiation of a favorable peace treaty with England
    B. establishment of a sound system of money and banking
    C. establishment of a policy for the development of western lands
    D. organization of the Northwest Territory as a national domain

    4._____

5. Which one of the following was NOT a part of the boundary line of the United States as established by the Treaty of Paris of 1783?
   The

    A. Mississippi River on the west
    B. St. Lawrence River, the Great Lakes, and Canada on the north
    C. Atlantic Ocean on the east
    D. Gulf of Mexico on the south

    5._____

6. Which one of the following was a CAUSE of all of the others in the period after the American Revolution?

    A. The uprising of debtors led by Daniel Shays in western Massachusetts
    B. Difficulties in negotiating commercial treaties with England and Spain
    C. Confusion in the finances of the states and the central government
    D. Reluctance of the states to surrender sovereignty to a strong central government

    6._____

7. Which one of the following statements pertaining to the ratification of the United States Constitution is TRUE?

    A. Two states did not ratify until after the first Congress had convened.
    B. Ratification received overwhelming majorities in the larger states
    C. Samuel Adams and Patrick Henry were prominent leaders of the ratification party.
    D. Rhode Island was the first state to ratify the new Constitution.

8. *Prudence, indeed, will dictate that Governments long established should not be changed for light and transient causes* is a quotation from

    A. the Fundamental Orders of Connecticut
    B. the Declaration of Independence
    C. Washington's Farewell Address
    D. Virginia and Kentucky Resolutions

9. In return for locating the Federal Capitol on the Potomac, Virginia agreed to the

    A. excise tax on whiskey
    B. funding of the domestic debts
    C. assumption of state debts
    D. establishment of the Bank of the United States

10. Which one of the following did NOT promote the doctrine of the supremacy of the Federal government and the Supreme Court over acts of the states?

    A. Martin v. Hunter's Lessee
    B. Marbury v. Madison
    C. Cohens v. Virginia
    D. McCulloch v. Maryland

11. The United States enjoyed its GREATEST diplomatic success during the Federalist Period in the conduct of its foreign affairs with

    A. England
    B. France
    C. Spain
    D. the Barbary pirates

12. Of the following, a MAJOR reason for the disappearance of the Federalist Party by 1820 was the fact that the

    A. Federalists had abandoned their original political and economic principles
    B. Republicans had adopted most of the Federalist policies on banking, the tariff, and manufactures
    C. Federalist policy of expansionism during the War of 1812 had proved unpopular
    D. uncompromising attitude of the Republicans on all controversial issues had won over the mass of Federalist politicians and voters

13. The Treaty of Ghent ending the War of 1812 provided that the

    A. territory of the United States be extended to the Rocky Mountains
    B. British territory in North America be extended to include the western bank of the Mississippi River
    C. British cease their interference with the freedom of the seas
    D. status quo be continued

14. Which one of the following was NOT included in the program advocated by Henry Clay?

    A. An independent treasury
    B. A protective tariff
    C. Federal aid for internal improvements
    D. A centralized banking system

15. Which one of the following arguments was NOT used by Jackson in his attack on the Second Bank of the United States?

    A. It enjoyed a monopoly position in banking circles.
    B. Much of its stock was held by foreigners.
    C. It maintained a stable currency.
    D. It was not provided for in the Constitution.

16. The memorial to the Massachusetts legislature in 1843 on the status of the *insane persons confined within this Commonwealth in cages, closets, cellars, stalls, pens, chained, naked, beaten with rods, and lashed into obedience* was submitted by

    A. Horace Mann   B. Dorothea Dix
    C. Julia Ward Howe   D. Henry Thoreau

17. Which one of the following parties reflected a wave of intolerance in the United States? The

    A. Locofocos   B. Hunkers
    C. Know-Nothings   D. Anti-Masonic Party

18. Which one of the following BEST states a principle established by the Dred Scott decision?

    A. Congress could abolish slavery in the territories.
    B. Congress could not legislate concerning slavery in the territories.
    C. Slaves residing in free territory automatically gained freedom.
    D. The territories, through popular sovereignty, had the sole right to decide the question of slavery within their limits.

19. Which one of the following boundary disputes was settled in a manner DIFFERENT from the others?
    _____ boundary

    A. Maine   B. Oregon
    C. Texan   D. Louisiana Territory

20. In which one of the following is a slogan CORRECTLY associated with the President during whose administration it became popular?

    A. *54-40 or Fight* - Andrew Jackson
    B. *Remember the Alamc* - Zachary Taylor
    C. *Remember the Maine* - William McKinley
    D. *Make the World Safe for Democracy* - Franklin D. Roosevelt

21. The United States attempted to keep out of both the War of 1812 and World War II by   21.____

    A. boycotting European goods
    B. placing an embargo on American shipping
    C. denying loans to European nations
    D. closing its ports to foreign ships

22. From 1875 to 1914, the diplomacy of the United States in Europe concerned itself   22.____
    CHIEFLY with the maintenance of

    A. friendly commercial and cultural contacts
    B. the rights of neutrals on the seas
    C. the preservation of the status quo
    D. economic and military aid to tottering regimes

23. The Monroe Doctrine was the basis for our intervention in the   23.____

    A. Rio Grande boundary dispute
    B. Oregon boundary dispute
    C. Venezuelan boundary dispute
    D. Panama revolt

24. The United States became the predominant naval power in the Caribbean area as a   24.____
    result of the

    A. Treaty of Ghent   B. Clayton-Bulwer Treaty
    C. Hay-Pauncefote Treaty   D. Treaty of Paris (1898)

25. The United States is practically sovereign on this continent, and its fiat is law.   25.____
    In American history, this statement is known as the

    A. Ostend Manifesto
    B. Olney interpretation of the Monroe Doctrine
    C. Teller Amendment
    D. Roosevelt Corollary

KEY (CORRECT ANSWERS)

1. B
2. C
3. B
4. B
5. D

6. D
7. A
8. B
9. C
10. B

11. C
12. B
13. D
14. A
15. C

16. B
17. C
18. B
19. C
20. C

21. B
22. A
23. C
24. C
25. B

TEST 3

DIRECTIONS: Each question or incomplete statement is followed by several suggested answers or completions. Select the one that BEST answers the question or completes the statement. *PRINT THE LETTER OF THE CORRECT ANSWER IN THE SPACE AT THE RIGHT.*

1. Huerta, Madero, Carranza, and Villa were Mexican leaders who created serious problems in the area of American foreign affairs during the administration of   1.____

    A. James Monroe
    B. Abraham Lincoln
    C. Woodrow Wilson
    D. Franklin D. Roosevelt

2. Which one of the following disputes did NOT involve the United States and Great Britain?   2.____

    A. The Trent Affair
    B. Venezuelan boundary
    C. Panama tolls
    D. Panay Incident

3. In 1906, Theodore Roosevelt involved the United States in the diplomatic problems of Europe when he helped settle the crisis over   3.____

    A. Albania
    B. The Berlin-to-Baghdad Railroad
    C. Fashoda
    D. Morocco

4. With respect to World War I, Theodore Roosevelt was   4.____

    A. eager to have the United States enter on the side of England
    B. sympathetic to Germany and strongly in favor of American neutrality
    C. active in attempting to stop the war through negotiation
    D. a consistent supporter of President Wilson's pre-war policies

5. Which one of the following events occurred FIRST?   5.____

    A. Manchurian Incident
    B. Rome-Berlin-Tokyo Axis
    C. Seizure of Austria
    D. Ethiopian Campaign

6. Which one of the following was substituted for the Anglo-Japanese Alliance of 1902 when it was scrapped in 1922?   6.____

    A. Four Power Pact
    B. Five Power Naval Treaty
    C. Nine Power Treaty
    D. Lansing-Ishii Agreement

7. The Lend-Lease Act of 1941 empowered the President of the United States to   7.____

    A. give England 50 overage destroyers in exchange for leases of 8 air and naval bases
    B. lend defense and war materials to foreign nations whose defense was considered necessary to the United States
    C. arrange for *cash and carry* exports of arms and ammunition
    D. make special trade agreements without submitting them to Congress

8. In the opening of Africa to civilization and commerce, the United States   8.____

    A. engaged in the imperialistic rivalries which developed
    B. assumed political responsibility over parts of the continent
    C. displayed a keen interest in the political and economic developments
    D. interested itself mostly in developments of a humanitarian and scientific nature

9. Which one of the following was NOT true of the Granger Movement? It

   A. led to legislation for the regulation of railroad rates
   B. led to the regulation of warehouse and elevator companies
   C. disapproved of the establishment of cooperatives for the sale of general merchandise and farm implements
   D. had for its original purpose the dissemination of information on scientific agriculture

10. Which one of the following is CORRECT regarding the Pullman Strike of 1894?

    A. The Governor of Illinois requested President Cleveland to send federal troops to Chicago to maintain order.
    B. President Cleveland sent federal troops to Chicago on the grounds that they were necessary to enforce the Interstate Commerce Act.
    C. The federal government's intervention included the use of the injunction as a weapon against labor.
    D. Debs was arrested for failing to obey the court order but the Supreme Court ordered his release on the grounds that a federal court had no right to issue a blanket injunction.

11. The Supreme Court upheld the constitutionality of which one of the following New Deal laws?

    A. Agricultural Adjustment Act (1933)
    B. National Labor Relations Act (1935)
    C. National Industrial Recovery Act (1933)
    D. Guffey-Snyder Bituminous Coal Act (1935)

12. The CHIEF opposition to the creation of the Tennessee Valley Authority was centered on its function of

    A. carrying out a program of flood control
    B. acting as a yardstick for rates of private utilities
    C. preventing soil erosion
    D. manufacturing fertilizers and explosives

13. Which one of the following terms has been used to characterize the social and cultural life in the United States during the period 1870-1900? The

    A. Tragic Era   B. Age of Hate
    C. New Freedom   D. Gilded Age

14. During which one of the following decades did immigration to the United States from Southern and Eastern Europe exceed that from Northern and Western Europe?

    A. 1870-1880   B. 1880-1890   C. 1900-1910   D. 1930-1940

15. Populism, the New Freedom, and the New Deal were all in favor of

    A. laissez-faire
    B. strict construction of the Constitution
    C. broad construction of the Constitution
    D. the exclusion of economic considerations from politics

16. Which one of the following groups lists the presidential programs in their CORRECT chronological order?

    A. The New Deal - the Fair Deal - the Square Deal - the New Freedom
    B. The New Freedom - the New Deal - the Square Deal - the Fair Deal
    C. The Square Deal - the New Freedom - the New Deal - the Fair Deal
    D. The Fair Deal - the Square Deal - the New Deal - the New Freedom

17. Which one of the following can be DIRECTLY associated with the development of the assembly line technique of mass production?

    A. John D. Rockefeller
    B. Andrew Carnegie
    C. J.P. Morgan
    D. Henry Ford

18. He was a gifted American architect whose view that form follows function has shaped the building of twentieth century skyscraper office buildings.
    This description refers to

    A. Augustus Saint-Gaudens
    B. Thomas Eakins
    C. Richard Morris Hunt
    D. Louis Sullivan

19. Which one of the following titles is NOT correctly paired with its author?

    A. THE NEW COLOSSUS - Emma Lazarus
    B. THE AMERICAN LANGUAGE - Henry L. Mencken
    C. THE VIRGINIAN - Owen Wister
    D. THE FRONTIER IN AMERICAN HISTORY - Hamlin in Garland

20. Which one of the following is NOT known primarily as an American historian?

    A. Henry Commager
    B. Henry James
    C. Arthur M. Schlesinger, Sr.
    D. Frederick J. Turner

21. The North Atlantic Treaty Organization (NATO) and the Southeast Asia Treaty Organization (SEATO) have the following members in common: United States,

    A. Great Britain, France
    B. Netherlands, Portugal
    C. Great Britain, India
    D. France, Australia

22. In which one of the following have military forces under United Nations supervision NOT been employed?

    A. Korean War
    B. Suez Canal Crisis (1956)
    C. Kashmir
    D. Congo

23. Which one of the following has NOT been true of the United Nations since its organization in 1945?

    A. Its membership has approximately doubled.
    B. The General Assembly has gained in stature and has been strengthened.
    C. The membership of the Security Council has been increased.
    D. The activities of the Economic and Social Council and of the Specialized Agencies have increased.

24. In which one of the following are the items regarding the United Nations INCORRECTLY paired?

   A. Uniting for Peace Resolution - Right of the General Assembly to act because of a Security Council veto
   B. UNESCO - Rehabilitation of Korea following the Korean War
   C. Procedural Matters - Vote of any 7 members of the Security Council
   D. Trusteeship Council - Supervision of designated territories whose peoples have not attained self-government

25. Which one of the following territories or possessions of the United States is INCORRECTLY identified with a terra designating its changed political status?

   A. Philippine Islands - independent country
   B. Puerto Rico - commonwealth
   C. Hawaii - state
   D. Virgin Islands - trust territory

KEY (CORRECT ANSWERS)

1.	C	11.	B
2.	D	12.	B
3.	D	13.	D
4.	A	14.	C
5.	A	15.	C
6.	A	16.	C
7.	B	17.	D
8.	D	18.	D
9.	C	19.	D
10.	C	20.	B

21.	A
22.	C
23.	C
24.	B
25.	D

TEST 4

DIRECTIONS: Each question or incomplete statement is followed by several suggested answers or completions. Select the one that BEST answers the question or completes the statement. *PRINT THE LETTER OF THE CORRECT ANSWER IN THE SPACE AT THE RIGHT.*

1. Many American colleges founded in the seventeenth and eighteenth centuries owe their origin to the

   A. initiative of wealthy planters and businessmen who sought to create institutions for the education of the less prosperous
   B. sponsorship of colonial and later of state governments which sought to provide educational opportunities for graduates of lower schools
   C. desire of the various churches in America to train young men for the ministry
   D. spirit of freedom that impelled Americans to sever all the bonds which tied them to European educational institutions

2. Britain's relations with her colonies in America were characterized by her

   A. failure to develop a machinery of colonial administration
   B. repudiation of the mercantile theory
   C. establishment of the Church of England in all the colonies
   D. establishment of a uniform type of government in all the colonies

3. Which one of the following men played an influential role in the formulation of the Albany Plan of Union, the Articles of Confederation, and the Constitution of the United States?

   A. Benjamin Franklin   B. Alexander Hamilton
   C. Thomas Jefferson   D. George Washington

4. The phrase *loose construction,* when applied to the United States Constitution, is GENERALLY understood to mean

   A. the laxity of enforcement of certain constitutional provisions
   B. the strictness with which Congress is held to its enumerated powers
   C. a Supreme Court decision invalidating an act of Congress
   D. a broad interpretation of the Constitution

5. From 1783 to 1795, Spain disputed the right of the United States to free navigation of the Mississippi River because

   A. for the greater part of its course the river flowed through Spanish territory
   B. the river had been discovered by Spanish explorers
   C. both banks of the river near its mouth were owned by Spain
   D. England had no right to cede the eastern bank of the river to any other power

6. Which one of the following statements is TRUE of Washington's Proclamation of Neutrality?

   A. Jefferson and Hamilton were in agreement on the need for issuing the Proclamation.
   B. The Proclamation brought to an end the treaties between the United States and France.

C. Genet precipitated the issuing of the Proclamation.
D. The Proclamation meant that the United States would not recognize the revolutionary government of France.

7. Hamilton's proposed plan for the payment of governmental debts was to pay

   A. only the foreign debt in full
   B. domestic, foreign, and state debts at their full value
   C. only the foreign and the state debts at their face value
   D. domestic, foreign, and state debts at their depreciated value

7._____

8. The PRIMARY purpose of the Virginia and Kentucky Resolutions was to

   A. repeal the neutrality laws of the 1790's
   B. defeat Hamilton's proposal for the payment of the national debt
   C. urge secession of the states which were dissatisfied with Federalist policies
   D. arouse public opinion against the Federalists' grant of excessive powers to the Federal government

8._____

9. The Hartford Convention adopted resolutions proposing

   A. New England's secession from the Union
   B. a separate New England peace treaty with Britain
   C. a Constitutional amendment requiring a two-thirds vote in Congress for a declaration of war
   D. the impeachment of President Madison

9._____

10. Which one of the following was the STRONGEST influence during the early decades of the nineteenth century in creating a legal structure within which capitalism could develop in the United States?

    A. The decisions of the Supreme Court under the leadership of John Marshall
    B. Federalist control of Congress
    C. The existence of the First and the Second National Banks
    D. The maintenance of protective tariffs

10._____

11. Which one of the following was NOT a reason for the issuing of the Monroe Doctrine? To

    A. restrict British trade in South America
    B. support the newly independent countries in South America
    C. deny the right of European nations to interfere in the Western Hemisphere
    D. bar Russian colonization in North America

11._____

12. Jackson's exercise of a vigorous executive leadership during his presidency is illustrated by each of the following EXCEPT his

    A. refusal to enforce a Supreme Court decision against the state of Georgia
    B. refusal to sign the *Force Bill* passed by Congress against the state of South Carolina
    C. use of the *pocket veto* for the first time in the history of the United States
    D. veto of more legislation than had been vetoed by all previous administrations combined

12._____

13. The 19th century American statesman who was the leading proponent of the theory of the concurrent minority, which guaranteed to large economic interests and geographic units a veto on the majority determination was

    A. John C. Calhoun   B. Henry Clay
    C. Stephen A. Douglas   D. Daniel Webster

14. Which one of the following permitted settlers in the Louisiana Territory to decide the question of slavery for themselves?
    The

    A. Dred Scott Decision   B. Missouri Compromise
    C. Wilmot Proviso   D. Kansas-Nebraska Act

15. Which one of the following terms has been frequently used to describe the group of New England idealists of the 1840's of which Ralph Waldo Emerson was a leading member?

    A. Demagogues   B. Jacksonians
    C. Transcendentalists D. Utopian Socialists

16. The election of Lincoln to the Presidency in 1860 was similar to that of Wilson in 1912 because, in each case, the

    A. Democratic candidate won
    B. election had to be decided by the House of Representatives
    C. winner benefited by a split in the opposition party
    D. winner scored a huge majority of the popular vote

17. Lincoln's Emancipation Proclamation

    A. contained a forceful indictment of slavery
    B. was based on military necessity
    C. declared all slaves in all the slave states to be free
    D. was issued after a succession of military victories by the North

18. Major attempts to suppress important civil liberties in the United States have generally come during periods of national fear.
    An example of this is the passage of the Alien and Sedition Acts during the

    A. French Revolution   B. War of 1812
    C. Period of Reconstruction D. First World War

19. The years immediately following the Civil War were similar to the years immediately following the War of 1812 because in both periods

    A. the executive and legislative branches were controlled by different parties
    B. the legislatures were unable to pass necessary laws
    C. the Presidents were successful military leaders but unsuccessful in civil office
    D. for practical purposes, no effective opposition groups operated in Congress

20. The Whiskey Rebellion in western Pennsylvania is famous in United States history because it marked the FIRST

    A. attempt to enforce a state prohibition law
    B. serious evidence of sectional differences between North and South
    C. demonstration by the new Federal government that it could enforce its laws

D. organized movement to challenge British authority in the American colonies

21. In which one of the following groups did ALL three persons contribute to regional literature?

    A. Kenneth Roberts, Sinclair Lewis, T.S. Eliot
    B. Eugene O' Neill, Edna St. Vincent Millay, Sherwood Anderson
    C. Archibald MacLeish, Robinson Jeffers, Thomas Wolfe
    D. Robert Frost, Carl Sandburg, Willa Cather

22. In which one of the following groups did ALL three persons attain prominence in the same field?

    A. William Cullen Bryant, Horace Greeley, Adolph Ochs
    B. John Jacob Astor, Andrew Carnegie, William H. McGuffey
    C. Josiah Royce, George Bancroft, John Wesley Powell
    D. Robert A. Millikan, Franz Boaz, Louis Sullivan

23. Which one of the following American journalists of the past century MOST closely resembled William Randolph Hearst in his conception of newspaper editing?

    A. James Gordon Bennet
    B. Charles A. Dana
    C. Horace Greeley
    D. Joseph Pulitzer

24. Which one of the following novels deals critically with governmental treatment of the American Indians in the 19th century?

    A. THE CALL OF THE WILD
    B. THE RISE OF SILAS LAPHAM
    C. RAMONA
    D. THE RED BADGE OF COURAGE

25. Edward Bellamy's *Looking Backward* is a

    A. muckraking sociological study of monopolies in the 1890's
    B. comparison of 20th century working conditions with medieval serfdom
    C. novel about a socialistic Utopia in the United States in the year 2000
    D. plan for a more humane treatment of the American Indian

KEY (CORRECT ANSWERS)

1. C
2. A
3. A
4. D
5. C

6. A
7. B
8. D
9. C
10. A

11. A
12. B
13. A
14. D
15. C

16. C
17. B
18. A
19. D
20. C

21. D
22. A
23. D
24. C
25. C

TEST 5

DIRECTIONS: Each question or incomplete statement is followed by several suggested answers or completions. Select the one that BEST answers the question or completes the statement. *PRINT THE LETTER OF THE CORRECT ANSWER IN THE SPACE AT THE RIGHT.*

1. In which one of the following groups do ALL three men closely approximate the appellation of the scholar-in-politics? 1.____

    A. Henry Cabot Lodge, Albert J. Beveridge, Theodore Roosevelt
    B. Oliver Wendell Holmes, Jr., James A. Garfield, Abraham Lincoln
    C. Alfred E. Smith, William Randolph Hearst, Ulysses S. Grant
    D. William McKinley, Warren G. Harding, Mark Hanna

2. Which one of the following groups was among the STRONGEST supporters of William Jennings Bryan in the campaign of 1896? 2.____

    A. Creditors
    B. Western mining interests
    C. Eastern propertied classes
    D. Workers in tariff-protected industries

3. Expressions such as *parity prices* and *codes of fair competition* are associated with the 3.____

    A. Square Deal   B. New Deal
    C. New Freedom   D. New Nationalism

4. An IMPORTANT twentieth century development affecting the use of private wealth for the support of education, medicine, and science in the United States has been the 4.____

    A. dependence of the American creative arts on old world styles
    B. rise of philanthropic family foundations
    C. gradual reduction of inheritance and estate taxes
    D. government sponsorship of research activities

5. *Czar* Thomas B. Reed and *Uncle Joe* Cannon at one time occupied the same position in the 5.____

    A. army   B. United States Senate
    C. House of Representatives   D. Cabinet

6. After a lapse of about a century, the personal appearance of the President to read his messages to Congress was revived by 6.____

    A. Theodore Roosevelt   B. William Howard Taft
    C. Woodrow Wilson   D. Franklin D. Roosevelt

7. Which one of the following incidents established the precedent whereby a President of the United States could send an American army to join an allied expeditionary force WITHOUT express Congressional authority? President 7.____

    A. Cleveland's dispatch of troops to Venezuela during the Venezuelan Boundary Dispute in 1895
    B. McKinley's intervention in the Boxer Rebellion of 1900
    C. Wilson's order to American troops to pursue Pancho Villa into Mexico in 1916

D. Truman's order to MacArthur to defend the Republic of Korea against invasion by North Koreans in 1950

8. The doctrine that the President may take any action in the general interest that is not specifically forbidden by the laws and the Constitution was enunciated by

   A. Grover Cleveland
   B. Theodore Roosevelt
   C. Woodrow Wilson
   D. Franklin D. Roosevelt

8.____

9. Which United States Senator was a MAJOR sponsor of both the Lame Duck Amendment and of the Anti-Injunction Act of 1932?

   A. Warren G. Harding
   B. Wayne Morse
   C. George W. Norris
   D. Harry S. Truman

9.____

10. The Hundred Days Congress of 1933 passed all of the following acts EXCEPT the _____ Act.

    A. Glass-Steagall Banking Reform
    B. National Industrial Recovery
    C. Social Security
    D. Tennessee Valley Authority

10.____

11. A feature of the Reciprocal Trade Agreements Act (1934) was that agreements negotiated under it would

    A. apply only to European countries
    B. need the approval of Congress
    C. need the approval of the Senate
    D. become effective without Senate approval

11.____

12. Which one of the following was NOT a provision of the Taft-Hartley Law of 1947?

    A. Union shop contracts permitted without prior polling of employees
    B. Ending of the check-off system
    C. A 60-day cooling-off period before a strike
    D. Public financial statements required of unions

12.____

13. All of the following recommendations of the second Hoover Commission have been accepted by the United States government EXCEPT the one which suggested the

    A. creation of a federal administrative court to reorganize the government's legal functions
    B. liquidation of the assets of the Reconstruction Finance Corporation
    C. elimination of duplicate hospital care by the various military services
    D. overhauling of military procurement procedures to permit the services to buy common items jointly

13.____

14. Governor Faubus's dispute with President Eisenhower arising out of the use of federal troops in Arkansas recalls a similar dispute between Governor

    A. Hughes of New York and President Taft
    B. Altgeld of Illinois and President Cleveland
    C. Cox of Ohio and President Wilson
    D. Stevenson of Illinois and President Truman

14.____

15. Which one of the following had to be approved by a two-thirds vote of the United States Senate in order to become effective?
The

    A. annexation of Hawaii in 1898
    B. Truman Doctrine
    C. Kellogg-Briand Peace Pact
    D. Lend-Lease Agreement with Great Britain

16. Which one of the following affected United States-Japanese relations in a way DIFFERENT from the others?

    A. Root-Takahira Agreement
    B. Hull-Kurusu Negotiations
    C. Lansing-Ishii Agreement
    D. Gentlemen's Agreement

17. During whose presidency was the Roosevelt Corollary officially repudiated by the State Department?

    A. Woodrow Wilson
    B. Calvin Coolidge
    C. Herbert Hoover
    D. Franklin D. Roosevelt

18. Which one of the following was the MOST immediate effect of the German invasion of Poland (1939) on American foreign policy?
Congress

    A. forbade the sale of arms to belligerents
    B. enacted a Neutrality Act permitting the sale of war materials on a *cash and carry* basis
    C. empowered the President to exchange fifty old destroyers for British bases in the Caribbean
    D. passed the Lend-Lease Act

19. Which one of the following World War II conferences is INCORRECTLY paired with the subject matter associated with it?

    A. Bretton Woods - plans for post-war international financial arrangements
    B. Casablanca - British-American war plans
    C. Dumbarton Oaks - tentative proposals for United Nations Charter
    D. Potsdam - Allied plans for military campaigns against Germany

20. United States troops were sent to assist South Korea against North Korean aggression in June 1950 under an action taken by the

    A. United Nations Security Council
    B. United States Congress
    C. United States Senate
    D. United States President

21. Which one of the following events prior to American participation in World War II had a CAUSATIVE effect on the others?

    A. Adoption of the Selective Service Act
    B. Exchange of American destroyers for bases in British possessions
    C. The fall of France to the German invasion
    D. The adoption of the Act of Havana by the Pan-American States

22. The Neutrality Acts of 1935 and 1937 reflected the desire of the American people to

    A. prepare defenses against possible aggression
    B. assert the traditional American doctrine of neutral rights
    C. maintain dollar trade
    D. remain out of any war originating in Europe or Asia

23. Place the following events in their proper chronological order:
    I. Hitler's invasion of Russia
    II. Japanese attack on Pearl Harbor
    III. Battle of Britain
    IV. Atlantic Charter

    The CORRECT answer is:

    A. I, II, III, IV
    B. III, I, IV, II
    C. IV, III, I, II
    D. III, IV, I, II

24. Which one of the following actions in foreign relations required ratification by the Senate?

    A. North Atlantic Pact
    B. Reciprocal Trade Agreement with Britain
    C. Atlantic Charter
    D. Yalta Conference Agreements

25. Canadian-American diplomatic relations during the past century have been comparatively tranquil as have been the relations of

    A. Chile and Peru
    B. Spain and North Africa
    C. Norway and Sweden
    D. Japan and Russia

KEY (CORRECT ANSWERS)

1.	A	11.	D
2.	B	12.	A
3.	B	13.	A
4.	B	14.	B
5.	C	15.	C
6.	C	16.	B
7.	B	17.	C
8.	B	18.	B
9.	C	19.	D
10.	C	20.	D

21. C
22. D
23. B
24. A
25. C

———

EXAMINATION SECTION
TEST 1

DIRECTIONS: Each question or incomplete statement is followed by several suggested answers or completions. Select the one that BEST answers the question or completes the statement. *PRINT THE LETTER OF THE CORRECT ANSWER IN THE SPACE AT THE RIGHT.*

1. The close relationship between railroad prosperity and the growth of the west was *clearly* understood by which builder of the Great Northern railway system? 1.____

   A. Cornelius Vanderbilt B. John Jacob Astor
   C. Andrew Carnegie D. James J. Hill

2. Uninterrupted passenger journeys and through shipments of freight were made possible by the 2.____

   A. generous government land grants given to railroad builders
   B. consolidation of short lines into great railroad systems
   C. invention of the automatic air brake
   D. passage of railway safety laws by Congress

3. Alexander Graham Bell exhibited his telephone at the Philadelphia Exposition in 3.____

   A. 1866 B. 1870 C. 1876 D. 1890

4. The time for sending trans-Atlantic messages was cut to practically nothing with the successful establishment of permanent cable service by 4.____

   A. Cyrus Field B. Samuel F.B. Morse
   C. James Watt D. George Pullman

5. Corporations may raise money by selling stocks or issuing 5.____

   A. bonds B. charters C. dividends D. trusts

6. Exclusive, or almost exclusive, control of an industry is called a 6.____

   A. monopoly B. proprietorship
   C. corporation D. pool

7. The American steel industry was dominated in its early years by 7.____

   A. William Kelly B. Andrew Carnegie
   C. J.P. Morgan D. Henry Ford

8. The Standard Oil Company was founded by 8.____

   A. John D. Rockefeller B. Edwin Drake
   C. Henry C. Frick D. Henry Bessemer

9. One of the arguments used by those who favored high tariff rates following the Civil War was that high tariffs would 9.____

   A. promote a greater volume of world trade
   B. encourage the development of new industries
   C. stop the growth of huge industrial combinations
   D. keep prices and wages low

10. In order to cut down the surplus supply of money which the United States Treasury had accumulated by the mid-1880's, President Grover Cleveland favored

    A. increased appropriations for internal improvements
    B. larger pensions for veterans
    C. tariff reduction
    D. payment of the national debt

11. The money surplus which the United States government had accumulated was NOT desirable because it meant that

    A. there was more money for industrial consolidation
    B. there was less money in circulation
    C. the national debt was reduced to nothing
    D. prices and wages must be reduced

12. The part of the McKinley Tariff of 1890 which, in effect, said to foreign nations, *I'll treat you as you treat me* was known as a

    A. reciprocity clause   B. bounty
    C. free trade agreement   D. mutual benefit pact

13. To make up for the expected loss of revenue, the Wilson Gorman Tariff Act provided for

    A. a federal sales tax
    B. graduated corporation taxes
    C. an income tax
    D. the reduction of defense spending

14. The theory of *laissez-faire* which dominated the national economic policy until the late 1800's held that

    A. business growth should be strictly controlled
    B. government control should extend beyond foreign and interstate commerce
    C. the government should not tamper with the economic system
    D. agricultural interests should be protected

15. The Missouri Compromise (1820), the Compromise of 1850, and the Kansas-Nebraska Act (1854)

    A. were a series of laws passed by Congress
    B. concerned the status of slavery in the Western territories
    C. dealt with sectional disputes which finally led to civil war
    D. all of the above

16. Identify the characteristic of the American free enterprise system.

    A. Private ownership of the means of production and distribution
    B. Absence of competition
    C. Prices of goods and services fixed by government regulation
    D. Government ownership of the means of production and distribution

17. Which tactic has NOT been used to achieve the aims of organized labor?

    A. Lockout   B. Strike   C. Picketing   D. Boycott

18. Which situation did NOT result from the rapid industrialization of the United States? 18.____

    A. The American standard of living was raised.
    B. New job opportunities encouraged immigration.
    C. Workers demanded higher wages and better working conditions.
    D. America became increasingly isolated in international affairs.

Questions 19-20.

DIRECTIONS: Questions 19 to 20 refer to the following chart.

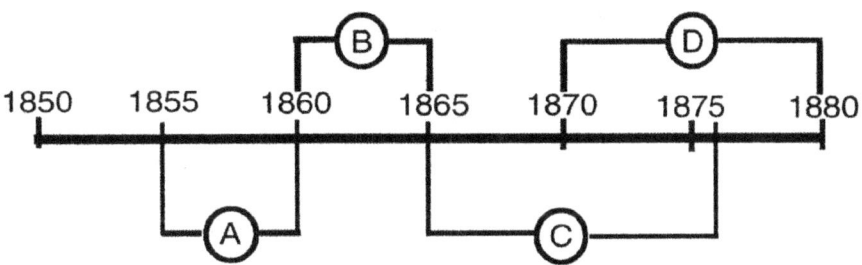

19. During Period _____ on the time line above, the Civil War occurred. 19.____

    A. A   B. B   C. C   D. D

20. The Reconstruction Era *generally* refers to Period _____ on the time line above. 20.____

    A. A   B. B   C. C   D. D

21. In which period did the MOST dramatic change in public manners and morals occur? 21.____

    A. The Federalist Era (1789-1800)
    B. The Age of Jackson (1825-1850)
    C. *The Jazz Age* (1920's)
    D. The Great Depression (1930's)

Questions 22-25.

DIRECTIONS: Questions 22 to 25 refer to the following map.

22. Which name is associated with the shaded portion of the map shown above? 22.___
    A. Napoleon Bonaparte   B. Thomas Jefferson
    C. Lewis and Clark   D. All of the above

23. Which of the territory areas above did Mexico cede to the United States after losing the   23.___
    Mexican War?
    A. A   B. B   C. C   D. D

24. Which of the territory areas above became an independent republic before it was *finally* 24.___
    annexed to the United States?
    A. A   B. B   C. C   D. D

25. In which section of the map shown above was the so-called Northwest Territory located? 25.___
    A. A   B. B   C. C   D. D

KEY (CORRECT ANSWERS)

1. D   11. B
2. B   12. A
3. C   13. C
4. A   14. C
5. A   15. D

6. A   16. A
7. B   17. A
8. A   18. D
9. B   19. B
10. C   20. C

21. C
22. D
23. A
24. B
25. C

TEST 2

DIRECTIONS: Each question or incomplete statement is followed by several suggested answers or completions. Select the one that BEST answers the question or completes the statement. *PRINT THE LETTER OF THE CORRECT ANSWER IN THE SPACE AT THE RIGHT.*

1. The United States foreign policy until the end of the nineteenth century was *generally* one of 1.____

    A. expansion
    B. colonization
    C. liberalism
    D. isolation

2. The man who was chiefly responsible for making the motor car popular in America was 2.____

    A. George B. Seidon
    B. Henry Ford
    C. Wiley Post
    D. E. I. du Pont

3. The FIRST solo flight across the Atlantic Ocean was made in 1927 by 3.____

    A. Charles Lindbergh
    B. Richard Byrd
    C. Samuel Langley
    D. Howard Hughes

4. American scientists R. A. Fessenden and Lee De Forest played important roles in experiments with wireless telephony which led to the development of the 4.____

    A. radio
    B. duplex telegraph
    C. multiplex telegraph
    D. motion pictures

5. A corporation which does NOT operate a business of its own but exists *only* to buy and keep shares in other corporations is called a 5.____

    A. pool
    B. trust
    C. holding company
    D. cartel

6. The WORST depression the United States has ever experienced occurred after the stock market crash of 6.____

    A. 1893 B. 1907 C. 1929 D. 1987

7. Public opinion against big business and corruption in government was aroused by a group of twentieth century writers called 7.____

    A. mugwumps
    B. local color writers
    C. stalwarts
    D. muckrakers

8. Because of his efforts to break up large business combinations, the title *trust-buster* was given to President 8.____

    A. William McKinley
    B. Theodore Roosevelt
    C. Woodrow Wilson
    D. Chester A. Arthur

9. The Federal Trade Commission Act and the Clayton Antitrust Act were intended to 9.____

    A. break up monopolies and trusts after they had been formed
    B. limit the size of all business combinations
    C. change the state laws about corporation charters
    D. prevent unfair competition and unlawful business combinations from developing

10. During the years following World War I, federal control of business was

    A. increased
    B. declared unconstitutional
    C. encouraged by President Harding
    D. relaxed

11. In regard to the depression which engulfed the United States during his administration, President Hoover felt that the government should

    A. not concern itself with the problems of business
    B. let the economy stabilize itself
    C. continue its policy of non-interference
    D. use its power to fight hard times and to improve business conditions

12. The Interstate Commerce Commission was made a *really* effective means of regulating the railroads by the passage in 1906 of the

    A. Wheeler-Rayburn Act   B. Glass-Steagall Act
    C. Hepburn Act   D. Taft-Hartley Act

13. President Theodore Roosevelt justified his interference in the coal strike of 1902 by

    A. finding a constitutional basis for it
    B. forcing an amendment through Congress
    C. using the special powers given to a President in time of war
    D. declaring that the *public interest* demanded his action

14. During the early 1900's, a new and radical labor union called the Industrial Workers of the World made a special effort to organize

    A. professional and clerical workers
    B. agricultural workers
    C. unskilled industrial workers
    D. skilled laborers

15. The Clayton Act and the policies of President Woodrow Wilson

    A. placed many legal restrictions on organized labor
    B. were helpful to organized labor
    C. favored employers at the cost of employees
    D. had little effect on labor

16. The term *Golden Twenties* is applied to the period from 1920 to 1929 because of the

    A. cultural advancements that took place
    B. scientific progress which was made
    C. great prosperity which the nation enjoyed
    D. discovery of gold in several western states

17. The FIRST president of the Congress of Industrial Organization was

    A. Eugene V. Debs   B. John L. Lewis
    C. William Z. Foster   D. William Green

18. Strikes arising from the rivalry between A.F. of L. and C.I.O. unions were called 18.____

    A. sit-down strikes
    B. lockouts
    C. secondary boycotts
    D. jurisdictional strikes

Questions 19-21.

DIRECTIONS: Questions 19 to 21 are based on the following paragraph.

America has a long tradition of religious freedom. Throughout our history, we have, with few exceptions, allowed people to worship as they choose. This right is protected in the Constitution. Indeed, the founding fathers could scarcely have done otherwise. Many Colonists had settled here for the very purpose of finding havens from religious persecution. Therefore, they would NOT have welcomed the establishment of a state religion with all its accompanying demands.

19. Which part of the Constitution guarantees religious freedom? 19.____

    A. Preamble
    B. Bill of Rights
    C. Section describing presidential duties
    D. Section listing congressional powers

20. One of the few exceptions referred to in this passage could be the practice of banishing dissenters. 20.____
    Which group had this policy?

    A. Puritans
    B. Roman Catholics
    C. Anglicans
    D. Quakers

21. Which of these was NOT founded as a haven from religious persecution? 21.____

    A. Maryland
    B. New York
    C. Pennsylvania
    D. Rhode Island

22. _____ did NOT help to make Oregon part of the United States. 22.____

    A. Fur traders
    B. Missionaries
    C. Lewis and Clark
    D. The Walla Walla Indians

23. The invention of new farm machinery after 1850 contributed to 23.____

    A. the growth of New York as a manufacturing city
    B. the introduction of several new crops
    C. an increase in the size of farms
    D. a decline in farm production

24. The strategy of the North for winning the Civil War was to 24.____

    A. hold out until the South tired of war
    B. gain foreign aid
    C. conquer by dividing the Confederacy in two
    D. capture General Lee

25. _____ FIRST set forth the terms of territorial government MOST commonly used by the United States territories.

    A. The Ordinance of 1787
    B. The Constitution of the United States
    C. Laws passed by the First Congress under the Constitution
    D. The treaty of 1783 with Great Britain

KEY (CORRECT ANSWERS)

1.	D	11.	D
2.	B	12.	C
3.	A	13.	D
4.	A	14.	C
5.	C	15.	B
6.	C	16.	C
7.	D	17.	B
8.	B	18.	D
9.	D	19.	B
10.	D	20.	A

21. B
22. D
23. C
24. C
25. A

TEST 3

DIRECTIONS: Each question or incomplete statement is followed by several suggested answers or completions. Select the one that BEST answers the question or completes the statement. *PRINT THE LETTER OF THE CORRECT ANSWER IN THE SPACE AT THE RIGHT.*

1. The rapid growth to statehood of the Rocky Mountain areas was due in a *large* part to the   1.____

    A. discovery of gold and silver
    B. westward movement of farmers
    C. Civil War
    D. removal of the Indian menace

2. The *long drive* of cattle from the western plains to railroad terminals was organized because of a demand in northern and eastern cities for more   2.____

    A. leather
    B. civilized government in the West
    C. free land for farming
    D. beef

3. Early settlers on the Great Plains lived in dugouts and sod houses because   3.____

    A. they offered more protection from rain than wooden houses
    B. timber was very scarce on the prairies
    C. the temperate climate made more permanent housing unnecessary
    D. there was little need for protection against wind or rain

4. The Plains Indians were stripped of their chief means of support by the killing of large numbers of   4.____

    A. deer   B. buffaloes
    C. prairie chickens D. antelope

5. Little Crow, Red Cloud, and Crazy Horse were all leaders of the   5.____

    A. Apaches   B. Pawnees   C. Sioux   D. Cherokees

6. The leader of the detachment which was wiped out by the Indians at the Little Big Horn in 1876 was   6.____

    A. William Cody   B. Yellowstone Kelly
    C. Davy Crockett   D. George Custer

7. The Indian policy of the United States government from the end of the Indian Wars until the passage of the Wheeler-Howard Act in 1934   7.____

    A. proved to be extremely successful
    B. led to a great increase in the Indian population
    C. was NOT very successful
    D. made no provision for the education of Indian children

8. From the end of the Civil War until 1900, the pace of industrial change in the United States

   A. grew faster and faster
   B. was unchecked by panics or depressions
   C. remained relatively slow
   D. was halted by the growth of labor unions

9. The inventions of Thomas A. Edison are an example of the

   A. application of scientific principles to practical purposes
   B. value of theoretical scientific research
   C. superiority of mass production methods
   D. close relationships between business organizations and industrial growth

10. The spectacular growth of industry following the Civil War was

    A. limited almost entirely to the Northeast
    B. not evident in the Midwest
    C. not confined to any one section of the country
    D. based on a very unstable foundation

11. The two railroad companies which were licensed to build the first transcontinental railroad were the Union Pacific and the

    A. New York Central   B. Central Pacific
    C. Northern Pacific   D. Great Western

12. The construction of the first transcontinental railroad was

    A. encouraged and aided by the Federal government
    B. financed entirely by the railroad companies
    C. completed without the use of Federal money
    D. financed by the states through which the right of way was built

13.

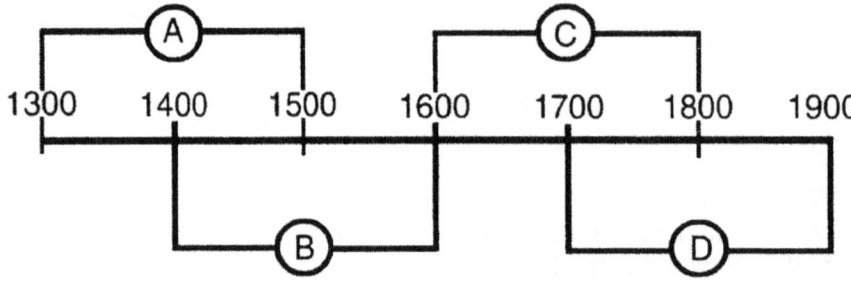

During Period _____ on the time line above, the English settlement of the thirteen colonies took place.

    A. A   B. B   C. C   D. D

14. Which event marked the beginning of representative government in America?

    A. Virginia House of Burgesses
    B. Articles of Confederation
    C. Mayflower Compact
    D. The election of Andrew Jackson

15. Which point is NOT a basic principle stated in the Declaration of Independence?

    A. All persons are born with certain God-given rights.
    B. Governments are created to protect certain God-given rights.
    C. When a government is unjust, the people have the right to overthrow it.
    D. People are the servants of governments.

16. The FALSE statement about the Northwest Ordinance is that it

    A. was a law which told how U.S. territories should be governed
    B. told how new states would be admitted to the Union
    C. guaranteed the personal liberties of people living in the territories
    D. told how states could peacefully leave the Union

17. The American Revolution is considered to be one of the MOST significant political developments of the _____ century.

    A. sixteenth   B. seventeenth
    C. eighteenth   D. nineteenth

18. The introduction to the Constitution says: *We, the people of the United States ... do ordain and establish this Constitution for the United States of America.*
    What basic principle of United States government is *clearly* stated in this introduction?

    A. Representative government
    B. Limited government
    C. Separation of powers
    D. Democratic self-government

19. One of the important causes of the War of 1812 was that Americans were angered when British vessels fired upon, searched, and seized neutral American ships at sea. The_____ was also prompted by interference with neutral American shipping.

    A. Mexican   B. First World   C. Korean   D. Vietnam

20. In which famous case did the Supreme Court establish the principle of judicial review by declaring an act of Congress to be unconstitutional?

    A. Marbury v. Madison
    B. Dred Scott v. Sanford
    C. McCulloch v. Maryland
    D. Gibbons v. Ogden

21. San Juan Hill and Manila Bay were sites of famous battles fought during the _____ War.

    A. Mexican   B. 1812
    C. Spanish-American   D. Korean

22. Which point was NOT stated in the Monroe Doctrine? 22.___

    A. North and South America are closed to future European colonization.
    B. The United States will NOT interfere with any European colony already established.
    C. The U.S. will consider further European intervention in the Americas as a threat to its safety.
    D. If its own vital interests are at stake, the U.S. has the right to interfere in the internal affairs of any country.

23. Identify the term for the nineteenth-century belief that the United States had the right and duty to expand its boundaries as far as possible on the North American continent. 23.___

    A. Manifest Destiny   B. The Frontier Theory
    C. The *American System*   D. The Good Neighbor Policy

24. Prior to the Civil War, which of these sections of the country *opposed* a high protective tariff? 24.___

    A. Northern states   B. Southern states
    C. Western states   D. Western territories

25. The Virginia and Kentucky Resolutions (1798), the Hartford Convention (1814), and the South Carolina Exposition and Protest (1828) all 25.___

    A. claimed that federal laws took precedence over state laws
    B. argued for the States' Rights Theory
    C. contributed to the development of nationalism
    D. all of the above

KEY (CORRECT ANSWERS)

1. A		11. B	
2. D		12. A	
3. B		13. C	
4. B		14. A	
5. C		15. D	
6. D		16. D	
7. C		17. C	
8. A		18. D	
9. A		19. B	
10. C		20. A	

21. C
22. D
23. A
24. A
25. B

TEST 4

DIRECTIONS: Each question or incomplete statement is followed by several suggested answers or completions. Select the one that BEST answers the question or completes the statement. *PRINT THE LETTER OF THE CORRECT ANSWER IN THE SPACE AT THE RIGHT.*

1. In the years *immediately* following both World War I and World War II, the number of strikes

    A. increased
    B. was controlled by federal law
    C. decreased
    D. remained relatively unchanged

    1.____

2. The Taft-Hartley Act of 1947 was

    A. opposed by management
    B. opposed by organized labor
    C. declared unconstitutional
    D. repealed in 1951

    2.____

3. By the passage of a law by Congress in 1900, the standard of value upon which all forms of currency was based became

    A. silver and gold
    B. gold
    C. silver
    D. government and corporate bonds

    3.____

4. The purpose of the Federal Reserve Act of 1913 was to

    A. vary the amount of currency in circulation according to the needs of the country
    B. build up the gold reserves in the United States Treasury
    C. allow the unlimited coinage of silver at a ratio of sixteen to one
    D. grant loans to business concerns and individuals

    4.____

5. The Securities and Exchange Act of 1934 gave the government the power to regulate

    A. national and state banks
    B. public utility companies
    C. stocks and bonds
    D. the national debt

    5.____

6. During World Wars I and II and the great depression, the national debt

    A. increased
    B. decreased slowly
    C. was reduced by high taxes
    D. was reduced by high tariffs

    6.____

7. Both the Dingley Tariff and the Payne-Aldrich Tariff provided for

    A. sharp reductions in tariff rates
    B. high protective tariff rates
    C. gradual lowering of the tariff wall
    D. the eventual end of protective tariffs

    7.____

8. In regard to the tariff, President Woodrow Wilson favored

   A. maintaining high protective rates
   B. doing away with it entirely
   C. lowering existing rates
   D. raising existing rates

9. The purpose of the Trade Agreements Act of 1934 was to

   A. cut down American trade
   B. revive foreign trade
   C. reduce the national debt
   D. provide a more flexible currency

10. The American agricultural specialist who became known as the *plant wizard* because of his success in producing new and better varieties of vegetables, fruits, and flowers was

    A. Charles Dana Gibson
    B. Carl Schurz
    C. Luther Burbank
    D. Louis Brandeis

11. During the *early* part of the great depression, the government tried to help the farmer by

    A. improving farming methods
    B. encouraging scientific methods
    C. retraining farmers for other jobs
    D. limiting farm production

12. The FIRST real start toward conservation of natural resources was made under the leadership of President

    A. Theodore Roosevelt
    B. Calvin Coolidge
    C. Franklin Pierce
    D. Warren Harding

13. The *Teapot Dome Scandal* forced the resignation and imprisonment of Secretary of the Interior

    A. Gifford Pinchot
    B. Richard A. Ballinger
    C. Oakes Ames
    D. Albert B. Fall

14. The Civilian Conservation Corps served the double purpose of helping to conserve America's natural resources and

    A. estimating the damage which had been done to American land by erosion
    B. reporting on the damage which had been done by floods
    C. finding new sources of coal and petroleum
    D. providing jobs for young men during the depression of the 1930's

15. The right of eminent domain is the power of the government to

    A. sell public lands
    B. provide adequate methods of flood control
    C. take private property for public use if the owners are reasonably compensated
    D. operate essential industries in time of national emergency

16. The INCREASE in the average age of Americans from 1900 to 1940 was due in part to the

    A. increase in the number of immigrants
    B. increase in the birth rate
    C. advances in medical science and public health
    D. settlement of the last American frontier areas

    16.____

17. By 1950, over sixty percent of the population of the United States lived in

    A. rural areas
    B. the western third of the nation
    C. cities and towns
    D. cities of 100,000 people or more

    17.____

18. Immigration restrictions of the early 1900's were *especially* insulting to the government of

    A. Mexico
    C. Canada
    B. Japan
    D. Great Britain

    18.____

19. The cartoon at the right portrays widespread social reforms FIRST adopted during the _____ era.

    A. Jeffersonian
    B. Jacksonian
    C. Populist
    D. New Deal

    19.____

20. _____ have been interested in restricting immigration.

    A. Farmers
    C. Manufacturers
    B. Professionals
    D. Trade unionists

    20.____

21. Immigration to the United States was at its HEAVIEST from _____ to _____.

    A. 1900; 1920
    C. 1941; 1960
    B. 1921; 1940
    D. 1961; 1980

    21.____

22. The Great Depression occurred from _____ to _____.

    A. 1900; 1920
    C. 1941; 1960
    B. 1921; 1940
    D. 1961; 1980

    22.____

23. The United States entered World War II between _____ and _____.

    A. 1900; 1920   B. 1921; 1940
    C. 1941; 1960   D. 1961; 1980

24. The Cold War between the United States and the Soviet Union began during which time period?

    A. 1900 to 1920   B. 1921 to 1940
    C. 1941 to 1960   D. 1961 to 1980

25. The Nobel Peace Prize in 1950 was won by an outstanding American Black:

    A. George Washington Carver
    B. Booker T. Washington
    C. Ralph J. Bunche
    D. Jesse Owens

KEY (CORRECT ANSWERS)

1. A   11. D
2. B   12. A
3. B   13. D
4. A   14. D
5. C   15. C

6. A   16. C
7. B   17. C
8. C   18. B
9. B   19. D
10. C   20. D

21. A
22. B
23. C
24. C
25. C

TEST 5

DIRECTIONS: Each question or incomplete statement is followed by several suggested answers or completions. Select the one that BEST answers the question or completes the statement. *PRINT THE LETTER OF THE CORRECT ANSWER IN THE SPACE AT THE RIGHT.*

1. The Crusades and the travels of Marco Polo contributed indirectly to the discovery of America.
   They helped the Europeans

   A. appreciate other religious beliefs
   B. strengthen their religious faith
   C. see that the world was round
   D. become more curious about the rest of the world

   1.____

2. The _____ gave important financial and military aid to the patriots in the Revolutionary War.

   A. Indians   B. French   C. Spanish   D. Russians

   2.____

3. The Battle of Gettysburg was considered a MAJOR turning point in the

   A. Revolutionary War   B. War of 1812
   C. Civil War   D. Spanish-American War

   3.____

4. The FIRST example of representative government in America was the

   A. First Continental Congress
   B. New England Confederation
   C. Virginia House of Burgesses
   D. Massachusetts town councils

   4.____

5. Identify the CORRECT statement concerning the Progressive movement.

   A. Progressives sought laws to protect working women and children.
   B. The Progressive movement was mainly rural.
   C. The Progressive movement achieved success because it was a wartime program.
   D. Progressives succeeded in ending corruption in city and state government.

   5.____

6. There was *little* manufacturing in the English colonies because

   A. most settlers refused to be shut up in factories
   B. not enough money could be made in manufacturing
   C. English factory workers did not want to come to America
   D. England placed restrictions on colonial manufacturing

   6.____

Questions 7-11.

DIRECTIONS: In answering Questions 7 to 11, use the following map.

115

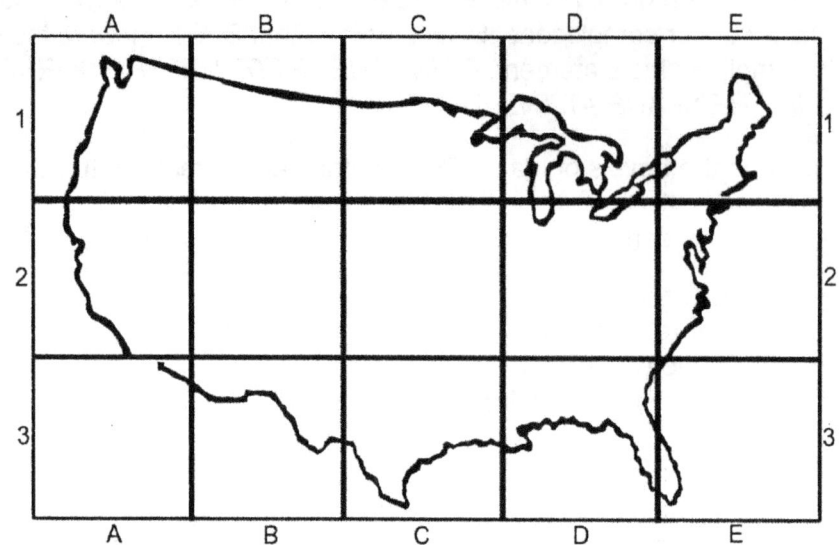

7. The Cumberland or National Road was located in which area?

   A. B-1   B. C-2   C. D-2   D. D-3

8. Which area was the destination of the forty-niners?

   A. A-1   B. A-2   C. B-2   D. C-3

9. The EARLIEST mark of Spanish civilization was left in which area?

   A. B-3   B. C-1   C. D-2   D. E-2

10. The cultivation of tobacco was largely responsible for the survival of early settlements in which of these areas?

    A. C-3   B. D-2   C. E-1   D. E-2

11. The Great Northern Railroad attracted many Scandinavians to settle in which area?

    A. A-2   B. B-2   C. C-1   D. C-3

12. In the 1890's, the United States was involved in a boundary dispute between Great Britain and

    A. Brazil   B. Mexico   C. Venezuela   D. France

13. The FIRST Pan-American Conference was brought about largely through the efforts of Secretary of State

    A. Richard Olney
    B. James G. Blaine
    C. Cordell Hull
    D. Charles Evans Hughes

14. American handling of a dispute with Chile in the late 1800's resulted in

    A. the creation of the International Bureau of American Republics
    B. a favorable impression of the United States among the republics of Latin America
    C. much ill-will among Latin-American countries toward the United States
    D. the abandonment of the Monroe Doctrine as a part of American foreign policy

15. The United States purchased Alaska from

    A. Great Britain
    B. Denmark
    C. Russia
    D. France

16. The successful settlement of the *Virginius* affairs ended the threat of an open break between the United States and

    A. Germany
    B. Great Britain
    C. France
    D. Spain

17. The *Alabama* claims grew out of

    A. American attempts to annex Hawaii
    B. the refusal of the Senate to purchase Santo Domingo
    C. British relations with the South during the Civil War
    D. a Cuban rebellion which occurred in 1868

18. Attempts by the United States to protect the Bering Seal herd led to a controversy with

    A. Great Britain
    B. Russia
    C. Japan
    D. Spain

19. Which invention had the GREATEST impact upon the political institutions of nineteenth-century America?

    A. Airplane
    B. Atomic bomb
    C. Cotton gin
    D. Automobile

20. Which invention has had the GREATEST impact upon the lifestyle of twentieth-century America?

    A. Airplane
    B. Atomic bomb
    C. Cotton gin
    D. Automobile

21. Which invention has had the GREATEST impact upon the foreign policy of twentieth-century America?

    A. Airplane
    B. Atomic bomb
    C. Cotton gin
    D. Automobile

22. Teheran, Yalta, and Potsdam were

    A. important Allied victories in World War II
    B. important Axis victories in World War II
    C. sites of wartime conferences at which Allied leaders developed military strategy for winning World War II
    D. provisional, or *puppet,* governments established in several nations conquered by Nazi Germany

23. _____ has NOT been a significant trend in recent American society.

    A. National Socialism
    B. Longevity
    C. Mobility
    D. Specialization

24. S.A.L.T., *peaceful coexistence,* and détente were terms associated with relations between the United States and

    A. the Soviet Union   B. Middle Eastern nations
    C. Communist China   D. Latin American nations

25. The _____ lunched a reform movement in the years 1900-1920 to correct social and political abuses caused by immigration, industrialization, and urbanization.

    A. Rough Riders   B. Progressives
    C. New Dealers   D. Suffragettes

KEY (CORRECT ANSWERS)

1. D   11. C
2. B   12. C
3. C   13. B
4. C   14. C
5. A   15. C

6. D   16. D
7. C   17. C
8. B   18. A
9. A   19. C
10. D   20. D

21. B
22. C
23. A
24. A
25. B

EXAMINATION SECTION
TEST 1

DIRECTIONS: Each question or incomplete statement is followed by several suggested answers or completions. Select the one that BEST answers the question or completes the statement. *PRINT THE LETTER OF THE CORRECT ANSWER IN THE SPACE AT THE RIGHT.*

1. Unequal freight rates established by many railroads were MOST damaging to

    A. eastern manufacturers
    B. western and mid-western farmers
    C. railroad stockholders
    D. foreign financial interests

2. The principle that railroads were subject to regulation by the national government was established by the passage in 1887 of the

    A. Sherman Anti-trust Law
    B. *Granger laws*
    C. Clayton Act
    D. Interstate Commerce Act

3. The founder of the American Federation of Labor was

    A. Uriah S. Stephens
    B. Terence Powderly
    C. John L. Lewis
    D. Samuel Gompers

4. Labor's MOST powerful weapons in the industrial conflict of the late 1800's were the strike and the

    A. lockout
    B. boycott
    C. blacklist
    D. closed shop

5. Violent methods used by some labor unions during the late 1800's led to

    A. the outlawing of all labor unions by the Supreme Court
    B. strict federal control of organized labor
    C. a decline in the use of state and federal troops to end strikes
    D. popular hostility toward labor unions

6. An effective legal device used to break strikes in the late 1800's was

    A. the injunction
    B. arbitration
    C. collective bargaining
    D. mediation

7. Large-scale farming was made possible through the use of labor-saving machinery and

    A. the introduction of specialized agriculture
    B. farm subsidy programs
    C. the passage of the Agricultural Adjustment Act
    D. a world-wide depression of farm prices

8. The Granges were local units of an organization called the

    A. Molly Maguires
    B. Farmers' Alliance
    C. Farmers' Union
    D. Patrons of Husbandry

9. In the dispute over money which took place in the United States for thirty years after the Civil War, the debtor group was opposed by the

   A. farmers
   B. creditor group
   C. small businessmen
   D. Greenback Party

10. Money which was made from something valuable or was backed by the government's promise to exchange it at anytime for something valuable was called

    A. greenbacks
    B. hard money
    C. shinplasters
    D. cheap money

11. The *Crime of 1873* refers to the

    A. omission of silver dollars from a coinage law
    B. failure of the federal government to retire greenbacks
    C. bargain made between President Cleveland and financier J.P. Morgan
    D. abandonment of the gold standard by the United States

12. The *Cross of Gold* speech was made in 1896 by the Democratic presidential candidate

    A. William McKinley
    B. Grover Cleveland
    C. William Jennings Bryan
    D. Oliver Wendell Holmes

13. The westward shift of the population is indicated by the fact that in 1880 the second LARGEST city in the United States was

    A. Philadelphia
    B. Detroit
    C. Chicago
    D. Los Angeles

14. The National Woman Suffrage Association was organized in 1869 under the leadership of

    A. Jane Addams
    B. Susan B. Anthony
    C. Frances E. Willard
    D. Clara Barton

15. The Chautauqua movement was

    A. an attempt to revive interest in Indian culture
    B. a program of slum clearance
    C. an education enterprise popular during the late 1800's
    D. a political organization for southern farmers

16. Who wrote the popular and controversial book UNCLE TOM'S CABIN?

    A. Harriet Tubman
    B. Willa Cather
    C. Harriet Beecher Stowe
    D. Elizabeth Cady Stanton

17. The _____ War was the contest for power between Communist nations headed by the Soviet Union and Western nations headed by the United States.

    A. Second World
    B. Cold
    C. Korean
    D. Vietnam

18. The _____ was organized for the purpose of protecting Western Europe and the United States.

    A. League of Nations
    B. United Nations
    C. Organization of American States
    D. North Atlantic Treaty Organization

19. The Cuban Missle Crisis occurred during the administration of President

    A. Dwight D. Eisenhower   B. John F. Kennedy
    C. Richard M. Nixon   D. Gerald R. Ford

20. In view of current social, political, and economic trends, which of these is *least likely* to occur during the remainder of this century?

    A. Women will become co-equal participants in all aspects of American life.
    B. The problem of caring for the elderly will decrease.
    C. More Spanish-speaking Americans will be elected to important offices in state and federal government.
    D. Increasing numbers of Black Americans will become involved in all occupations and professions.

21. Which headline has traditionally meant good news for the American economy?

    A. *GNP Down 10%*
    B. *Unemployment Rate Up*
    C. *U.S. Imports Exceed Exports*
    D. *U.S. Exports Exceed Imports*

22. Which President succeeded to office upon the assassination of John F. Kennedy?

    A. Dwight D. Eisenhower   B. Harry S. Truman
    C. Lyndon B. Johnson   D. Richard M. Nixon

23. Who made the following statement?
    I have a dream that one day this nation will rise up and live out the true meaning of its creed: "We hold these truths to be self-evident: that all men are created equal..."

    A. Abraham Lincoln   B. John Brown
    C. Susan B. Anthony   D. Martin Luther King, Jr.

24. The term *Watergate* belongs in which of these lists?

    A. The Haymarket Riot, the Pullman Strike
    B. *Credit Mobilier,* Teapot Dome
    C. John Wilkes Booth, Lee Harvey Oswald
    D. The Maximilian Affair, the U-2 Incident

25. The _____ was the EARLIEST goal of the American feminist movement.

    A. right to vote
    B. right to receive an education
    C. right to equal opportunity in all aspects of American social, economic, and political life
    D. right to elect a woman President

KEY (CORRECT ANSWERS)

1.	B	11.	A
2.	D	12.	C
3.	D	13.	C
4.	B	14.	B
5.	D	15.	C
6.	A	16.	C
7.	A	17.	B
8.	D	18.	D
9.	B	19.	B
10.	B	20.	B

21. D
22. C
23. D
24. B
25. A

TEST 2

DIRECTIONS: Each question or incomplete statement is followed by several suggested answers or completions. Select the one that BEST answers the question or completes the statement. *PRINT THE LETTER OF THE CORRECT ANSWER IN THE SPACE AT THE RIGHT.*

1. Women's suffrage became nation-wide with the ratification of the _____ Amendment. 1._____

    A. Seventeenth
    B. Eighteenth
    C. Nineteenth
    D. Twentieth

2. National prohibition of liquor proved unsuccessful because 2._____

    A. no law was passed to put it into effect
    B. it was almost impossible to enforce
    C. only one-third of the states ratified the prohibition amendment
    D. there were no state prohibition laws at the time of its enactment

3. A man whose philosophy of education has GREATLY influenced American schools in the twentieth century was 3._____

    A. James B. Duke
    B. George Eastman
    C. Henry L. Mencken
    D. John Dewey

4. An example of constructive fiction which appeared in America in the 1930's was THE GRAPES OF WRATH by 4._____

    A. Frank Norris
    B. John Steinbeck
    C. Sinclair Lewis
    D. Ernest Hemingway

5. Grant Wood and Thomas Hart Benton are famous for their contributions to American 5._____

    A. architecture B. music C. art D. science

6. The MOST powerful of the American playwrights to excite admiration following World War I was the author of *Mourning Becomes Electra*, 6._____

    A. Eugene O'Neill
    B. Aaron Copeland
    C. Robert Frost
    D. Jerome Kern

7. Near the end of the 1800's, Americans became interested in a revolt against Spanish rule in 7._____

    A. Panama B. Hawaii C. Cuba D. Colombia

8. The publication of the de Lome letter in 1898 8._____

    A. aroused American public opinion against Spain
    B. seemed to eliminate the possibility of war with Spain
    C. encouraged the United States to help Spain put down Caribbean revolutions
    D. led to a declaration of war with Spain within a week

9. American public opinion against Spain was aroused in February, 1898 by the sinking of the battleship 9._____

    A. Maine B. Oregon C. Missouri D. Arizona

10. Early in the Spanish-American War, a great naval victory was won in Manila Bay by American ships under the command of

    A. George Dewey   B. Winfield Scott
    C. J.D. Sloat   D. Matthew Perry

11. A colorful volunteer regiment composed *mostly* of cowboys, Indians, and athletes which took part in the Spanish-American War adopted for its name the

    A. Fighting 69th   B. Rough Riders
    C. Flying Tigers   D. Seabees

12. In the treaty ending the Spanish-American War, Spain ceded to the United States Guam and

    A. Puerto Rico   B. Hawaii
    C. Samoa   D. the Virgin Islands

13. One reason why the Spanish-American War is considered a landmark in American history is that it marked the

    A. end of America's policy of overseas imperialism
    B. beginning of new sectional rivalry between the North and the South
    C. end of a period of growing friendship between the United States and Great Britain
    D. emergence of the United States as a leading naval power

14. The Platt Amendment of 1901 stated the conditions under which the United States would give up its control of

    A. the Philippine Islands   B. Midway Island
    C. Cuba   D. American Samoa

15. Puerto Rico was a territory of the United States until 1952 when it became

    A. an independent republic
    B. a free commonwealth under American protection
    C. the forty-ninth state in the Union
    D. a socialistic republic

16. President McKinley was given the power to govern the Philippine Islands by the passage in 1901 of the

    A. Foraker Act   B. Spooner Amendment
    C. Roosevelt Corollary   D. Hay-Pauncefote Treaty

17. On July 4, 1946, the United States

    A. made the Philippine Islands an American Commonwealth
    B. granted complete independence to the Philippine Islands
    C. removed all American armed forces from the Philippines
    D. granted American citizenship to all Filipinos

18. The method by which the United States acquired the Panama Canal Zone   18.____

    A. met with little criticism in the United States
    B. caused indignation and alarm in Latin America
    C. was vigorously opposed by President Theodore Roosevelt
    D. helped foster good relations between this country and Latin America

19. The construction of the Panama Canal was an army project under the control of Colonel   19.____

    A. Leonard Wood   B. W.D. Gorgas
    C. G.W. Goethals   D. John J. Pershing

Question 20.

DIRECTIONS: Question 20 is based on the following passage.

Convinced that the old parties had only tried to sidestep the burning issue of the day, they believed that the time had come to organize a new party. By joining with the Free-Soilers party, they were confident that they could march to victory in 1856 or certainly in 1860.

20. The "burning" issue which had been sidestepped was   20.____

    A. free and unlimited coinage of silver
    B. the extension of slavery into the territories
    C. the annexation of Oregon
    D. civil service reform

21. Thomas Jefferson is responsible for the   21.____

    A. purchase of the Louisiana Territory
    B. formation of the Federalist Party
    C. defeat of the British at New Orleans
    D. announcement of the Monroe Doctrine

22. The Monroe Doctrine was expanded into a positive doctrine permitting the United States   22.____
    to assume a position of leadership in the western hemisphere by the addition of the

    A. Platt Amendment   B. Spooner Amendment
    C. reciprocity clause   D. Roosevelt corollary

23. By _____, Congress started a great tide of westward migration.   23.____

    A. placing Indians on reservations
    B. passing the Reconstruction Acts
    C. promoting soil conservation
    D. passing the Homestead Act

24. The _____ was NOT associated with the Cold War.   24.____

    A. Marshall Plan
    B. blockade of Berlin
    C. Cuban missle crisis
    D. sinking of the Lusitania

25. The Missouri Compromise was dead and a new act, which would let the territories decide for themselves whether to be slave or free, would take its place. The basic principle of this new act is called

    A. states' rights
    B. direct democracy
    C. Manifest Destiny
    D. popular sovereignty

26. When the framers of the Constitution agreed that the President could veto a bill passed by Congress, they were attempting to provide for

    A. checks and balances
    B. basic human rights
    C. federalism
    D. representative government

Questions 27-30.

DIRECTIONS: Questions 27 to 30 are based on the following map.

27. _____ was the FIRST nation to explore in Area 5.

    A. Spain   B. France   C. Portugal   D. Great Britain

28. By 1750, emigrants from several different nations had started colonies in Area

    A. 2   B. 3   C. 5   D. 7

29. Columbus, who is credited with discovering America, actually landed in Area

    A. 2   B. 6   C. 7   D. 8

30. _____ proved to be the great source of wealth in Area 5 during the seventeenth and eighteenth centuries.

    A. Gold   B. Iron   C. Furs   D. Timber

KEY (CORRECT ANSWERS)

1. C	11. B	21. A
2. B	12. A	22. D
3. D	13. D	23. D
4. B	14. C	24. D
5. C	15. B	25. D
6. A	16. B	26. A
7. C	17. B	27. B
8. A	18. B	28. D
9. A	19. C	29. D
10. A	20. B	30. C

TEST 3

DIRECTIONS: Each question or incomplete statement is followed by several suggested answers or completions. Select the one that BEST answers the question or completes the statement. *PRINT THE LETTER OF THE CORRECT ANSWER IN THE SPACE AT THE RIGHT.*

1. For twenty-five years, the Caribbean policy of the United States followed the line of development begun by President Theodore Roosevelt and was *commonly* called 1.____

    A. watchful waiting   B. dollar diplomacy
    C. shirtsleeve diplomacy   D. manifest destiny

2. The Virgin Islands were purchased by the United States in 1917 as a 2.____

    A. source of sugar and coffee
    B. source of petroleum
    C. refueling stop for trans-Atlantic planes
    D. link in the defense of the Panama Canal

3. The United States *gradually* surrendered its control over the Caribbean area with the development in the 1930's of the 3.____

    A. International Trade Organization
    B. Organization of American States
    C. Good Neighbor policy
    D. Open Door policy

4. President Woodrow Wilson accepted the offer of the ABC powers, Argentina, Brazil, and Chile, to mediate the differences the United States was having with 4.____

    A. Nicaragua   B. Haiti   C. Mexico   D. Venezuela

5. American troops were sent to Mexico in 1916 to capture the rebel leader 5.____

    A. Pancho Villa   B. Porfirio Diaz
    C. Santa Anna   D. Victoriano Huerta

6. American relations with Mexico were improved following 1927 *largely* through the efforts of the ambassador to Mexico 6.____

    A. James G. Blaine   B. Cordell Hull
    C. Mackenzie King   D. Dwight W. Morrow

7. The Open Door policy in China was proclaimed in 1900 by Secretary of State 7.____

    A. John Hay   B. Philander Knox
    C. William Jennings Bryan   D. Henry L. Stimson

8. Acting as mediator between Russia and Japan at the peace conference ending the Russian-Japanese War was President 8.____

    A. Theodore Roosevelt   B. William Howard Taft
    C. Woodrow Wilson   D. Warren G. Harding

9. The Root-Takahira Agreement of 1908 and the Lansing-Ishii Agreement of 1917 were attempts to settle differences between the United States and   9.____

   A. Japan   B. China   C. Korea   D. Manchuria

10. Following the outbreak of World War I in Europe, American citizens   10.____

    A. could trade only with neutral European nations
    B. sold supplies only to Great Britain and her allies
    C. restricted trade to Latin America and the Orient
    D. sold munitions and supplies to both the Central Powers and the Allies

11. The German practice which particularly angered Americans prior to the entrance of the United States into World War I was the unrestricted use of   11.____

    A. poison gas   B. submarines
    C. aerial bombing   D. germ warfare

12. The United States entered World War I on April 6,   12.____

    A. 1915   B. 1916   C. 1917   D. 1918

13. In order to raise an army for use in World War I, Congress passed   13.____

    A. an Espionage Act
    B. a Selective Service Act
    C. a law creating the Department of War
    D. the National Security Act

14. During World War I, an agency led by Herbert Hoover regulated   14.____

    A. the consumption and conservation of food
    B. prices of vital material
    C. American trade and shipping
    D. the settlement of labor disputes

Questions 15-16.

DIRECTIONS: Questions 15 and 16 each show a newspaper headline from the first half of the nineteenth century. Decide which man's actions might have led to that headline.

15. VICE PRESIDENT CHARGES THAT NEW TARIFF BENEFITS NEW ENGLAND FACTORY OWNERS AT EXPENSE OF SOUTHERN PLANTERS AND WESTERN FARMERS   15.____

    A. Henry Clay   B. Andrew Jackson
    C. Daniel Webster   D. John C. Calhoun

16. ELECTION OF A PRESIDENT SEEN AS TRIUMPH FOR THE WEST AND VICTORY FOR THE COMMON PEOPLE   16.____

    A. Henry Clay   B. Andrew Jackson
    C. Daniel Webster   D. John C. Calhoun

17. The 1954 ruling against segregation marked an important change in the Supreme Court's interpretation of the Constitution.
    This court decision referred to segregation practiced in

    A. voting
    C. parks and playgrounds
    B. schools
    D. restaurants and motels

17.____

18. After the French and Indian War, Britain

    A. continued to neglect the American colonies
    B. began encouraging complete self-rule for the American colonies
    C. tightened the enforcement of laws regulating the trade of the American colonies
    D. urged the American colonies to trade with other countries

18.____

19. America's emergence as a MAJOR industrial country occurred between

    A. the War of 1812 and the Mexican War
    B. the Mexican War and the Civil War
    C. the Civil War and World War I
    D. World War I and World War II

19.____

20. The immigrant famous for founding a company that later became part of the United States Steel Corporation was

    A. Jacob Riis
    C. David Dubinsky
    B. Samuel Gompers
    D. Andrew Carnegie

20.____

21. The immigrant who became the FIRST president of the American Federation of Labor was

    A. Jacob Riis
    C. David Dubinsky
    B. Samuel Gompers
    D. Andrew Carnegie

21.____

22. _____ wrote about the crowded, filthy conditions of slum life.

    A. Jacob Riis
    C. David Dubinsky
    B. Samuel Gompers
    D. Andrew Carnegie

22.____

Questions 23-26.

DIRECTIONS: The following discussion might have taken place in the 1880's or 1890's among three friends. Two were farmers and one was a laborer. Use this discussion to answer Questions 23 to 26.

Speaker I: These past few years have been hard ones. There was a time when a man could talk to his boss about wages, but not now. With all this new machinery, these big companies hire thousands of workers. Whether a man has a particular skill doesn't even matter anymore.

Speaker II: It looked for a while like better times lay ahead for us farmers, but it hasn't turned out that way. I'm raising more wheat than I have ever raised, and yet I can't make enough on my crops to pay my debts.

Speaker III: We have tried forming farm organizations, but it looks as if we are going to have to set up our own political party and, get our own candidates in office in order to solve our problems.

23. The situation of which Speaker I complains had been brought about because of the   23._____

    A. standardization of work required of factory workers
    B. decrease in output by factory workers
    C. improvement in working conditions
    D. agitation of labor leaders

24. Speaker II's difficulty resulted, in part, from   24._____

    A. withdrawal of federal price supports
    B. falling agricultural prices
    C. importation of large quantities of farm products from Europe
    D. poor farming methods

25. When Speaker III referred to farm organizations, he *probably* did NOT have in mind   25._____

    A. the Department of Agriculture
    B. cooperative associations
    C. the Farmers' Alliance
    D. the Grange

26. Speaker III *probably* became a member of the _____ party.   26._____

    A. Whig   B. Populist   C. Socialist   D. Federalist

Questions 27-30.

DIRECTIONS: Read the following viewpoints about United States,States' policy toward Latin America. Then, answer Questions 27 to 30.

Speaker I: European nations henceforth should NOT attempt to establish colonies in the Western Hemisphere, nor should they interfere in the affairs of this hemisphere.

Speaker II: When a Latin American nation is unable to keep its house in order, the United States has the responsibility to send in troops, if necessary, and set things right. Regardless of what the Latin Americans think,this is the only way to keep the European powers out of this hemisphere.

Speaker III: The United States does NOT have the right to intervene in this fashion. What happens in this hemisphere is the joint responsibility of all the nations of the hemisphere.

Speaker IV: The United States MUST go even further. We MUST be willing to provide economic assistance to the nations south of the border. But we MUST do so in cooperation with them.

27. Speaker _____ advocates the policy which did the MOST to arouse Latin American opposition to the United States.   27._____

    A. I   B. II   C. III   D. IV

28. Speaker II expresses a viewpoint MOST similar to that of President   28._____

    A. Thomas Jefferson   B. Abraham Lincoln
    C. Theodore Roosevelt   D. John Kennedy

29. The viewpoint of Speaker III FIRST became the United States' policy during which of these periods? 29.____

    A. 1861 to 1880   B. 1881 to 1900
    C. 1901 to 1920   D. 1921 to 1940

30. The viewpoint of Speaker _____ is MOST similar to the provisions of the Monroe Doctrine. 30.____

    A. I   B. II   C. III   D. IV

KEY (CORRECT ANSWERS)

1.	B	11.	B	21.	B
2.	D	12.	C	22.	A
3.	C	13.	B	23.	A
4.	C	14.	A	24.	B
5.	A	15.	D	25.	A
6.	D	16.	B	26.	B
7.	A	17.	B	27.	B
8.	A	18.	C	28.	C
9.	A	19.	C	29.	D
10.	D	20.	D	30.	A

TEST 4

DIRECTIONS: Each question or incomplete statement is followed by several suggested answers or completions. Select the one that BEST answers the question or completes the statement. *PRINT THE LETTER OF THE CORRECT ANSWER IN THE SPACE AT THE RIGHT.*

1. During the late 1800's, 1.____
    A. most Americans had the equivalent of a high school education
    B. illiteracy in America increased sharply
    C. educational standards were the same in all sections of the country
    D. public school attendance increased

2. The great American *middle class* which emerged during the late 1800's was made up MOSTLY of 2.____
    A. farmers
    B. persons engaged in professional, business, and white collar jobs
    C. immigrants and unskilled factory workers
    D. eastern industrialists and financiers

3. The *poet of democracy* is the name given to the author of LEAVES OF GRASS: 3.____
    A. Joaquin Miller B. Bret Harte
    C. John Greenleaf Whittier D. Walt Whitman

4. The great American local color writer, Samuel Langhorne Clemens, used as a pen name 4.____
    A. O. Henry B. Jack London
    C. Mark Twain D. Saint-Gaudens

5. From 1860 until 1885, national politics in the United States were controlled by the _____ Party. 5.____
    A. Progressive B. Democrat
    C. Republican D. Whig

6. The gold conspiracy of 1869 was due, in part, to the over-trusting nature of President 6.____
    A. Andrew Johnson B. Ulysses S. Grant
    C. Rutherford B. Hayes D. James A. Garfield

7. The Credit Mobilizer Scandal centered about the 7.____
    A. Tweed Ring of New York City
    B. construction of the first transcontinental railroad
    C. illegal leasing of government oil reserves
    D. attempt to corner the gold market by Wall Street financiers

8. In the election of 1872, Ulysses S. Grant was opposed by New York editor 8.____
    A. Horace Greeley B. Samuel J. Tilden
    C. Jay Gould D. William Lloyd Garrison

9. The disputed election of 1876 was settled by

   A. an Electoral Commission
   B. the Supreme Court
   C. the Electoral College
   D. the House of Representatives

10. President Rutherford B. Hayes was opposed in his reform program by a group of conservative Republicans known as

    A. Stalwarts B. Mugwumps
    C. Half-Breeds D. Scalawags

11. Civil service reform was *greatly* aided by the passage in 1883 of the _____ Act.

    A. Pendleton B. Morrill
    C. Bland-Allison D. Wagner

12. The adoption of the *Reed rules* brought about a change in the procedure followed by the

    A. Senate B. House of Representatives
    C. Supreme Court D. Electoral College

13. The MOST outstanding accomplishment of Grover Cleveland's first administration was the

    A. removal of Union troops from the South
    B. passage of the Interstate Commerce Act
    C. beginning of an effective conservation program
    D. vigorous prosecution of industrial trusts

14. Widespread discontent among farmers in the west and south and silver miners of the west led to the formation in 1891 of a political organization which became known as the _____ Party.

    A. Prohibition B. Greenback
    C. American D. Populist

15. One of the MAJOR problems which Grover Cleveland faced during his second administration was

    A. a surplus in the United States Treasury
    B. the severe depression which followed the panic of 1893
    C. the possibility of war with Mexico
    D. the discovery of a *whiskey ring* in the Middle West

16. The nomination of William McKinley for the Presidency in 1896 was *largely* the result of the effort of Republican leader

    A. Mark Hanna B. James G. Blaine
    C. Roscoe Conkling D. Thomas Nast

Questions 17-20.

DIRECTIONS: Which of the four leaders shown below is described by each of Questions 17 to 20? Mark the CORRECT answer in the space at the right.

A. Washington   B. Hamilton   C. Jefferson   D. Jackson

17. He is the man responsible for solving the MAJOR financial problems which confronted the new nation. 17.____

18. He warned against permanent alliances with foreign nations. 18.____

19. He believed that any citizen was intelligent enough to hold public office. 19.____

20. He stated, *That government is BEST which governs LEAST.* 20.____

21. The adoptions of the initiative, referendum, recall, and direct primary are examples of which of the following? 21.____

    A. Governmental attempts to regulate *big business*
    B. The growth of democratic participation in government.
    C. Power shifting from the people to the political *bosses*
    D. Laws passed to reduce the number of foreign immigrants

22. Which date is significant in American economic history? 22.____

    A. July 4, 1776   B. April 12, 1861
    C. October 24, 1929   D. December 7, 1941

23. Which event triggered American entry into World War II? 23.____

    A. Attack on the U.S. Pacific fleet
    B. Capture of the U.S.S. Pueblo
    C. Sinking of the U.S.S. Maine
    D. Sinking of the H.M.S. Lusitania

24. The program for economic recovery and reform introduced during the administration of Franklin D. Roosevelt was the 24.____

    A. New Deal   B. Marshall Plan
    C. New Frontier   D. Great Society

25. What is the political practice of publicizing accusations of disloyalty or subversion WITHOUT sufficient regard to evidence called? 25.____

    A. McCarthyism   B. Logrolling
    C. Muckraking   D. Filibustering

KEY (CORRECT ANSWERS)

1. D
2. B
3. D
4. C
5. C

6. B
7. B
8. A
9. A
10. A

11. A
12. B
13. B
14. D
15. B

16. A
17. B
18. A
19. D
20. C

21. B
22. C
23. A
24. A
25. A

EXAMINATION SECTION
TEST 1

DIRECTIONS: Each question or incomplete statement is followed by several suggested answers or completions. Select the one that BEST answers the question or completes the statement. *PRINT THE LETTER OF THE CORRECT ANSWER IN THE SPACE AT THE RIGHT.*

1. Which one of the following groups contains the names of people famous for their achievements in unrelated field of endeavor?

    A. Benjamin Lovejoy and Wendell Phillips
    B. Frances Wright and the Grimke Sisters
    C. George Goethals and Ferdinand DeLesseps
    D. Maxwell Anderson and Edward MacDowell
    E. Walter Reed and William Gorgas

    1.____

2. Which one of the following problems did NOT accompany the *end* of the frontier in the United States?

    A. Growing sense of job insecurity among factory workers
    B. Need for a changed viewpoint in our economic thinking
    C. Rapid decline of interest in imperialistic enterprises
    D. Rapid rise of disease in large cities
    E. Recognition of the need for conservation of natural resources

    2.____

3. Which one of the following economic policies is NOT consistent with the other four?

    A. Decrease of the rediscount rates by the Federal Reserve Banks
    B. Government appropriations under the European Recovery Program
    C. Increase in individual income taxes
    D. Increase in open-market buying operations by the Federal Reserve Banks
    E. Increase in time permitted for paying installment buying obligations

    3.____

4. The principle of *unanimous consent* is illustrated in the

    A. decisions of the United States Supreme Court
    B. method of admitting new states to our Union
    C. procedures in the General Assembly of the United Nations
    D. provision for amending the Articles of Confederation
    E. vote of the House of Representatives in impeachment proceedings

    4.____

5. In which one of the following groups are the terms NOT arranged in correct chronological order?

    A. Alien and Sedition Acts, Kentucky and Virginia Resolutions, Personal Liberty Laws
    B. Bland-Allison Act, Sherman Silver Purchase Act, Gold Standard Act
    C. Granger Laws, Wabash Railroad Case, Interstate Commerce Act
    D. Hawley-Smooth Tariff, Underwood Tariff, Payne-Aldrich Tariff
    E. Maximilian Affair, Venezuela Boundary Dispute, Venezuela Debt Dispute

    5.____

6. Which one of the following was NOT true of both the League of Nations and the United States under the Articles of Confederation?

    A. Members might have several representatives, but only one vote.
    B. Membership was declined by some who were eligible.
    C. Membership was held by states, not by individuals.
    D. The power to collect taxes was lacking.
    E. The sovereignty of the states was retained.

7. A MAJOR cause for the decrease in farm exports from the United States immediately after World War I was that

    A. production in the United States declined
    B. competition with other agricultural nations increased
    C. domestic demands increased
    D. Europe quickly regained her economic self-sufficiency
    E. exports shifted to factory goods

8. Which one of the following statements regarding the periods after both World War I and World War II is TRUE?

    A. American investment bankers loaned huge sums to European countries to aid in recovery.
    B. Germany was forced to sign a peace treaty which weakened her whole economy.
    C. Heavy cash reparations were exacted from Germany.
    D. The Union of Soviet Socialist Republics took an active part in the postwar conferences.
    E. The exchange reserves in Europe were low.

9. Since 1900, which one of the following has been the MOST consistent trend in the United States?
    A(n)

    A. *decline* in mortality rates
    B. *decline* in population
    C. *decrease* in emigration
    D. *increase* in mortality rates
    E. *increase* in the birth rate

10. An IMPORTANT argument for the United States Presidential Succession Act in 1947 was that

    A. conditions which caused the passage of the original act no longer applied
    B. the president of the Senate should succeed to the Presidency
    C. only an elected official should be the nation's chief executive
    D. there was no law providing for succession to the Presidency in case of the death of the Vice President
    E. it would make it possible for a President to resign by delivering his resignation to the office of the Secretary of State

11. An example of the use of an implied power by the Congress of the United States is the

    A. declaration of war in 1941
    B. adoption of the Gold Standard Act, 1900
    C. imposition of the present federal income tax
    D. repeal of the national prohibition amendment
    E. enactment of the Securities and Exchange Act, 1934

12. The Marshall proposal offered United States aid in the economic recovery of Europe if the European countries FIRST

    A. abolished discriminatory trade practices
    B. outlined a reconstruction program for Europe as a whole
    C. drew up a plan for a United States of Europe
    D. outlawed communism in their countries
    E. signed a pact guaranteeing civil liberties in each nation

13. A large deficit in a national budget is MOST likely to result in

    A. inflation
    B. deflation
    C. high interest rates
    D. low profits
    E. an unfavorable balance of trade

14. In the first half of the twentieth century, the BEST evidence of social mobility in the United States as a whole is found in the increase in the

    A. number of new millionaires from decade to decade
    B. average per capita income from decade to decade
    C. percentage of white collar workers whose fathers worked at blue collar industrial jobs
    D. percentage of agricultural workers who migrated to the cities

15. English colonization differed from Spanish and French colonization in that the English

    A. were the first to understand and act upon the economic potential of New World colonies
    B. came to the New World mainly as settlers rather than soldiers, missonaries, and trappers
    C. controlled vaster lands and large populations
    D. established better relations with the Indians and Blacks

16. Which of the following contributed MOST to the development of religious toleration in the British colonies? The

    A. stand of Roger Williams in defense of liberty of conscience
    B. Puritan guarantee of religious freedom to settlers in the Massachusetts Bay Colony
    C. common interest of each of the numerous sects in preventing domination by any of the others
    D. attitude of religious indifference that permeated the colonial aristocracy

17. The Preamble of the Declaration of Independence appeals to which of the following principles?

    A. Governments founded in popular consent
    B. Strict majoritarian rule
    C. The right of all men to protection of their property
    D. The right of all citizens to vote

18. The Federal Constitution EXPLICITLY authorized the

    A. creation of presidential nominating conventions
    B. power of federal courts to declare acts of Congress unconstitutional
    C. creation of the Cabinet
    D. power of Congress to regulate interstate commerce

19. The Bill of Rights explicitly provides for all of the following EXCEPT

    A. freedom of speech and of the press
    B. freedom of enterprise
    C. freedom of assembly and of petition
    D. the right of trial by jury

20. The aim of the Monroe Doctrine, as it was proclaimed in 1823, was to

    A. prevent the outbreak of democratic revolutions in Latin America
    B. guarantee preferential trading rights to the United States in Latin America
    C. secure a territorial outlet for American slavery in Latin America
    D. ensure that the United States, rather than Europe, would be the dominant power in the Western Hemisphere

21. All of the following characterized the Jacksonian Democrats EXCEPT

    A. hostility toward the institution of slavery
    B. support for freedom of economic opportunity
    C. opposition to special privilege and large business corporations
    D. opposition to internal improvements at federal expense

22. In the politics of the decade after the Civil War, the issue of slavery focused on whether

    A. racial equality should be the foremost national priority
    B. slavery should be permitted to exist in the territories
    C. slavery should be eliminated where it already existed in the states
    D. the foreign slave trade should be reopened

23. Republican policies toward the South during the post-Civil War Reconstruction Era can be described MOST accurately as

    A. aiming consistently to protect the interests of postwar big business at the expense of the newly freed slaves
    B. leading to unparalleled corruption among the entrenched carpetbagger governors and their allies in the Black dominated legislatures of the defeated states
    C. leading to significant but only partially implemented constitutional changes on the state level in the South and also on the national level
    D. leading to an effective program of land redistribution that gave to large numbers of newly freed slaves *forty acres and a mule*

Questions 24-25.

DIRECTIONS: Questions 24 through 25 are to be answered on the basis of the following business leaders:
I. John D. Rockefeller
II. Andrew Carnegie
III. J. Pierpont Morgan
IV. Henry Ford

24. Which business leader adapted the trust as a device for large-scale industrial organization? 24.____

    A. I B. II C. III D. IV

25. Which business leader mobilized the power of the banks to curb industrial competition and to facilitate corporate mergers and reorganizations? 25.____

    A. I B. II C. III D. IV

KEY (CORRECT ANSWERS)

1.	D	11.	E
2.	C	12.	B
3.	C	13.	A
4.	D	14.	C
5.	D	15.	B
6.	B	16.	C
7.	B	17.	A
8.	E	18.	D
9.	A	19.	B
10.	C	20.	D

21. A
22. B
23. C
24. A
25. C

TEST 2

DIRECTIONS: Each question or incomplete statement is followed by several suggested answers or completions. Select the one that BEST answers the question or completes the statement. *PRINT THE LETTER OF THE CORRECT ANSWER IN THE SPACE AT THE RIGHT.*

Question 1.

DIRECTIONS: Question 1 is to be answered on the basis of the following business leaders:

   I. John D. Rockefeller
   II. Andrew Carnegie
   III. J. Pierpont Morgan
   IV. Henry Ford

1. Which business leader pioneered in the mass production assembly line?
    A. I   B. II   C. III   D. IV

Questions 2-5.

DIRECTIONS: Questions 2 through 5 are to be answered on the basis of the following groups:

   I.   Northern and Western Europeans (e.g., Germans and Irish)
   II. Southern and Eastern Europeans (e.g., Italians and Russians)
   III. African slaves
   IV. Mexicans

2. For which group were the peak years of entry into the United States 1700-1800?
    A. I   B. II   C. III   D. IV

3. For which group were the peak years of entry into the United States 1840-1880?
    A. I   B. II   C. III   D. IV

4. For which group were the peak years of entry into the United States 1885-1915?
    A. I   B. II   C. III   D. IV

5. For which group were the peak years of entry into the United States 1910-1930?
    A. I   B. II   C. III   D. IV

6. The defeat of the Versailles Treaty in the Senate after the First World War was due to the

   A. growing conviction in the United States that the Kellogg-Briand Pact outlawing war posed a better alternative for the future conduct of foreign affairs
   B. widespread view in the United States that proposed neutrality legislation to prohibit citizens from traveling on belligerent ships except at their own risk would suffice to keep the United States out of future European wars
   C. inability of President Wilson and his political opponents to reach a compromise on the issue of United States participation in the collective security arrangements of the League of Nations
   D. widespread view in the United States that the League of Nations had been tainted by its admission of the Soviet Union to membership

7. Which of the following BEST describes the domestic changes brought about by the New Deal?

    A. The enactment of a number of new economic regulations, joined with new relief and welfare measures
    B. A vast increase in governmental ownership of business
    C. A major redistribution of income and wealth in favor of the poorest segment of the population
    D. The restoration of a free market as a result of effective antitrust action

8. In the years immediately after the Second World War, the United States assumed

    A. the dominant role in an alliance of Western nations for the purpose of containing Soviet power
    B. its traditional policy of non-involvement in world affairs
    C. the burden of arming friendly democratic nations with atomic weapons
    D. the leadership of Third World countries seeking independence from their colonial rulers

9. Before the Supreme Court's decision in 1954 that racial segregation in the public schools was unconstitutional, the Court had

    A. refused to consider cases about racial segregation
    B. justified racial segregation in public facilities by the *separate-but-equal* doctrine
    C. been prevented from considering cases about racial segregation by Southern filibusters in Congress
    D. required desegregation of public facilities *with all deliberate speed,* but stopped short of ordering the President to enforce the decision

10. Even in areas where the right to vote was widespread, voters in the British colonies consistently returned a relatively small number of wealthy and prominent men to office. This indicates that

    A. the British government suppressed the idea of democracy in the colonies until just before the American Revolution
    B. the colonists generally did not regard deference to one's *betters* as being incompatible with political liberty
    C. the wealthy and prominent controlled the colonial electorate
    D. apathy was the prevailing characteristic of colonial politics

11. From 1763 to 1776, the CHIEF aim of colonial resistance to British policies was to

    A. bring about a long-suppressed social revolution against the colonial aristocracy
    B. achieve in America the ideals proclaimed in the French Revolution
    C. ensure that the colonists were represented in Parliament
    D. restore what the colonists perceived to be the rights of Englishmen

12. All of the following contributed to Great Britain's defeat in the American Revolution EXCEPT

    A. an initial tendency to underestimate the scope and intensity of the rebellion
    B. the rapid defection of loyalists to the patriot cause after the battle of Bunker Hill
    C. the indecisiveness of General Howe in exploiting colonial military weaknesses
    D. the French decisions to provide money, supplies, and military and diplomatic support to the colonists

13. The Articles of Confederation were MOST severely criticized in the 1780s for their lack of

   A. a plan for the admission of new states
   B. equal representation of the states in Congress
   C. a bill of rights
   D. a national taxing power

14. In the decade after the ratification of the Constitution, the American political party system developed from all of the following EXCEPT

   A. the belief of the founding fathers that a two-party system was crucial to the maintenance of a stable political order
   B. the conflict engendered by Secretary of the Treasury Alexander Hamilton's proposed economic policies
   C. the conflict engendered by the foreign policies of George Washington's administration in relation to Great Britain and France
   D. ideological differences between Hamilton and Thomas Jefferson over the nature of republican government

15. The feminist movement, which originated in the second quarter of the nineteenth century, succeeded in accomplishing all of the following before the Civil War EXCEPT

   A. broadening the right of married women to hold property in their own names
   B. gaining the right of women to vote in national elections
   C. expanding the opportunity for women to receive a college education
   D. improving the job opportunities for women in the teaching profession at the elementary level

16. The strategy of the Confederacy at the start of the Civil War was based on all of the following assumptions EXCEPT:

   A. Cutting the North in two by seizing Washington and thrusting northward into Maryland and Pennsylvania would force the North to sue for peace
   B. The dependence of Great Britain and France on Southern cotton would lead them to grant diplomatic recognition and give military aid to the Confederacy
   C. Arming the slaves would help the South to offset superior Northern manpower
   D. Southern control of the port of New Orleans would induce the states in the upper Mississippi Valley to join the Confederacy

17. Federal policy toward Indians between the 1880s and the 1930s was based MAINLY on the assumption that

   A. the Indians should be assimilated into white society
   B. Indian culture and tribal organization should be nurtured
   C. interference with Indian culture and tribal organization should not be permitted
   D. the Indians should be removed from their homeland areas and relocated in Indian Territory

18. The aim of the Open Door policy of 1900 was to

   A. guarantee American industry a supply of cheap labor from China
   B. protect American commercial interests against discrimination in China

C. establish China as a buffer against Russian and Japanese expansion
D. encourage the forces of liberalism in China to throw off the yoke of European domination

19. In the first decade of the twentieth century, Black leaders debated the issues of direct political action to obtain civil rights and the type of training or education Blacks should seek.
    The CHIEF figures in these debates were

    A. Benjamin Banneker and Frederick Douglass
    B. Booker T. Washington and W.E.B. DuBois
    C. Marcus Garvey and Father Divine
    D. A. Philip Randolph and the Rev. Martin Luther King, Jr.

19.____

20. A MAJOR issue debated among progressives during the first two decades of the twentieth century was whether

    A. labor unions should be organized by craft or by industry
    B. the federal government should establish a social security system
    C. the federal government should permit the free coinage of silver
    D. the federal government should abolish economic monopolies or permit them to exist under regulation

20.____

21. Collective bargaining between labor and management became widespread in American industry AFTER

    A. the voluntary acquiescence of large industries that had suffered major strikes in the late nineteenth century
    B. a Supreme Court decision written by Justice Holmes in the early twentieth century
    C. legislation enacted during the administration of President Wilson before the First World War
    D. legislation enacted during the administration of President Franklin D. Roosevelt in the 1930s

21.____

22. President Harry S. Truman's decision to have the atomic bomb dropped on Japan was influenced by all of the following considerations EXCEPT the

    A. desire to counter Republican charges that the Democrats were the party of appeasement and defeat
    B. desire to avoid the large number of casualties that would occur in a United States invasion of Japan
    C. desire to prod the Soviet Union to be more cooperative as it began to formulate its postwar plans
    D. difficulty of devising a test demonstration of the atomic bomb that would unfailingly impress the Japanese government

22.____

23. The Korean and Vietnam Wars were similar in all of the following respects EXCEPT:

    A. Warnings were voiced by some respected military leaders against the United States becoming bogged down in a land war in Asia
    B. Domestic support of the war declined as the possibility of a quick and decisive United States military victory grew remote

23.____

C. United States troops were engaged against an essentially guerilla enemy force
D. The war remained limited rather than leading to war directly between, or among, the major powers

Question 24.

DIRECTIONS: Question 49 is to be answered on the basis of the following statement.

...3 saddlers, 3 hatters, 4 blacksmiths, 4 weavers, 6 boot and shoemakers, 8 carpenters, 3 tailors, 3 cabinet makers, 1 baker, 1 apothecary, and 2 wagon makers' shops—2 tanneries, 1 shop for making wool carding machines, 1 with a machine for spinning wool, 1 manufactory for spinning thread from flax, 1 nail factory, 2 wood carding machines. Within the distance of six miles from the town were—9 merchant mills, 2 grist mills, 12 saw mills, 1 paper mill with 2 vats, 1 wooden factory with 4 looms and 2 fulling mills.

24. The diversity of local manufacturing shown in the census above for a small town in Ohio in the early nineteenth century was characteristic of an area that had yet to

   A. adopt the system of rectangular land surveys and establish credit facilities for persons buying land at public auction
   B. make the transition from a barter to a cash economy
   C. accumulate as adequate supply of skilled labor to facilitate industrial growth
   D. be made accessible as a market for Eastern manufactures by the construction of canals and railroads through the Appalachian barrier

25. Presidential elections in the United States that had to be settled by the House of Representatives were those of

   A. 1876 and 1916   B. 1800 and 1900
   C. 1800 and 1916   D. 1800 and 1824

KEY (CORRECT ANSWERS)

1. D
2. C
3. A
4. B
5. D

6. C
7. A
8. A
9. B
10. B

11. D
12. B
13. D
14. A
15. B

16. C
17. A
18. B
19. B
20. D

21. D
22. A
23. C
24. D
25. D

———

EXAMINATION SECTION
TEST 1

PASSAGE

By far, the best-known industry in Steuben County is the manufacture of glass. Just after the Civil War, the Flint Glass Company moved from Brooklyn to Corning, One reason why the company chose to settle in Corning was that the railroad from Pennsylvania to Corning brought coal for fuel at a low cost. In the early days, the company made lantern chimneys, bottles, and such familiar products. Later, it began making electric light bulbs. Now it manufactures all kinds of glass products. It makes Pyrex, a kind of glass that resists heat so well that it is used for cooking and baking. The company also makes glass wool, which is used for insulation and other purposes, and glass bricks, out of which the walls of some modern buildings are built.

1. The Flint Glass Company moved to Corning because it

   A. would be exempt from local taxes
   B. had been promised free land for its buildings
   C. could obtain coal cheaply
   D. could make glass bricks there

2. Glass wool, made in Corning, is used for

   A. insulation
   B. low cost fuel
   C. manufacturing lantern chimneys
   D. making electric blankets

3. Since its early days in Corning, the number and variety of the products of the glass industry have

   A. decreased
   C. increased slightly
   B. remained about the same
   D. increased greatly

4. The county in which Corning is located is

   A. Chautauqua   B. Cortland   C. Seneca   D. Steuben

5. Pyrex is used for

   A. antifreeze
   C. curtain material
   B. cooking utensils
   D. refrigeration

KEY (CORRECT ANSWERS)

1. C
2. A
3. D
4. D
5. B

TEST 2

PASSAGE

While Admiral Dewey was waiting in Manila Bay, exciting events were happening in the Atlantic. Soon after the start of the war, a Spanish fleet under Admiral Pascual Cervera set sail from the coast of Spain. An American fleet under Admiral William T. Sampson set out to give battle to Cervera's fleet. On May 19, Cervera's fleet came to anchor in the Cuban harbor of Santiago. Sampson's fleet quickly took up its position just outside the channel in order to blockade the harbor, which was too well defended by forts for the Americans to sail in. An American army was landed on the coast a few miles south of Santiago. On July 1-2, this force captured the outer defenses of the city at San Juan Hill and began a siege of Santiago. One of the regiments of volunteers that took part in the charge at San Juan Hill had been recruited by Theodore Roosevelt, who was second in command. The victory of the American army caused the Spaniards to give up hope. The Spanish commander in Cuba ordered Admiral Cervera to put to sea and save his fleet if he could. On July 3, Cervera, with his ships under full steam, started out of Santiago Harbor.

1. The paragraph describes a campaign in the

    A. War of 1812
    B. Mexican War
    C. Civil War
    D. Spanish-American War

2. At the time of the Cuban campaign, a new regiment was recruited by

    A. Cervera B. Dewey C. Roosevelt D. Sampson

3. The American victory at San Juan Hill caused the enemy to

    A. lose confidence
    B. surrender unconditionally
    C. retreat to San Juan Hill
    D. enter Santiago

4. The war was fought

    A. only in the Atlantic Ocean
    B. only in the Pacific Ocean
    C. on both land and sea
    D. off the coast of Tripoli

5. Sampson's fleet tried to

    A. keep Cervera's fleet from entering the harbor
    B. blockade Santiago Harbor
    C. attack San Juan Hill
    D. prevent the United States regiment from entering the battle

KEY (CORRECT ANSWERS)

1. D
2. C
3. A
4. C
5. B

TEST 3

PASSAGE

In the generation after Appomattox, the pattern of our present society and economy took shape. Growth - in area, numbers, wealth, power, social complexity, and economic maturity - was the one most arresting fact. The political divisions of the republic were drawn in their final form, a dozen new states were admitted to the Union, and an American empire was established. In a space of forty years, population increased from thirty-one to seventy-six million, fifteen million immigrants - an ever-increasing proportion of them from southern and eastern Europe - poured into the Promised Land, and great cities like New York, Chicago, Pittsburgh, Cleveland, and Detroit doubled and redoubled their size. In swift succession, the Indians were harried out of their ancient haunts on the high plains and in the mountains and valleys beyond and herded into reservations, the mining and cattle kingdoms rose and fell, the West was peopled and farmed, and by the end of the century, the frontier was no more. Vast new finds of iron ore, copper, and oil created scores of great industries; small business grew into big business.

1. Which one of the following terms BEST describes the period discussed?

    A. Expansion   B. Conservation   C. Regulation   D. Isolation

2. The policy of the Federal government toward the Indians was to

    A. break up the tribal governments
    B. disenfranchise the Indians
    C. educate all Indian children in public schools
    D. remove them to reservations

3. An IMPORTANT factor in the industrial development that followed the Civil War was the

    A. diversification of agriculture
    B. development of new mineral resources
    C. rapid transformation of farmers into industrial workers
    D. development of a colonial empire

4. The last stage in the development of the West was accomplished by

    A. Indians   B. farmers   C. ranchers   D. miners

5. Which one of the following statements is made concerning the United States during the period described in the paragraph? The United States

    A. established an empire
    B. secured special interests in the oil wells and copper mines of Mexico
    C. developed a policy of dollar diplomacy
    D. advocated the open-door policy

6. Which one of the following statements concerning the frontier is made in the paragraph?

    A. After the admission of twelve states, expansion ceased.
    B. An outstanding characteristic of the frontier people was their intense nationalism.
    C. At the end of the 19th century, the frontier came to an end.
    D. The frontier was most important in shaping our present society.

KEY (CORRECT ANSWERS)

1. A
2. D
3. B
4. B
5. A
6. C

TEST 4

PASSAGE

If George Washington could have visited the United States in the 1840's, his thoughts might have run somewhat like this:

"I find it hard to believe that over 20,000,000 people now live in the United States, and that towns have been built beyond the Mississippi River. In my day, there were only 4,000,000 people, and most of these lived along the Atlantic Coast. Can this great city be New York, where I took the oath of office as President? The city I knew had 60,000 inhabitants; today, they tell me, it is the largest city in the New World and has a population of 500,000. What is this engine belching smoke and sparks which carries people across the countryside? When I traveled from Mount Vernon to New York in 1789, I depended on horses. I see factories where machines spin thread to weave it into cloth. Who ever heard in my day of a machine that could spin eighty threads at one time? Here is a boat run by steam which travels against the current of a river! In my time, we depended on the wind to drive our boats. Who would have believed that this country could change so greatly in fifty years!"

1. How much GREATER was the population of the United States in 1840 than in 1789?

    A. Twice as great
    B. Five times as great
    C. Twelve times as great
    D. Twenty times as great

2. George Washington was inaugurated in

    A. Boston
    B. Mount Vernon
    C. New York
    D. Philadelphia

3. A method of transportation used in the 1840's but not in Washington's time was the

    A. airplane   B. automobile   C. sailboat   D. railroad

4. The changes described in the paragraph took place within a period of about _____ years.

    A. 10   B. 20   C. 50   D. 70

5. In Washington's time, MOST of the people in the United States lived

    A. beyond the Mississippi
    B. along the eastern seaboard
    C. in the deep South
    D. in the Northwest

KEY (CORRECT ANSWERS)

1. B
2. C
3. D
4. C
5. B

TEST 5

PASSAGE

In philosophy, the New Deal was democratic, in method evolutionary. Because for fifteen years legislative reforms had been dammed up, they now burst upon the country with what seemed like violence but when the waters subsided, it was clear that they ran in familiar channels. The conservation policy of the New Deal had been inaugurated by Theodore Roosevelt; railroad and trust regulation went back to the eighties; banking and currency reforms had been advocated by Bryan and partially achieved by Wilson; the farm-relief program borrowed much from the Populists, labor legislation from the practices of such states as Wisconsin and Oregon. Even judicial reform, which caused such a mighty stir, had been anticipated by Lincoln and Theodore Roosevelt. And in the realm of international relations, the policies of the New Deal were clearly continuations of the traditional policies of strengthening national security, maintaining freedom of the seas, supporting law and peace, and championing democracy in the Western world.

1. All of the following are suitable titles for the selection EXCEPT

    A. The New Deal - an Evolution
    B. The Radical Program of the New Deal
    C. Precedents for the New Deal
    D. Conservatism in the New Deal

2. Many students of history do not agree that legislative reforms had been *dammed up* during the fifteen-year period preceding the New Deal.
All of the following legislative measures were passed during this fifteen-year period EXCEPT the _____ Act.

    A. Norris-LaGuardia
    B. Reconstruction Finance Corporation
    C. Sherman Antitrust
    D. Agricultural Marketing

3. This selection traces the origin of many of the policies of the New Deal to all of the following EXCEPT

    A. former Presidents
    B. legislation of the Western states
    C. minority parties
    D. the Supreme Court

4. All of the following were indications of isolationism in the New Deal period EXCEPT the

    A. *cash-and-carry* policy
    B. Johnson Debt-Default Act
    C. Lima Conference
    D. *America First* organization

5. Abraham Lincoln, Theodore Roosevelt, and Franklin Roosevelt had all of the following policies in common EXCEPT

    A. trust regulation
    B. expansion of executive powers
    C. land reforms
    D. economic betterment of the common man

6. According to the selection legislative reforms of the New Deal are characterized by all of the following adjectives EXCEPT

    A. democratic
    B. evolutionary
    C. reactionary
    D. traditional

7. All of the following Presidents were associated with banking reforms EXCEPT

    A. Warren Harding
    B. Andrew Jackson
    C. Abraham Lincoln
    D. Woodrow Wilson

8. According to the selection, some legislative precedents for the New Deal were furthered in the United States by all of the following Presidents EXCEPT

    A. Abraham Lincoln
    B. Theodore Roosevelt
    C. Calvin Coolidge
    D. Woodrow Wilson

9. The student seeking primary source material on the New Deal farm program should consult

    A. THE WORLD ALMANAC
    B. the CONGRESSIONAL RECORD
    C. an encyclopedia of the social studies
    D. WHO'S WHO IN AMERICA

KEY (CORRECT ANSWERS)

1. B
2. C
3. D
4. C
5. A
6. C
7. A
8. C
9. B

TEST 6

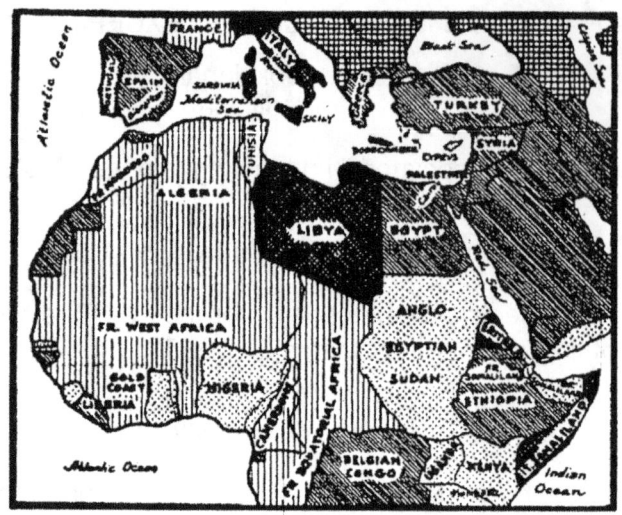

PASSAGE

London, August 14, 1948. A bankrupt empire was put for disposal in London this week. Although the empire, once the property of Italy, has few assets, bidding for the properties was spirited. Italy, despite her present domestic problems, was bidding strongly. Only Italy seemed to want the whole lot; others were angling for bits and pieces and odd parcels of the colonies. On the other hand, Great Britain, which wants the properties almost as badly as Italy, was bidding timidly as if she were afraid of running up the price too fast and too far.

The international auction sale was arranged last year when the winning powers in the recent war settled accounts with Italy. In the Italian peace treaty, Italy renounced all rights to her colonies. The Dodecanese promptly were ceded to Greece. In an annex to the treaty, the Big Four agreed that their Foreign Ministers should decide on the disposal of the other three colonies - Eritrea and Italian Somaliland on the east coast of Africa and Libya in North Africa. Failing a decision within one year, that is, by September 15, 1948, the Big Four agreed that they would hand over the problem to the United Nations General Assembly and abide by its verdict.

That year was nearly out when the deputies of the Big Four Foreign Ministers met, not to decide finally the future of the colonies, but merely to pass on recommendations to the Council of Foreign Minis- ters. When these deputies met last October, they sent out a four-power commission to investigate the situation in the colonies and the wishes of the inhabitants. Reports of that commission were in the hands of the deputies when they met this week.

1. The writer believes that the former Italian colonies

    A. have many fine resources
    B. are desired by some of the great powers
    C. are financially sound
    D. are strategically important to Russia

1.____

2. The Italian colonies in Africa include

   A. Ethiopia, Eritrea, Libya
   B. Italian Somaliland, Eritrea, Libya
   C. Eritrea, Libya, and the Dodecanese
   D. Ethiopia, Tripoli, and the Dodecanese

3. Italy's African colonies bordered on the

   A. Mediterranean Sea
   B. Indian Ocean
   C. Atlantic Ocean and Red Sea
   D. Red Sea, Mediterranean Sea, and Indian Ocean

4. The MOST appropriate title for the article would be

   A. PROBLEMS OF WORLD EMPIRES
   B. FATE OF ITALY'S AFRICAN EMPIRE UNDECIDED
   C. FOUR POWERS INVESTIGATE ITALY'S COLONIES
   D. ITALY'S WEALTH IN AFRICA

5. Libya lies

   A. east of Algeria
   B. east of Egypt
   C. north of Egypt
   D. west of Tunisia

6. The author of the article

   A. thinks that the colonies will be restored to the natives
   B. says the colonies will be given to the Arabs
   C. predicts that the colonies will be returned to Italy
   D. makes no prediction as to the action of the United Nations Assembly

7. MOST of Libya's boundaries bordered on

   A. possessions of the French Empire
   B. possessions of the British Empire
   C. the sea
   D. independent countries

8. If the Big Four cannot agree upon the disposition of the Italian colonies, they will refer the problem to the

   A. International Court of Justice
   B. Trusteeship Council
   C. General Assembly of the United Nations
   D. Security Council of the United Nations

9. The author of the article states that

   A. the colonies were disposed of in the Italian peace treaty
   B. Greece received all the Italian colonies
   C. the Big Four were first assigned disposal of the colonies
   D. the United Nations Assembly would have to approve the disposal of the colonies

10. The author names the following countries as bidders in the disposal of the remaining colonies

    A. France and the Netherlands
    B. Great Britain and France
    C. Italy and Portugal
    D. Great Britain and Italy

10.____

11. By a study of this map, a student could determine the

    A. number of air miles from Rome to Cairo
    B. most densely populated areas
    C. notable topographic features of Ethiopia
    D. boundaries and comparative areas

11.____

12. Of the following statements selected from the article, the one that is CLEARLY a statement of opinion is that

    A. the Dodecanese were ceded to Greece
    B. the Big Four agreed to hand over the problem to the United Nations under certain conditions
    C. the deputies met in October, 1947
    D. Great Britain was afraid of running the price up too fast and too far

12.____

KEYS (CORRECT ANSWERS)

1. B   6. D
2. B   7. A
3. D   8. C
4. B   9. C
5. A   10. D
       11. D
       12. D

TEST 7

PASSAGE

"We hold these truths to be self-evident: that all men and women are created equal; that they are endowed by their Creator with certain inalienable rights; that among these are life, liberty, and the pursuit of happiness...

"The history of mankind is a history of repeated injuries and usurpations on the part of man toward woman, having in direct object the establishment of an absolute tyranny over her. To prove this, let facts be submitted to a candid world.

"He has never permitted her to exercise her inalienable right to the elective franchise.

"He has compelled her to submit to laws, in the formation of which she had no voice...

"He has so framed the laws of divorce, as to what shall be the proper causes, and in case of separation, to whom the guardianship of the children shall be given, as to be wholly regardless of the happiness of women - the law, in all cases, going upon a false supposition of the supremacy of man, and giving all power into his hands...

"He has monopolized nearly all the profitable employments, and from those she is permitted to follow, she receives but a scanty remuneration. He closes against her all the avenues to wealth and distinction which he considers most honorable to himself. As a teacher of theology, medicine, or law, she is not known.

"He has denied her the facilities for obtaining a thorough education, all colleges being closed against her..."

RESOLUTIONS ADOPTED AT THE SENECA FALLS CONVENTION, 1848

1. This selection appeals for support of the movement for

    A. temperance
    B. women's rights
    C. social security
    D. child labor legislation

2. Which served as a model for this selection?

    A. Federal Bill of Rights
    B. Emancipation Proclamation
    C. Mayflower Compact
    D. Declaration of Independence

3. An *inalienable right* is BEST defined as a right that

    A. cannot be taken away
    B. is granted to women only
    C. is granted to all except aliens
    D. is guaranteed by the preamble to the Federal Constitution

4. Which right did women enjoy at the time of the Seneca Falls Convention?

    A. The right to serve on juries
    B. The right of assembly
    C. Equal vocational opportunities
    D. Equal rights before the law

5. Which problem of the Seneca Falls Convention remains a legal issue in the United States today?

    A. A voice in making laws
    B. College admission
    C. Equal pay for equal work in industry
    D. Exclusion from the practice of medicine

5.____

6. About how long after the Seneca Falls Convention was the right to the elective franchise (referred to in the selection) achieved by a constitutional amendment? _____ years.

    A. 5   B. 50   C. 75   D. 100

6.____

KEY (CORRECT ANSWERS)

1. B
2. D
3. A
4. B
5. C
6. C

TEST 8

FROM THE FOUR CORNERS OF THE COUNTRY

1. The cartoon suggests that in the 82nd Congress

   A. harmony prevailed
   B. more agreement existed on domestic issues than on foreign policy
   C. only the reactionary Democrats opposed Truman's foreign policy
   D. there was disagreement within both the Democratic and the Republican parties

2. The cartoon specifically refers to division within the Republican party over

   A. foreign policy   B. inflation
   C. civil rights   D. taxation

3. Which of the following are leaders of the two Republican groups represented in the cartoon?

   A. Taft and Acheson   B. Dewey and Hoover
   C. Austin and Dulles   D. Stassen and Lehman

4. We can conclude from the cartoon that in the 82nd Congress, there was

   A. little prospect that either group in the Democratic party will take a world-minded view
   B. no possibility of any important legislation
   C. no possibility that the President's recommendations will receive favorable consideration
   D. little likelihood of settling significant foreign policy issues on strict party lines

5. Which of the following conclusions drawn from the cartoon can be readily proved?

   A. There was a reaction group in the Democratic party.
   B. All isolationists came from the same part of the country.
   C. The 82nd Congress was evenly divided between Republicans and Democrats.
   D. The Republicans were more interested in foreign policy than in domestic issues.

KEY (CORRECT ANSWERS)

1. D
2. A
3. B
4. D
5. A

TEST 9

FAMILY INCOME BEFORE TAXES
United States, 1946 and 1953

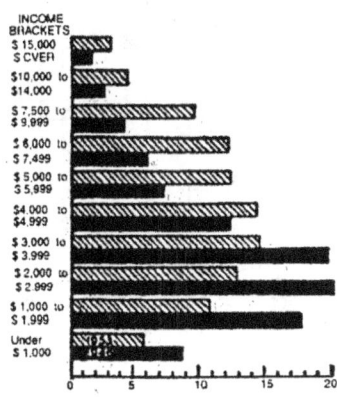

PERCENT OF FAMILIES

1. In 1953, the percent of families with incomes between $3000 and $3,999 was APPROXIMATELY

   A. 5% B. 10% C. 15% D. 20%

2. In 1946, which income bracket included the largest percentage of families?

   A. $1,000 to $1,999
   B. $2,000 to $2,999
   C. $3,000 to $3,999
   D. $4,000 to $4,999

3. Which of these income brackets included a larger percentage of families in 1953 than in 1946?

   A. $1,000 to $1,999
   B. $2,000 to $2,999
   C. $3,000 to $3,999
   D. $4,000 to $4,999

4. In 1953, the percent of families with incomes less than $3,000 was about

   A. 30 B. 45 C. 60 D. 75

5. The average family income in 1953 was CLOSEST TO

   A. $1,500 B. $2,500 C. $4,500 D. $6,000

KEY (CORRECT ANSWERS)

1. C
2. B
3. D
4. A
5. C

TEST 10

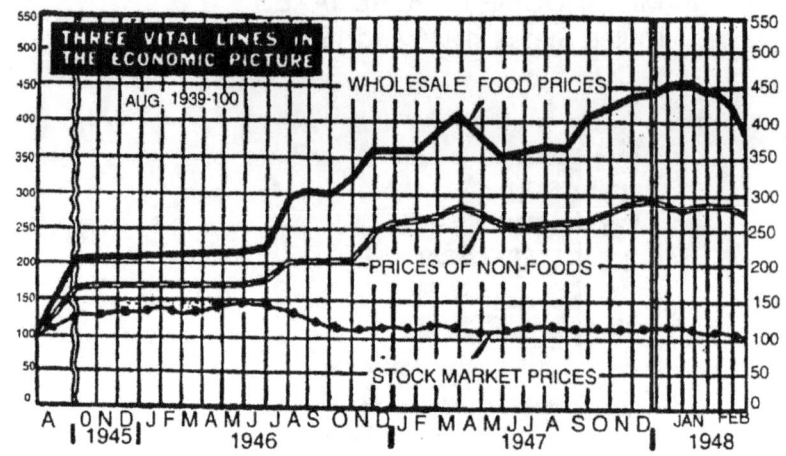

1. For the year 1948, the chart shows a _____ period.

   A. two-month B. six-week C. seven-week D. eight-week

2. Throughout the period from October 1945 to February 1948, stock market prices

   A. rose sharply
   B. declined sharply
   C. remained comparatively steady
   D. fluctuated greatly

3. A comparison of wholesale food prices at the end of the second week in February 1948 with wholesale food prices in October 1945 shows an increase of APPROXIMATELY _____ points.

   A. 50 B. 100 C. 200 D. 300

4. In the period covered by the graph, wholesale food prices declined sharply

   A. once B. twice C. three times D. four times

5. The prices of non-food items reached their highest peak in

   A. March 1946   B. December 1946
   C. March 1947   D. December 1947

6. For the period shown in 1948, all items

   A. rose   B. remained the same
   C. declined   D. fluctuated greatly

7. The month in which the GREATEST increase in wholesale food prices occurred was

   A. July 1946   B. October 1946
   C. September 1947 D. December 1947

8. The same wholesale order of groceries that cost $100 in August 1939 cost approximately $450 in

   A. November 1946   B. March 1947
   C. December 1947   D. January 1948

KEY (CORRECT ANSWERS)

1. C 6. C
2. C 7. A
3. C 8. D
4. B
5. D

www.ingramcontent.com/pod-product-compliance
Lightning Source LLC
Chambersburg PA
CBHW082036300426
44117CB00015B/2503